Here's what students say about Pleiadian Lightwork training:

"Pleiadian Lightwork is the most effective means for achieving personal growth and spiritual connectedness I have found in over fifteen years as a healing-arts professional. This has proven true not only for myself but for my clients as well."
—Harvey Caine, ergonomist, licensed massage therapist, and Pleiadian Lightwork practitioner, Gold Hills, CA

"The Pleiadian Lightwork Intensive held the space for a grand scale of transformative, nurturing energies to have timely interplay in my life. There are indelible reflections of the integrity of this body of work laced throughout my remembrances."
—Marquita Harris, RN, BSN, holistic care practitioner, Mt. Shasta, CA

"My experience with the Pleiadians and Amorah as my teacher has taken me to quantum leaps in my growth and transformation. This work is beyond awesome."
—Janice Schuelke, massage therapist, Medford, Oregon

"After studying the Pleiadian Lightwork with Amorah Quan Yin, I began to routinely use the various healing chambers described in this book to accelerate my own healing. I heartily recommend the Pleiadian Lightwork in its entirety as a way to feel totally loved and to speed you on your way to enlightenment."
—Rosemary DeCoursey, computer technician, licensed massage therapist, and Pleiadian Lightwork practitioner, Dolphin Song/Phoenix

"The Pleiadian Lightwork intensives have truly changed my life. I found that patterns that had ruled my life no longer seemed to have any hold on me. I've also noticed the more I work with the 'Ka' energy, the more my senses are heightened, and I have more awareness of the cellular structure of my body. It is much like opening another level of being aware so that when I check on a body part I can almost see the cells of that part and know exactly what it needs. It is a level that has been shown to me and that I can access when I need that depth of awareness."
—Cree Powell, systems analyst and Pleiadian Lightwork practitioner, Dolphin Song/Phoenix

"The Pleiadian Lightwork is a pivotal landmark where both personal and universal cosmology unite together through sacred geometry. All illusions stored in the body, mind, and emotions are exposed, revealed, and surrendered through grace. With the unifying forces of humans and our brothers and sisters from the Pleiades, this play is a must for those who desire to know their galactic inheritance and anchor it in everyday life."

—Andrea Miller, radiant teacher and learner, Mt. Shasta, CA

THE PLEIADIAN WORKBOOK

Awakening Your Divine Ka

Amorah Quan Yin

Bear & Company
Rochester, Vermont

133.93
Yin

Bear & Company
One Park Street
Rochester, Vermont 05767
www.InnerTraditions.com

Library of Congress Cataloging-in-Publication Data

Quan-Yin, Amorah.
    The pleiadian workbook : awakening your divine Ka / Amorah Quan-Yin.
       p.   cm.
    ISBN 978-187918131-1
    1. Parapsychology. 2. Pleiades—Miscellanea. 3. Spiritual life. 4. Mental healing. I. Title.
BF1031.Q36   1995
133.9'3—dc20   95–35437
                                                          CIP

Printed and bound in the United States

20 19 18 17 16

Cover design: © 1996 Lightbourne Images
Cover illustration: Preston Emery
Interior design and typography: Marilyn Hager
Editing: Gail Vivino

*To my beloved godchildren, who rarely saw or heard from me
during the writing and editing of this book.
Wisper, Zack, and Kiva, I love you.*

CONTENTS

ILLUSTRATIONS

ACKNOWLEDGMENTS

Throughout many ages, cultures, dimensions, and experiences, my beloved friends, the Pleiadian Emissaries of Light, have always kept their promises. They show up at the right time, help me *remember*, and remain dedicated to this solar system, to all its people, and dimensions, until the Divine Plan here is fulfilled. They also honor my free will and never push me beyond where I have pre-chosen to go. These Pleiadians have also been patient and loving toward me, even on those rare occasions when I have not responded to their requests quickly or readily. I am grateful for the opportunity to share with them in the presentation of this book, and in camaraderie in the Light.

I also acknowledge with deep thankfulness the Ascended Masters Jesus Christ, Quan Yin, Mother Mary, Saint Germain, and the many others who have guided and led me both personally and in my spiritual service. I also offer heartfelt thanks to the angels and devic beings who have aided me, inspired me, and given to me along the way. Their love and omnipresences are cherished always.

Next, I would like to acknowledge and thank Shahan Jon for her foresight, her commitment to following guidance, her selfless dedication to this project, her many wonderful skills, and her friendship. Her fresh viewpoint in the preliminary editing phase, responsiveness and availability in the last-minute crunch to assist with the illustrations, and overall spiritual selflessness are greatly respected and appreciated.

After all the horror stories I had heard about publishers' deadlines, pressure, lack of sensitivity, and unreasonable contracts, I can say that my experiences with Barbara and Gerry Clow at Bear & Company have been just the opposite. Barbara and Gerry are caring, enthusiastic, generous, accessible, humane, spiritually sincere, and generally delightful people with whom to work. They always make sure business is well taken care of, and that deadlines and time crunches are met. But, I always felt cared about as a person first—and when the pressure is on, that really matters. Thank you both for the opportunity to experience your sacred approach to people, business, and life in general.

Steven Chase eloquently guided and facilitated the past-life regression work referenced in the text. I am truly grateful to you, Steve, for the privilege of working with you and for being blessed with the quality of presence and safe, sacred space you create.

I thank Gail Vivino for providing another lens through which to look at my manuscript more objectively than I could have done on my own. Your skill and persistent loyalty to the accelerated time demands for copyediting are deeply appreciated.

The painting that is used on the cover of this book was conceived and birthed by Preston Emery several years ago. When I bought it from him in 1991, neither of us knew its destiny. So, Preston, I thank you a second time for creating this inspirational piece of art and beauty to enrich my life and the lives of those who buy this book. Also, I thank you for the preliminary drawings from which the illustrations were done.

To all my friends who had to put up with my lack of availability, my hugs on the run, and my self-absorption with this creative process, I thank you. Please start inviting me to do things with you again. I miss you and I promise to talk about something other than the book. I especially want to thank Andrea, Harvey, Pat, Carlye, and John for their genuine enthusiasm, support, and belief in me and my work—and for not taking my singular focus personally.

I would also like to honor and express gratitude to the participants in the Pleiadian Lightwork Intensives who followed their guidance and took a chance on committing to twenty-day programs based on previously-unheard-of spiritual and healing practices. You are a source of inspiration to me, and have proven over and over again the credibility of this work through your willingness to trust, to give it your best, to go beyond your previous limits, and to allow it to make a difference in your spiritual life and overall well-being. It is a privilege to know you and to grow with you in the spirit of dedication to impeccability.

And to you, the readers, may you attain your goals, become spiritually impeccable, and benefit as much as I have from the materials offered in this book. Thank you for your support and spiritual dedication.

FOREWORD

This book was born of clear vision. You may use it as a window through which to view a new perspective of the past and an expanded vista of your current opportunity. In these pages, you will meet the Pleiadian Emissaries of Light, remarkable beings who will assist you to express your Christ Presence—the joyful, wise, healthy, spontaneous, loving, immortal individual you are—and they will guide you through an experience of Pleiadian Lightwork. It is an opportunity to awaken.

My experience of *The Pleiadian Workbook: Awakening Your Divine Ka* began on a golden spring day on the western slopes of Mt. Shasta. I had gone to "the place where ladybugs come to dance," as I call the small medicine wheel I helped build near my home. On dry days, hundreds of ladybugs emerge from the cushion of pine needles on the forest floor as I beat my drum; their flight fills the air with hard orange bodies. They walk about my arms and legs eagerly greeting me, and cover a small cedar tree. I often go to this place for pipe ceremonies with a friend to pray for the unfolding Divine Plan on Earth; I also pray that I may know the most appropriate steps to take each moment to assist the unfolding plan. Here with the dancing ladybugs, the delicious scent of warm pine, and the music of clear rushing water playfully slapping stoic gray boulders, I "saw" that my friend Amorah would write her first book and that I would assist the birthing by editing her first-draft manuscript and helping prepare her materials for submission to a publisher.

Several days later I broached the subject with Amorah. Silence. More silence. I could see the faint flush of pink rising in her face, embarassment at contemplating something "so grand." A nervous laugh. "We'll see," she stated in that I'm-changing-the-subject-now tone of voice. Within weeks, confirmation came from other unexpected sources. The project was conceived.

By the time Amorah began to write and I began to edit, I was working with the Pleiadian Emissaries of Light every day, especially during sleep, with the intention of transmuting anything—beliefs, thought-forms, genetic encoding, karmic imprints, behavioral patterns—that in any way hindered my full expression and embodiment of my Christ Presence. With the assistance of these Pleiadians, I carefully scrutinized my own life and body to determine what patterns I carried; then I applied the techniques of Pleiadian Lightwork to make the needed transformation.

I noticed that I was beginning to "read between the lines," so to speak. I seemed to have access to new information and knowing that was not "in print" in the book which I could immediately apply to my life. Much of this new knowing was very practical and basic information for my physical well-being. An example was the intuition I received regarding indigenous plants. I began to understand that in order for my Christ Presence to be fully expressed on Earth, certain adjustments in the genetic coding of my body would be necessary; I began to understand that specific native plants in my environment had the ability to make those adjustments.

One day, when I began to work the soil and prepare my garden for spring planting, the thought of native plants came forcefully into my awareness. I stood transfixed. Earlier in the morning, huge, feathery snowflakes had fallen and disappeared into the dark brown earth. Later, a cold glistening rain beat down on the community of plants inhabiting the grounds within the garden fence. Now, the air was wet and cold and vital, and every plant stood in vibrant green contrast to the dense gray sky. Native plants, I thought, surely there must be some here for me now. I began to notice the variety of wild plants. I noted how some species emanated a powerful vitality and were very abundant. I reached down and picked a handful of chickweed and placed it in my mouth; the taste was mild and sweet. Shaking the raindrops free, I selected a young dandelion leaf and carefully bit into it; a pungent bitter taste satisfied me. A beautiful mullein plant, tender in its softness, caught my eye; I thought of tea.

As I stood in my garden that morning, I began to understand something of the relationship between my body and the indigenous plants; I knew what was provided for me now and why; I perceived the cycles of the plants and understood how other plants would have similar purposes for me in their time, too. Indescribable joy filled me. Only the song of an occasional robin broke the silence, but I think every cell in my body and all the plants in the meadow were singing in chorus. Later that day, I referred to a book of herbs and confirmed that chickweed is a blood purifier, as are the tops of red clover that bloom in the summer, and the roots of Oregon grape that can be found in the winter. Later I verified that young dandelion greens are a powerful liver cleanser, and that in the spring humans produce a secretion for liver cleansing. And I was left with a subtle intuitive sense that these properties of plants are simply the easily observed side effects of a deeper effect that science has not measured. My knowledge of native plants continues to unfold.

The artful balance of idea and application is much of the genius of *The Pleiadian Workbook*. Ultimately, it is not enough to read about something, to think about certain ideas. The way to know something is to experience it. The material in this book is carefully arranged. If you read it from the beginning to the end and do the processes as they are presented, you will be surprised and delighted by the results.

I have had some remarkable and profound experiences with the techniques in this workbook. Sometimes the simplest techniques proved to have powerful and far-reaching effects when I applied them at specific times in my life. One example was "blowing roses." I first learned this technique several years ago while on a walk with Amorah through Far Meadow to an area where the larkspur bloomed. We had come in search of the sapphire blue flowers that hid in the sage. It was that magical time of warm afternoon when all the trees seemed to radiate light and you could "float" through the soft golden air. Despite the splendor of the setting, as I walked I began to feel increasingly weak and nauseous. "Try blowing roses," offered Amorah. "Create an image of a large, beautiful rose before you. Now put the face of that anxiety-ridden client you saw before our walk in the center of the rose. Simply allow the rose to absorb this person's energy from you; when it's complete, dissolve the rose." As we walked, I did as she suggested. I could feel the pain and nausea lifting. Within minutes they were completely gone. I was grateful and amazed.

I have used this simple technique with wonderful results innumerable times since learning it. This may seem to be a small thing, but considering my past experiences, it has important ramifications for my life. Since birth I have been very clairsentient. As a child, when I saw someone hurt, I yelled "ouch!" because I could feel the pain. I have always been able to feel everyone's emotions and sensations in my body. Very frequently I have unconsciously absorbed them. This has quite literally been a sickening experience. While living in San Francisco, I would sometimes be caught in gridlock traffic during rush hour; I would sit patiently and gulp big mouthfuls of lemon-cream antacid directly from the large economy-size bottle I kept in my car at all times, and practice deep breathing exercises to release the pain. As early as kindergarten I learned that before I slept at night I would probably vomit; but when I did, I would feel strong and well again. As an adult, I sought the advice of medical doctors and alternative healers, but almost daily I still experienced at least a few hours of extreme discomfort and vomiting. That is, until at age forty-four when I was searching for larkspur and I discovered "blowing roses."

This book has the potential to assist the spiritual awakening of many, many people at this crucial time. It is to Amorah's credit that she has so freely given these materials. You do not need to attend expensive workshops to awaken spiritually. You do not need to place yourself in secluded retreats to achieve your spiritual opening. You do not need to struggle for years to express your spiritual mastery. Because "It's time now" and a great deal of assistance is available for you. The simple tools provided here, and in other works that are being brought forth now, will help you catapult yourself into new awareness and expression of your Christ Presence.

You will be supported. The Pleiadian Emissaries of Light and Ascended Master Jesus Christ are giving you a beautiful opportunity. It is a gift. If you choose, they will assist you in your growth as you consciously work with the materials in this book. If you choose and are ready, they will work with you during your sleep time to open your Ka Channels so that you may fully embody your Christ Presence.

The Pleiadian Emissaries of Light have worked with me, especially during sleep, and have brought a grace, an ease, and a sense of nurturing and support to my growth that I had not previously known. As I began an active spiritual opening in my twenties, I participated in some long meditation retreats. The longest retreat was nine months, and it was a highly-structured time to practice advanced meditation techniques in residence. Phenomena were not discussed, and I felt very alone with my new experiences. By the time I was in my thirties and a graduate student studying East/West psychology, my awakening process became overwhelming. I thought perhaps I was very ill, or maybe becoming psychotic. Sometimes my body would violently shake as it attempted to hold the increasing energies pouring through me; I would lie in the center of the living room and let myself go limp as I involuntarily shook and my body was tossed about the room like a rag doll, sometimes for more than an hour. Other times my body would "light up" and heat would radiate from me; my body would be rigid and paralyzed, my skin somehow too small and stretched taut across my frame as all my cells imitated miniature volcanoes and erupted simultaneously. Sometimes I felt the sensation of hundreds of buzzing bees swarming over my skin and then lifting off, or the full force of every known emotion raging simultaneously through me.

This was my path, and I will not discredit it. However, an opening process does not need to be so dramatic and painful. The Pleiadian Emissaries of Light will assist you to clear any obstacles in your being that hinder your full expression of your Christ Presence. They will assist you to regulate your awakening so that your transformation is easy and graceful. In some of the Chamber of Light sessions, I felt as if I were floating in a serene ocean of peace; occasionally I felt a ripple, and I simply observed my thoughts at that time to note what was being released. Very often, upon going to bed, I made arrangements with the Pleiadian Emissaries of Light to work with me on my body while I slept. Upon waking in the morning, I very much felt changes in myself, and what is more, I possessed new insight and wisdom. I have been extremely blessed to receive such grace.

This incredible opportunity is offered to you at this time, not because of what you lack, but because of who you already are and because of what you bring to this time of planetary, galactic, and universal transformation. I am reminded of a wonderful line from the Sufi poet Rumi: *"Let the beautiful one come into existence; his light is better than the Sun's."* Ra, a spokesperson for the Pleiadian Emissaries of Light, says, "It's time now." And it is. Let your Christ Presence come forth and walk on this Earth. You may use this book as a tool to assist in that birth. It's time now to dance in the radiance you are.

Shahan Jon
Mt. Shasta, California
May 1995

PROLOGUE

Have you ever looked back over your life and realized that everything you experienced was leading to something? That this process called life is not just a random series of events but follows an intelligent, divine order? The Pleiadian Lightwork has been such an unfolding for me.

As a child, I saw fairies and miniature spaceships made of blue light in the flowers and bushes. When I closed my eyes in a darkened room, I saw swirling mandalas of multiple bright colors, images, and scenes. Upon awaking or falling into sleep, past-life movies played before me. I did not have names for all these experiences then, but they were an important part of me—a part I knew I could share with no one.

Throughout the years, occasional psychic phenomena, which I prefer to call Full Sensory Perception phenomena, haunted my otherwise "ordinary" days and nights. I simply learned to live with them. However, by the late 1970s and my Saturn Return, the experiences had become more and more frequent, as well as emotionally unnerving. I considered myself an atheist by then, disillusioned with organized religion; but I *knew* past lives were real because of my lucid, recurring experiences.

In my very first past-life healing session with a regressionist, much to my chagrin, I found myself on a mountainside meadow with thousands of others as Jesus delivered a sermon. I had told Mr. Brown, the therapist, "I'm here to heal my past lives so I can get on with this one. But don't you try and convince me of any religious crap because I'm an atheist. I just want these past-life memories to stop invading my life."

I have often wondered how I might respond to a client who came to a first session with such an arrogant, non-spiritual attitude. Hopefully, I would have the patience and tolerance Mr. Brown did as he simply replied, "That's fine," and began the session.

In my "sermon on the mount" regression experience, as Jesus spoke, there suddenly appeared a gigantic spaceship made of stellar blue light just above the woods to his right. Then another spaceship appeared, and another—until six of the huge craft had come and gone. All around me people fell to the ground, covering their heads and whimpering. But I stood, hands above my head in ecstasy, silently repeating, "Home, home," and weeping tears of joy.

With a tug on my garment, my husband cried, "Samantha, get down!" I stood transfixed, unable to move, until I felt a magnetic pull at my third eye and found myself eye to eye with Jesus Christ. My third eye was lasered with a beam of the most intense light I had ever seen, followed by a cellular flood of light and energy. I burst into tears of spiritual awakening and joy. I had experienced a cellular awakening, my soul's remembrance of itself, and enlightenment all at once.

The scene replayed itself from beginning to end, complete with all the sensations and knowing, and then ended. Immediately, I reexperienced myself as pure consciousness in the form of a blue ball of light falling through space to Earth from a large blue star. This was the beginning of my spiritual awakening in this lifetime. At that time, I had no reference points as to the meaning of enlightenment. I had never heard of spaceships having any connection with spiritual or religious phenomena. I had never even heard of auras or oversouls or *shaktiput*—all of which I had experienced vividly during the regression.

I opened my eyes after the session and saw a clear green light around Mr. Brown's body. I remarked to him, "Mr. Brown, your aura is so green tonight! What does a green aura mean? In fact, what is an aura?" He looked at me rather suspiciously as he replied, "You obviously know what an aura is—you just talked about mine." I assured him that the words had come from my mouth but that I had no conscious knowledge of what I was talking about. I was seeing auras for the first time in this life, yet I had no understanding of what they were. Mr. Brown gave me a very basic definition of an aura, saying it was a person's energy field around his or her body.

It was years before I understood the connections between the Christ, Sirius, enlightenment, and the spaceships of light. I learned that the extraterrestrial Light Beings who taught and healed me while I slept were from the Pleiades, and that their work was to help bring about the Second Coming of Christ *en masse*: when many of us here on Earth become actualized, Christed Beings. I also came to know that spaceships from Sirius appear as blue light vessels, and that the Christ teachings for this galaxy originated on Sirius and are held there and impulsed to Earth.

All of these puzzle pieces put together have led to the Pleiadian

Lightwork, taught to me by the Pleiadian Emissaries of Light and the Ascended Master who was Jesus Christ when last embodied. Pleiadian Lightwork has several facets, including hands-on energy work, clairvoyant reading, Dolphin Brain Repatterning, Dolphin Star-Linking, and Higher Self alignment. The main purpose of Pleiadian Lightwork is to open and activate your *Ka Channels*, which pull high-frequency energy and light from your multidimensional holographic self to your physical body. This activation opens the necessary pathways in your body for your Master Presence, or Christed Self, to come in, as well as making the possibility of ascension versus physical death. The alignment of your divine self and your physical body raises your vibratory rate, energizes your acupuncture meridians for physical balance and rejuvenation, accelerates your spiritual evolution, activates your electrical light body, increases the flow of cerebrospinal fluid throughout your central nervous system, clears neural pathways, and stimulates emotional healing.

Much of this healing and spiritual transformation work can be done without a human practitioner. If you know how to call on the Pleiadian Emissaries of Light healing teams, what to ask for, and appropriate self-care methods for assisting in your own process, sessions can be set up in your own home. That is why I have been guided to write this book: to enable you to receive guidance, healing, and spiritual assistance from the Pleiadian Emissaries of Light as it is appropriate for you.

The Pleiadians have told me that the knowledge and healing practices of the Divine Ka, which are the heart of Pleiadian Lightwork, were key ingredients of ancient Lemurian, Atlantean, and Egyptian healing-temple practices. Once, while I was talking to a woman on the telephone about the Pleiadian Lightwork Intensives I teach, I had a vision of the two of us, along with several other women dressed in white priestess robes, standing in a circle in an ancient Egyptian temple. Some of the women were crying, and all were very sad. We had just learned that soldiers were on their way to destroy the temples and take us prisoner. The political and spiritual hierarchies had been defeated, and the temples of Set, a fear-based dark religious order, were to replace the sacred light temples.

As a group we decided to burn the temple belongings and take poison—a gentle suicide seemed a better destiny than the rape, violence, and oppression that was our other option. I said to the women, "When the cycle of darkness has ended, we will return and reawaken the memories of the temple teachings." One of the younger women said through her sobs, "But how can it be? Everything we've loved and worked so hard for will be lost." I replied, "Dear One, if I dreamed it before and brought it to our people, then I will do it again when the time is right."

Several lifetimes before that one, I had been a priestess with the gift of dreaming. I had worked multidimensionally through lucid dreamtime doing healing and spiritual teaching, while bringing through teachings from the Pleiadian Emissaries of Light to the temples. In the Egyptian temples that were about to be destroyed, I had begun a new avenue of healing. It was basically the Pleiadian Lightwork that has now been reintroduced in this life. And so my promise has been kept. Because of Earth's position in her evolutionary cycle, the Pleiadian Emissaries of Light have said to me, "*It's time now* for this work to be remembered."

The process of writing this book has been an amazing life experience in and of itself. I deliberately decided, once I was asked to do the book by the Pleiadians, not to read any other remotely related materials until the manuscript was completed. So any similarities of information are totally coincidental, except for a few cross references to Barbara Hand Clow's newest book that were added afterward.

I had no idea prior to sending in the book proposal and partial manuscript to Bear & Company that Barbara Hand Clow and her husband own this publishing house. Since reading several of her books—*Heart of the Christos, Liquid Light of Sex,* and *Chiron: Rainbow Bridge Between the Inner and Outer Planets*—and hearing her speak in Seattle a few years before, I had held her in deepest respect and considered her to be a very clear person of high integrity. To have the opportunity to work with her directly was like icing on the cake. So, when I came home one evening to find a message from Barbara on my answering machine saying Bear wanted to publish my book, I was doubly ecstatic. When the Pleiadian Emissaries of Light had first told me about writing the book, they had shown me the back cover with Bear & Company's name on it.

Five days after receiving Barbara's message, before reaching her by phone, I received a letter from her that began, "Are you as excited about this as I am?" I could not help but laugh and feel honored at the same time as I went on to read that she had a new book coming out in the fall called *The Pleiadian Agenda: A New Cosmology for the Age of Light,* to which my book was the perfect companion. Her book included information about the Ka and about the pressing need for healing and activating it, but the Pleiadians had told her that someone else would be channeling and writing the workbook on how to do so. Barbara and I were completing each other's vision and information without any conscious direct collaboration. We agreed that we would not see each other's manuscripts until both were complete so that we would not be influenced by each other, and yet even in our phone conversations it was obvious that we were working with exactly the same Pleiadian source. The natural complementary nature of the two works is simply a direct product of Pleiadian ingenuity. After completing my manuscript and reading parts of Barbara's new book, I added a couple of references from *The Pleiadian Agenda* into my text and Glossary.

Just prior to completion of this book—after my morning meditation—I was guided to the living room to pick up another of Barbara's books, *Signet of Atlantis*. I had recently purchased it to read after my book was complete but was told that morning to open it and read the Preface. It contained Barbara's story of how her trilogy, of which *Signet* was the third book, had come about; all the delays, the distractions, the time constraints, and so on were outlined. Her story was so similar to mine that I thought, "Maybe this is just how the Pleiadians do things. I wish I'd known before; then I might have been less anxious about getting it done on time." During the six months of writing this book, I went through separation and finally divorce from my recent marriage, kept up my full-time teaching and private healing practice, was ill for two-and-a-half weeks, moved, and taught a twenty-one-day Pleiadian Lightwork Intensive. Prior to that time, I had seldom worked more than three days in a row without a day or two off; for those six months that schedule seemed like an ancient dream. However, I gained a new level of confidence in my ability to keep going in an effective and consistent way.

Eight weeks prior to the completion of this book, near the end of my morning meditation time, the Pleiadians came in and took me through several new energy and frequency experiences. Afterward they asked me to go to the computer and open a new file. I did so, and they proceeded to give me a rough outline for the next book on Pleiadian Lightwork. I guess my new lesson is that the river continues to flow without ceasing or hesitation.

Partly this continuing rapid flow is accelerated by the fact that Earth is in the Photon Band and will continue to move deeper into it without going retrograde. As the year 2013 approaches, there will be no major "let-ups" in the intensity and acceleration; the shifts have begun physically, emotionally, spiritually, and mentally and will only get bigger and more obvious as humanity moves through time and space over the next seventeen years. You may feel called to learn healing modalities, take spiritual trainings, see healers for assistance, or seek out sacred ceremonial experiences. You have your own individual role in the upcoming times, and your urges need to be examined and followed through on when they feel divinely inspired and are not just reactionary fears about being left out. Many people will just be beginning to awaken to the concept of spiritual evolution during the upcoming times, while others will choose to leave the planet or resist change to the last breath. If you have a role during these accelerated days as a healer, teacher, counselor, or knowledgeable friend, do not hesitate to prepare yourself to fill that role.

The Pleiadians' and my hope and intent are that this book will contribute to the grace and deepening of your healing, clearing, and spiritual evolution, as well as that of the planet. With unity of purpose, we shall individually and collectively give birth to a new way of being and living, and the goal of planetary ascension will be achieved.

WHY THE PLEIADIANS?

WHY NOW?

Chapter 1

IN THE BEGINNING . . .

A s I lay on the floor at the end of three days of Feldenkrais guided floor movement work, a human-size Light Being named Pa-La held out his hand for me to take. The trust and familiarity were immediate, and as I let go and reached for his hand, I bilocated beside my own body. Holding Pa-La's hand all the while, I floated with him out of the room, above the house, and quickly beyond Earth's atmosphere. Moving effortlessly through and beyond layers of murkiness, followed by areas of soft radiant blue and milky white, we broke through into open space. The vision of a vast and beautiful multicolored nebula of mostly red with splotches of blue and smaller amounts of yellow and white was the only thing that interrupted the seemingly endless skyscape of deep blue-black expansiveness dotted holographically with stars. Today, the exquisite memory of passing beneath the nebula is as vivid in my mind's eye as if I were still there watching.

Just beyond the nebula, we seemed to slow down and approach a structure made of dozens of bright gold pyramids with equilateral golden crosses on top. It was the roof of a space station, which, as we lowered to approach it from beneath the pyramids, proved to be quite large. From inside the warehouse-size building, the pyramids were about forty feet above us and hollow, yet emanating clear colors of light from an unknown power source. The room itself was mostly white, very sterile in appearance, and also lit from an unapparent source. I was so taken by the beauty of the pyramids and the incredible blend of love and intelligence flowing from the four Light Beings who greeted us that I noticed nothing else about the place. These beings were each a solid color: red, golden yellow, green, and blue.

They appeared to be about half again my height and were shaped like elongated triangles that were rounded on top. They had no obvious limbs or faces, and yet the tops of the tall triangular-shaped bodies seemed to contain semblances of eyes and communication centers, as if the beings were hooded, robed figures with bodies inside. Pa-La, on the other hand, was humanoid in shape, and completely made of sparkling bluish-silver light.

The golden being at some point telepathically asked if I would like to receive an energy balancing. Contrary to my usual cautious nature, I answered, "Yes!" with no questions asked. The smaller, silvery-white being who had guided me there lifted me to the ceiling and deposited me in one of the pyramids with my head in the very top. I was surrounded and filled with sparkling, yet clear, colored light and energy until I felt overwhelming joy and lightness of being. Then the golden being asked telepathically if I was ready to have my Pleiadian astral body back. Without hesitation and with tears of great love and relief, I replied, "Oh, yes!" Energy and color began to accumulate and swirl rapidly; somehow this was an interplay between my body and the energy field inside the pyramid. A light body exactly like that of the tall triangular beings, red in color, was formed. It attached into my body with a silver cord like the one to my human astral body, and I could feel my consciousness simultaneously in the new form and my human one. This light body blended in and around my human body. My energy surged, and my joy and relief birthed a deep sense of peace and rightness of being. It was not another entity that was attaching itself and blending with me. It was a part of my own wholeness that was being given a light form and was returning to me: a part I had left behind a long time ago.

A deep bond of friendship, trust, and ancient love welled up inside me for these old refound comrades. I knew that when I had originally come to this galaxy, the Pleiadian form had been the first one I had taken to down-step my vibration in preparation for service here. I had dwelled in varying locations in the Seven Sisters, receiving instruction and experience pertinent to my future purpose. So, being with these cherished and ancient friends was natural and felt long awaited. When the tour and light body connections were complete, we parted with a silent exchange of mutual love, gratitude, and respect.

The return flight was very quick compared to the journey there. I have done many journeys since that time and they have always been faster. When I am blended with my Pleiadian light body, time and space restrictions are minimized. While hovering above the room before I returned to the floor with the other students, I was told that my Pleiadian light body would be away from me most of the time, but would maintain a constant connection with the Pleiadian Emissaries of Light, which is the name I later learned to call my friends. My Pleiadian light body would enable me to serve in two places at once and to be an intermediary between the higher dimensions and third-dimensional Earth, as well as between the Pleiadian central sun, Alcyone, and Earth. The Pleiadians told me they were closely studying the Neuro-Muscular-Cortical Repatterning training in which I was participating, because they were learning how to assist human beings in making the vibrational shifts necessary for our nervous systems to withstand the coming frequency changes on Earth. The key was in learning as many ways to heal the nervous system as possible.

For the purpose of studying and assisting us in deepening our healing experiences, one Pleiadian guide would be assigned to each person in the training who was willing. These guides would monitor us, study the effects of the work, and determine ways of utilizing the information to assist others as well. This would be done in upcoming times with many people on the higher astral planes while they slept. In addition, many people would receive work directly from human practitioners such as myself. I would be given healings and realignment work during my sleep in order to deepen my own benefits from the Neuro-Muscular-Cortical Repatterning training, as well as participate in experiments on how to etherically work on others most effectively. The Pleiadian Emissaries of Light would also teach me advanced techniques during sleep. While in the third-dimensional class learning on the teacher's level, I would simultaneously be instructed telepathically on ways of improving the work as these Pleiadians deemed appropriate. With these last preparations, my Pleiadian guide, Pa-La, brought me back to my body. I had virtually no sense of travel time by Earth standards of measurement as I awoke back in the room.

That night was the first astral class in which I *consciously* partici-pated. When I awoke the next morning my body was moving invol-untarily. Immediately the telepathic message from Pa-La was, "Relax and allow the body to complete the movement pattern and then write it down." As I did so, my body performed a series of elegant yet subtle moves. When I wrote them down sequentially, they became what I entitled The Cradle. This type of guided movement work as a whole is called Dolphin Moves and is part of Dolphin Brain Repatterning. Its roots are in the principles of Moshe Feldenkrais' Awareness Through Movement exercises. The Pleiadian version of guided movement work is the next evolutionary step for that modality.

In fact, that same night of my first astral class I was with Moshe Feldenkrais and several others in a laboratory setting. Computers were there with a capability of monitoring "psychic" or nonphysical input. Moshe, whom I had never met in the physical world, was explaining and demonstrating the work he had developed in his physical life and how it could be expanded and improved with the willing assistance of people like me. Moshe's body had died a few years before, but his genius and commitment were alive and well, so to speak.

I met with Moshe and the Pleiadian Emissaries of Light together many times on the astral planes. The times spent with Moshe and the group were wonderful. Moshe tended to be straightforward and to the point, offering little unnecessary communication—an occasional heart-warming comment or joke was rare and precious. Sometimes I was given Dolphin Moves. Sometimes the group taught me the phi-losophy and theory behind the work. Sometimes laser technology for healing was included—or hands-on sessions, which are the other aspect of Dolphin Brain Repatterning. I always wrote down what I remembered in the mornings. For an entire month, I kept two jour-nals: one for the Pleiadian work and the other for the Neuro-Muscular-Cortical Repatterning training intensive I was taking.

A few times during the intensive, I spent time on Pleiadian light-ships or at other space stations. These occurrences took place both in my astral body while I was lucid dreaming and while I was awake during class or meditating. Without exception, the experiences were loving, respectful of my boundaries, and honoring of my free will. To this day, I have never had a psychic cord or implanted device of any kind placed in me by the Pleiadians, nor have I witnessed these occurring in others. I have personally had problems in the past with extreme invasion by other, not so ethical, extraterrestrials, and have depossessed many clients from these extraterrestrials and their implants.

After the intensive, I spent a couple of days in Anaheim, California, to go to Disneyland with friends from the training. The first afternoon there, I was lounging by the motel pool with mellow music playing on my Walkman when my Pleiadian guide came and asked me to go with him. As I lifted out of my body, I was startled and immediately on guard at the sight of two other beings whom I recognized as from Orion. My guide quickly reassured me they were okay, which I soon sensed was true, for I felt compassion from these Orion beings. A silent communication from them let me feel and know their regret that some of their kind had gone awry. They also let me know that they were serving the Light, and the Galactic Federation of Light, specifically.

The four of us moved quickly together to a large space station just inside Earth's atmosphere. It was huge—many levels high, with each floor appearing to have a complete function of its own. However, I was not in any one place long enough to examine it until we arrived at our destination. There, in the center of an approximately twenty-by-twenty-foot room, was a dark, cobalt-gray cylinder made of what appeared to be a strange metal. I can describe it no further at this time. This particular group of Light Beings from Orion told me that they have the ability to reverse nuclear waste and nuclear energy out of existence with the use of this chamber, which they created. In fact, they assured me that no residue will exist anywhere when this device is used. They went on to explain that they will never use it unless enough humans awaken to the recognition of the darkness that has permeated this planet and choose to take responsibility for cocreation here according to divine law. As Earth's people, we must become aware of our impact on the planet and on each other and future generations. We human beings must ask for divine intervention to remove the threat of nuclear annihilation from the planet. Without this threat we will have a chance to start over as cocreators with one another, God/Goddess/All That Is, Earth, all lifeforms on Earth, and our intergalactic friends.

Since that time, St. Germain further explained to me that we must all take responsibility for working within what he calls the "harmonics of cocreation." With cocreation, *win-win* is the attitude employed as well as the result of all action and creation of reality.

Needless to say, I was very grateful when I returned to my body that day in Anaheim, and a bit humbled by the meeting with the Orion beings whom I had previously presumed to be "all bad." They had so impressed me with their sincere dedication to Earth and to the Light that ever since that meeting I have attempted to remove all such negative and judgmental labels from my attitudes and vocabulary. My intent is simply to see everything from a standpoint of evolutionary development levels. All of existence is in an ongoing process of learning and evolving. Along the way we may get caught up in power trips or black magic, drugs or abuse of some kind, but eventually all lifeforms evolve into being cocreators with God/Goddess/All That Is in harmony with the Divine Plan of Light, Love, and Truth. We will all naturally care deeply for all of creation. To judge anything or anyone for its present level in that evolutionary process is both counterproductive and in error. We are responsible for teaching by example, first and always, as we grow and become more conscious. It certainly helps us to feel and honor the connectedness of all things by choosing to see that way.

After that trip with my three escorts, all of my Pleiadian friends seemed to vanish into thin air. I called on them. I established dream intents for rendezvous times. But nothing happened. Daily I became more and more frustrated and lonely, until one afternoon while meditating I began sobbing loudly, crying out, "Why have you deserted me? Where are you? Have I done something wrong?" (The automatic human conclusion, right?) I felt the warm glow of the familiar loving presence I had come to know as Ra, the golden being, touching my arm. Again I asked, "Why did you disappear? I've missed you.

You've made my life so much more meaningful and I just can't bear it if you go away."

Very compassionately, Ra replied, "Beloved, we will never be far from you. And if you really need us, we'll always make our presence known to you. But, for now, you must get on with your life here on Earth. When we are in contact with you regularly, you tend to make us more important and more real than the rest of your life. And we would never do anything to usurp your learning and growth and service here on Earth. We love and respect you too much for that. When the time is right, we'll be together again in your conscious awareness as well as in the unconscious realms." Sending a last wave of love and compassion that flowed through me and helped me relax, Ra left.

After that, with the exception of a small number of channeling sessions, most of my conscious contacts with Ra and the others happened during sessions with clients. In these sessions, the Pleiadian Emissaries of Light sometimes instructed and assisted me in the healing process. This was almost exclusively during Dolphin Brain Repatterning and Dolphin Move sessions until the late summer of 1993 when the next phase began.

Chapter 2

MY INTRODUCTION TO PLEIADIAN LIGHTWORK

August of 1993 found me taking a much-needed rest at Breitenbush Hot Springs, a resort in central Oregon. Surrounded by old-growth forest and the sounds of the rushing Breitenbush River, I sat at a wooden picnic bench on an outside deck leisurely having an organic vegetarian meal prepared by the incredible kitchen staff. I had been at the resort for six days and had managed to do enough hot mineral soaks, saunas, cold plunges, and hikes, not to mention long sleep periods and a few naps, to begin to feel replenished. By that time I was wearing a contented smile and as little else as I could get away with on that hot summer evening.

As I got up to take my tray inside the lodge, a pendant worn around a woman's neck took my interest. I continued on my busing mission, but came back out and, without conscious intent, walked over to the wearer of the pendant and said, "Hello, I couldn't help noticing the unusual design of your pendant. Did you design it?" She answered with an explanation that I have now forgotten, but it served the purpose of allowing us to meet. She identified herself as a practicing chiropractor living in the Laguna Beach area. She went on to say that lately she had been doing something other than chiropractic that she could not explain, except that it was dramatically enhancing the results with her clients. It was totally intuitive and never the same twice. She was in a little bit of an identity crisis as to how to advertise herself now, but knew the changes were positive.

Less than two minutes into the conversation, I became so distracted by visionary experiences that I said, almost apologetically, "Excuse me, but something is happening that requires me to go into a trance. I'm a clairvoyant, you see, and I don't usually do this with people I've just met, but for some reason this seems to be important. Is that okay with you?" Her curious eyes brightened and she quickly gave me the okay to proceed. What I saw took me completely by surprise. In a bubble just to the upper right of her aura was a miniature scene of the two of us with several Pleiadian Emissaries of Light aboard a spaceship learning about and observing a Dolphin Star-Linking session. I opened my eyes and said something to the effect of, "Does this new work you're doing involve placing fingertips on various spots on the body that need to be energized by connecting them to one another? And when you do it, does the electrical circuitry between those points reconnect and activate? And do people experience immediate pain or pressure release?"

Looking quite surprised, she said, "Why, yes! But, I've never been able to explain it so well. How did you know?" I replied, "Because we learned it on the same Pleiadian lightship. I've been doing this type of hands-on work since the early 1980s. But I didn't know until just now that the Pleiadians had taught it to me." There was a pause while my Pleiadian guide, Pa-La, popped in and said to tell her they had been working with her for the last six months during her dreamtime. When I relayed that message to her, she simply replied, "That's about how long it's been since I started doing this new work. For some reason I can't say I'm surprised."

From that point, I shared with her some of my own conscious experiences with the Pleiadian Emissaries of Light. Pleiadian Lightwork, which I later learned to call the Pleiadian healing techniques, was originally intended to replace the type of chiropractic work that deals only with symptoms instead of clearing the source of structural pain. She agreed that she had felt a need for a deeper way of working prior to beginning to use the new approach, and she felt there was still more to come. I continued to tell her about my early experiences with Dolphin Star-Linking, and she shared her experiences as well. Then, Pa-La initiated a new twist in our conversation.

Pa-La asked me to get some paper and a pen, which I did. For the next hour and a half, he told me about Ka Channels, which are described in more detail in Section II of this book. He showed me the general pathways of these channels, which are a whole "new" old meridian-type system. He also informed me about something called the Ka Template that serves to regulate the flow of Ka energy in the body. The Ka energy was described as the basic cosmic light and life force that, when flowing properly in our physical and etheric bodies, replenishes the other meridian systems such as those used in acupuncture and Shiatsu, and keeps them open and flowing. This energy source essentially consists of stepped-down light frequencies from our own Higher Selves in their multidimensional holographic alignment. When we are reconnected to our Higher Selves and have our Ka Channels open and receiving the higher-dimensional Ka energy, the opportunity for uniting our spirits with our physical bodies is greatly increased. What this basically provides for those of us who are spiritual seekers of Truth is assistance with the full process of descension of spirit into matter for the purpose of transfiguration and enlightenment. When spirit fully descends into matter, we become the bodies of Christ here on Earth. This could be called the Second Coming of Christ en masse. The final Ka activation is that of ascension.

So much for light after-dinner meetings and conversation! My new friend and I were both very delighted with the information we had received as well as the energy boost that came with it. I was particularly energized by the past-life visions and feelings that spontaneously came into my awareness. There were scenes in Lemuria, Atlantis, and ancient Egypt in which I was among the healers who were using the same healing processes I was now being reminded of again. I reexperienced activities in temples of ancient cultures that were much more spiritually attuned, in general, than our world is today. It was as if I were there again. And yet, the knowing that these advanced civilizations had all ultimately fallen was fresh in my memories, too.

The Pleiadians [my shortened name for the Pleiadian Emissaries of Light] say that as Earth cycles around Alcyone, as Alcyone and the Pleiadian system orbit around the Galactic Center, and as our galaxy does its ongoing spiral dance through time and space, there are points in the sacred spiral when we enter into grace periods. During those times, there is great opportunity for individual and planetary spiritual awakening and evolution. *Now* is one of those times: a time to remember and go beyond where we have gone before. We have a window of opportunity during which we can learn from our past mistakes, forgive, and take responsibility for all we have created and experienced—and *will* create and experience. By doing so, we will open the door to the unfolding of this ancient future.

At Breitenbush, my new acquaintance and I were deeply inspired by the sharing and remembering. After exchanging phone numbers and addresses and making a copy of the notes for her, my new "old" friend and I parted for the evening, agreeing to stay in touch.

Later that same evening in my cabin, I received another transmission—this time from Ascended Master Jesus Christ [whom I will refer to as "Christ" or "the Christ" in future references; I use "Jesus Christ" when referring to the historical incarnation of Christ]. This transmission was about the seven rays and the role of the divine couples who are keepers and dispensers of ray energies for couples on Earth. This transmission was explained that the transformation of male/female relationships into what they are intended to be is essential now, and part of the overall Christ and Pleiadian plan. [More details about the new male/female paradigm are included in chapter 10, entitled "Love Configuration Chamber."] The information brought up a little sadness for me since I was not in a relationship at the time and dearly wanted to be. But it also planted the seed of hope that a relationship would soon be forthcoming. I had waited a long time for my spiritual partner and helpmate. Still, I fell asleep mostly contented and grateful.

Two weeks or so after my return home, two important events happened back-to-back. First, I was given a twenty-four-hour "enlightenment" period, as Ra called it when he instructed me to go to Sand Flat on Mt. Shasta at a certain time the following afternoon and sit under "the Christ Tree." This tree had first been shown to me by the Christ in his etheric form a few years previously as a place to meet with him. For a few months, every time I went there, the Christ would welcome me. He would give me spiritual teachings and discourses to help me have compassion for myself, or to direct my life and spiritual growth in some way. After an especially joyful sharing with him one day, he informed me that he would not be meeting me there any more, except on rare occasions. He said he wanted me to be an equal friend and not to rely on him too much. The spot under the tree would become a place to sit in peace and connect with my own Christed Presence in a stronger way than I was usually able to at that time. So when Ra asked me to go there, I went.

I barely had time to get comfortable under the tree when a group of Pleiadians—as well as the Christ, Quan Yin, many angels, and Light Beings—surrounded me. I was taken into an expanded state that they called an enlightenment reference point.

The first words I heard were from Ra: "You will be teaching a twenty-day program called the Pleiadian Lightwork Intensive. It will be held in late November and December of this year and will be in three parts. Section 1 will be called 'Neuro-Muscular-Cortical Repatterning' [now called Dolphin Brain Repatterning] and will free the spine and skeletal system of the most basic holding patterns in order to allow and encourage the cerebral-spinal fluid to flow more fully. This will help open the neural transmitters in the body to the new light frequencies.

"These new frequencies will be introduced in Section 2, which will be entitled 'Ka Channels and Ka Template Activation.' Within this section of the intensive, you will also be teaching Higher Self connection, higher ethics, and the basic spiritual responsibility necessary to keep the Ka energies flowing once opened. Section 3 will be called 'Electrical Light-Body Reactivation and Realignment' [now called Dolphin Star-Linking]. In order to have this work have a fuller and more lasting effect, the Ka Channels must be opened prior to electrical work. The Ka energy is needed to keep the electrical pathways clear once the initial work is done."

I was more than a little surprised. To begin with, I had tended toward the conservative approach in my networking and advertising. To blatantly call this new program the Pleiadian Lightwork Intensive was a big stretch for me. But I did not question it because in the state I was in, I felt the rightness of it. So be it.

The next stretch came when Ra went on to outline a couple of things I did not even know about yet. With a slight touch of amusement, he said I would be well prepared by the time I needed to be. He outlined many more details and plans at that time, which, I must say, I had no trouble at all remembering when I got home. This was not my usual experience; generally, my memory is not much to brag about.

The second important event that occurred after I returned from Breitenbush was the return of my ex-fiancé into my life. This was an even bigger surprise, since I had considered myself complete with that relationship. And yet there he was—ancient soul partner and beloved—complete with all the deep feelings.

I went back to my teaching and healing practices. At first, not much seemed to be happening toward the Pleiadian Lightwork Intensive. The only continuum was that the Pleiadians and the Christ together were doing regular healing sessions for me to open my Ka Channels as much as they could be opened without physical hands-on work. They told me the results would be deeper for me when I had students trained who could do the healing work hands-on. At times the Pleiadian Emissaries of Light would clairvoyantly show me where the channel they were working on was located in my body and have me erase pain, which, for some reason, they are unable to do. At other times I would just relax and feel subtle energies or fall asleep.

The most noticeable change from their work on me was a balancing of my energy level throughout the day. The highs and lows I was used to diminished to almost nonexistence. In general, a feeling of lightness and resilience formed. Later, clients receiving the Pleiadian Lightwork reported almost identical results. The Pleiadians seemed to find my tendency to measure the value of the work by its immediate results humorous; they told me the real purpose of the work was only vaguely connected with what I was experiencing directly. It would be two years after the Ka Channels were opened before most recipients would be available for the true Ka function to begin: the connection throughout the higher dimensions with our own Higher Selves. This connection would open multidimensional communications with our Higher Selves and with other Light Beings, allowing us to receive direct communications from the star systems involved with our solar system and galaxy. Even after the two years, the Ka's range of functions would continue to expand in ways we could not yet imagine.

Still happy with the changes the work was making in my own life and the promises of greater things to come, I began my first series of Ka sessions with a close friend who was also a student and healing client. Each time the sessions began, I had no idea what I would be doing. Inevitably, I would be shown a channel, one activation point at a time, which I would note on paper afterward. Another friend and student came for a three-day private healing intensive and became the source of three more sets of channels being revealed. Between these sessions and the private meetings with the Pleiadians, all the channels were shown to me. The pieces of the puzzle began to fit together.

There were thirty-two meridians, or sixteen pairs of meridians, all together. All had several activation points. Sometimes there was a form of what I would call psychic surgery needed to heal the channels. Other times the techniques for opening Ka Channels were much simpler, though very specific; and these were only the most obvious aspects of the Pleiadian Lightwork.

In a reading with one client, I was shown the role of the neural pathways in the brain to spiritual growth and honesty. In a nutshell, if our response in *every* life situation is not 100 percent spontaneously truthful and correct, the spirit cannot live in the body. The frequency of even the most minor deception, even by omission, is below the minimum frequency level necessary for spirit to embody fully. [The details of this are explained in "Clearing Erroneous Neural Pathways" in chapter 12.] For now, just ponder the implications in your own life of being spontaneously 100 percent truthful. How would that change everything in your life?

November, and the first Pleiadian Lightwork Intensive, came. Now I can truthfully say it far surpassed my own expectations of what it would be. Every day the lightship would superimpose itself around the house, and all present would be accelerated at once. After only three days my observation was: "Now I know why they call it an 'intensive'." It was certainly that! Without exception, everyone in the group went through the emotional wringer at least once; some students did so repeatedly. That partially had to do with tendencies toward resistant and reactionary response patterns. However, for the most part, the Pleiadian Lightwork Intensive simply involved deep healing and opening that happened consistently enough to help people go beyond their prior limits. In other words, everyone, including me, grew incredibly during those twenty days.

My biggest challenge was having my partner in the group, because our relationship was rocky, at best, much of the time. There I was, leading this group and teaching about spontaneous truthfulness as a spiritual responsibility for Pleiadian Lightwork Intensive-level work, and some days I could not hold back the tears. Having my mate in a group I was leading would have had its challenges in the best of situations. Added to that was the painful state of our relationship—it was hard to even look at him without crying at times. So what did I do? I was totally honest with the group, without blaming, just like I was teaching them to be in their lives.

At morning check-in, I would simply state where I was. Sometimes I was balanced, open, and loving; sometimes I was tearful; and at other times I was frustrated. The one consistent thing was that I always shared with the group honestly. Each day I recommitted to giving the group my best, regardless. And I did. I dare say that group probably learned more about being painfully honest and exposed by witnessing my own day-to-day process of just being there than they did any other way. I went through self-judgment about not being more collected on a consistent basis, about not being in a more fulfilling relationship, and about choosing to allow him in the group. Each day I dealt with my own expectations and judgments of myself, and each day I transformed them into self-acceptance and compassion for myself. In the end, without exception, the group members thanked me for having the courage to "walk my talk" and be so vulnerable with them. It had been a great part of the learning experience for all concerned. Their loving acceptance and appreciation made it a lot easier to accept myself. Still, at the end, I promised myself I would never repeat that part of the experience. True compassion for myself would mean not putting myself in that position ever again.

Now, don't misunderstand. I was not a basket case all day every day; I had clear and happy days as well. It was just that when the pain was there, I allowed it. Verbally, I let the intensive members know, without too many personal details about my partner, how I was feeling. Yet when the teaching began, I put my best foot forward and did my job. There is a great sense of personal strength and self-respect that comes when we mature enough to know we can always be there for others no matter what is going on in our lives. This was simply the biggest test of that capability I had ever undergone. My neural pathways must have been buzzing after that one.

Well, the relationship ended shortly after the Pleiadian Lightwork Intensive was over, and a personal recovery and healing ensued. As always, my own process was mixed with my ongoing private healing practice and teaching. It helped that I was finally getting some of my own Ka Channels opened in hands-on sessions with a Pleiadian Lightwork Intensive graduate, which was a great reward. The deeper the work went in my own body, the better I felt about sharing it with others.

One wintry night I came into the living room to read my mail and relax. In the mail was a newsletter from a friend I had not seen in over a year and a half. She was sharing in the newsletter about goals for a new healing center she was in the process of pulling together. As I read, I felt more and more strongly the role of the Pleiadian Lightwork Intensive in a shared future with this friend. Yet, in my state of tiredness, I went into self-doubt and began to think I was just projecting that onto her because it was my "latest thing" to be excited about. But the feelings were strong. Finally, I noticed a copy of *The Keys of Enoch* my roommate had left on the table. I had never been drawn to reading that book before, but suddenly I felt compelled to pick it up. As I did, the familiar voice of Ra said, "Open the book randomly and see what's there. It will either confirm your doubts or affirm your feelings about the future of Pleiadian Lightwork."

Randomly, I opened the book to Section 315, which proceeded to define Ka as the "divine double," calling it by name. My mouth dropped open as I read the next three sections. The passages described the function of this divine double in our own enChristment, which is to make way for our own Ascended Master selves to enter the physical form. "Axiatonal lines," which I believe are the same as Ka Channels, were described as corresponding to the acupuncture meridians. These lines, or meridians, were described as the keys not only to physical health but, when properly aligned with our higher-dimensional selves, as capable of regeneration of organs and the opening to the descension of our Christed Selves into our bodies. Basically, the book outlined what needs to be accomplished in order for the mass enlightenment to take place on a person-by-person level though it did not explain how it was to be done. The Pleiadian Lightwork is precisely about how to accomplish this worthy and timely task. That was as clear a confirmation as I could have ever imagined receiving, and my enthusiasm soared.

The next thing that came strongly into the foreground of my life, after weeks of hints, was the need to write. Within twenty-four hours of *The Keys of Enoch* experience, two friends approached me with the question, "When are you going to start your book?" I had not told either of these people that I had any ideas about writing. And yet, there they were, telling me. Shahan said that for weeks, every time she went to her medicine wheel at the lake to meditate, a book would float in the air above the circle. She said it was by me and edited by her and when would we start? Then Beth, a graduate of the first intensive, called. She had just done her first introductory evening to Pleiadian Lightwork in Georgia, and had been successful in having a great turnout. The majority of the attendees were interested either in classes or private work. But what had surprised her the most was that Ra had come into the presentation with a message for the group, announcing, "Keep an eye out for Amorah's book, which will be out in the next year to year and a half. The word Ka is scarcely known by a handful of people now. But in upcoming times it will be an important buzzword for many. . . ." After relaying Ra's message, Beth said to me, "I didn't know you were writing a book. When will it be out?" My honest reply was, "I didn't really know for sure either, but I guess I'd better get busy."

At that point in the conversation, I was given an image of the front cover of a book on which were written the words, "IT'S TIME NOW." At the time I assumed the words on the cover were the title;

later I realized they were a message to me. Years before, when the Pleiadians had disappeared, Ra had said, "When the time is right we'll be together again. . . ." Months before I had asked the Pleiadians why the healing work was being introduced at this particular time and not sooner. Ra had replied, "It's time now," simply and clearly that.

Chapter 3

IT'S
TIME NOW

The message that "It's time now" for the spiritual revolution and awakening of the evolutionary purpose of all of life seems paradoxical in a society that still values money and capital gain above human life, and "survival of the fittest" above integrity. Even the term *evolution* has had a very limited definition in this society. *Webster's New World Dictionary* defines *evolution* as the following: "1. an unfolding, opening out, or working out; process of development as from a single to a complex form, or of gradual progressive change, as in a social and economic structure 2. a result or product of this; thing evolved 3. a) a movement that is part of a series or pattern b) a pattern produced, or seemingly produced, by such a series of movements 4. a setting free or giving off, as of gas in a chemical reaction 5. a) the development of a species, organism, or organ from its original or primitive state to its present or specialized state; phylogeny or ontogeny b) Darwinian Theory." (Mathematical and military definitions excluded.)

In my understanding, evolution and spirit are inseparable, although not even remotely connected in *Webster's* or in modern life by the average person. Most people still believe that we live on the only inhabited planet in existence . . . where every human or other lifeform lives only once and dies forever . . . where the value of every lifeform and substance is measured in dollar signs . . . where only the smallest number of special people recognized by established churches are able to communicate and experience direct relationship with God, angels, or Ascended Masters . . . and where the idea of spiritual evolution to a state of self-realization, enlightenment, and ascension is considered either blasphemous or psychotic.

Across the planet, there has been steady growth in the number of people who have begun to believe differently. These people have awareness of, or communicate with, lifeforms from other places. They see a spiritual evolution that goes beyond this lifetime. The members of this current minority are aware of the inherent sacredness of all things. They are opening to their own God Presence as well as communication with angels, guides, and Ascended Masters. These awakening ones have chosen a path toward self-realization, enlightenment, and/or ascension. Though this group is by far a small minority, we who are members of this group are growing in numbers all the time, and we are finding a louder and louder voice in this world.

The paradox of spiritual evolutionaries living in a capitalistic evolutionary society is becoming more and more obvious. It will continue to become even more so as time marches on at an ever-accelerating pace. We have become a spiritual movement in a non-spiritual society.

This spiritual movement takes many forms: professionals leaving organized religions to discover meditation and introduce it in the workplace; societal drop-outs; alternative healing professions; spiritual workshops, tapes, books, and meditation groups; December 31 worldwide prayers and meditations for peace; and most importantly, individuals like you and me who are questioning the value of living in a world like this one and are exploring the alternatives both internally and externally in our lives. We are exploring these alternatives by examining our own thoughts, feelings, and actions. We are asking questions of ourselves: Does what I do harm anyone else or the planet in any way? Would I want my thoughts or judgments to create my reality or anyone else's? Am I ready to care more about my impact on Earth, people, and other lifeforms than I do about getting ahead at all costs? Am I trying to control the people and circumstances of my world, or am I living in alignment with the ideals of sovereignty for all—"win/win" instead of "may the best man win"? Do I genuinely care about and feel compassion (not sympathy) for others, whether I know them or not? Do I pray for my chosen enemies, or curse them and wish them harm? Do I forgive, or blame and hold grudges?

The list of questions could go on and on, but the point is that we all need to take responsibility for how we are creating and cocreating reality every moment of our lives with every thought and action. "It's time now" to take a spiritual inventory and plan where we go from here. Our impact on one another and the world in general is a fact. In order to spiritually evolve on our planet from this point forth, we must take that fact into consideration and let it matter deeply. We can no longer create autonomously at the expense of others without suffering ourselves. The spiritual laws have been changing and are continuing to change. We are now required not only to be "decent, good folks," but to live impeccably every moment of our lives. The time for psychic fascination, intellectual, or slow, "I'll worry about that tomorrow" spirituality is over. These comments are not intended to scare, judge, or intimidate anyone—just to offer some simple spiritual reality updates. This millennium is almost over. What we do now with ourselves, our relationships, and our lives will determine the next millennium's inheritance.

Who Are the Pleiadian Emissaries of Light?

Whenever we come to the end of a major evolutionary cycle, usually every 5200 years or 26,000 years, the Pleiadian Emissaries of Light make themselves known. They are a collective group with diverse responsibilities and roles, including that of guardians of Earth and this solar system. As guardians, they come to awaken us to where we are in our evolution and to what is needed in order to take the next steps. Their information applies not only to our planet as a whole, but to individuals who have a personal connection with the Pleiadians, as I do.

When my needs are genuine, my Pleiadian friends always seem to appear. Whether my needs are for personal healing and clearing, information, or, at times, simple reassurance—or perhaps for reawakening more of my memories of my purpose and service here on Earth—the Pleiadians always assist me in appropriate and meaningful ways. There are different kinds of beings with different functions within the Pleiadian Emissaries of Light, and they have met a wide variety of needs along the way. Not all Pleiadians are members of this group, however.

Ra, the being who always speaks to me instructionally and philosophically, is part of what is called the Pleiadian Archangelic Tribes of the Light. These archangels serve as wards of Earth and our solar system. There are four of these Archangelic Tribes that are delineated by the color they emanate: the golden yellow, the scarlet red, the clear sky blue, and the gentle emerald green. There are many beings of each color, and all beings of the same color share the same name.

All of the golden yellow Pleiadian Archangelic Tribe members are called Ra and are the keepers of divine wisdom, which is the product of all experience. The blue beings are named Ptah, and they are the protectors and preservers of the eternal nature of life. Ma-at is the title given to the red beings who are the spiritual warriors; they hold the energy of divine courage, which is beyond fear. There are more of the Ma-at beings incarnated on Earth at this time than any of the other three archangelic groups. The green beings are referred to as An-Ra, and they hold the energy of divine compassion and understanding.

Some of the Pleiadian Archangels make conscious links with human beings, as Ra has done with me. Others specialize in interstellar and planetary communications that are centralized in Alcyone, the central sun of the Pleiades. Still other Pleiadian Archangels work with humans during our dreamtime and show us possibilities beyond what we have presumed to be physical limitations. At times they orchestrate special healing dreams to help us release the past and continue growing, or to find new ways of expressing ourselves that are more commensurate with who we are becoming. Now they are beginning to facilitate the remembrance and teaching of ancient healing modalities, such as the Pleiadian Lightwork contained in chapters 5 to 14.

Another type of interface with humans and Earth occurred in the winter of 1992. The Pleiadian Emissaries of Light succeeded in making out-of-body space travel almost instantaneous between Earth and the Pleiadian cluster for those of us experiencing human lifetimes. There was a celebration at that time with a great gathering of human lightworkers and members of the Galactic Federation, including the Pleiadian Emissaries of Light, which I was privileged to attend. I was also blessed to experience this "no time and space" travel when I was taken to a planet in one of the solar systems of the Pleiades and back again. Going there and coming back each took place in a matter of seconds.

The planet I was taken to was incredible. The Pleiadians who inhabit it have created the equivalent of a planetwide museum where every species that has ever existed in this galaxy, including those extinct on Earth, still lives. There are groves of tree species that have been extinct on Earth since prehistoric times. Caretaking of the museum is one of the inhabitants' fondest responsibilities.

The list of specialties of the Pleiadian Archangelic Tribes and the Pleiadian Emissaries of Light has barely been touched upon, yet I have given you a general sense of the vast range of their expertise and dedication. The psychic surgeons and healers are the other members of the Pleiadian Emissaries of Light with whom I am privileged to work. They are not Pleiadian Archangels [my shortened name for the Pleiadian Angelic Tribes of the Light], but they do work closely with them. Loosely speaking, the Pleiadian Archangels are their instructors who delegate to them what is to be done. Just as we on Earth have a Higher Council of Twelve that oversees everything in our solar system, the Pleiadian Archangelic Tribes of the Light serve that function in the Pleiades. As we have angels, guides, Ascended Masters, and teachers working under our Higher Council of Twelve, likewise the Pleiadians have many groups serving the Pleiadian Archangels. These archangels in turn have a broader-based Supreme Being they serve, just as our Higher Council does.

These hierarchies are not ones of masters and servers in the sense of some being "better than" and some "less than." The structure is simply based on the particular essential nature of all beings who, when reaching certain levels of evolution, deeply desire to give to and serve others. From what I have been given to understand, this desire is based on Divine Love that is beyond most humans' ability to comprehend. It is also motivated by the same thing that keeps us growing: the desire for an end to separation and to be One with God/Goddess/All That Is. These higher beings long to be fully One with us again.

The Archangelic Tribe names—Ra, An-Ra, Ma-at, and Ptah—may be familiar to you as they were frequently used in ancient Egypt, especially for royalty. The Egyptians were more advanced spiritually in ancient times than they are currently. The Pleiadians, including the Archangelic Tribes, were commonly in communication with the ancient Egyptians who were able to respond to them during their height of spiritual advancement. The Pleiadians taught them much of their spiritual knowledge, healing practices, development of full sensory perception, and understanding of Earth's purpose within the solar system, galaxy, and far beyond.

Many Pleiadians took on human bodies in ancient Egypt, while others worked in higher dimensions with the dreamers, seers, healers, priests and priestesses, and even the royalty. Their common purposes were: the overall evolution of the planet and the human race; and to store enough higher knowledge here on Earth so that, when the time came for the Great Awakening, what would be needed would be here. Of course, Egypt was not the only civilization to receive such gifts.

The Pleiadian/Christ Connection and Purpose

While under hypnosis once, I recalled a Mayan past lifetime in 10 BC in which there was a large gathering of all the Mayan tribes to celebrate the completion of the largest pyramid ever built by their culture at that time. It was an extremely tall structure that had an opening in the upper chamber as well as an entryway at the base. The striking thing about this pyramid was that it was constructed of a white granite-type of rock with large veins of gold—so much gold that it looked marbleized with large glimmering streaks throughout.

As the Maya were beginning their ceremony and celebration, a transparent gateway with clear crystalline steps opened in the air just above the top of the pyramid. A group of the Pleiadian Archangels filed out and began to congratulate the people on their structural feat and share with them its true purpose. The temple itself was a higher-dimensional gateway and ascension chamber. We were all overjoyed to see our beloved Pleiadian friends, who had long been spiritual teachers and guardians for our people. So, when the Pleiadians instructed us to go into the pyramid, we did so without hesitation. After we were all inside, I saw a spiraling ramp that went all the way up to the windowlike opening near the top. Soon afterward the Sun began to shine through the opening until it lit up the interior of the pyramid, which gleamed golden. As the Sun entered, it exactly illuminated the ramp, which became overlighted with a scarlet red, writhing, etheric Quetzalcoatl, the feathered serpent deity. In its belly was the face of the Christ, who said, "Now you will know me."

The Pleiadian Archangels explained to us that the Christ would be born in only a few years and that we would know the timing of his birth by the appearance of a great new star in the sky. They further explained his role on Earth as a representative of the collective cosmic Christ and told about the 144,000 "chosen ones" from that collective who would be the minimum number to be awakened during his lifetime through meeting him. To prepare Earth vibrationally for the Christ's birth, many of the 144,000 who were on Earth at that time would either die consciously or ascend. This was to take place beginning that day and continue until his birth.

At that point, many of us began to levitate. We became lighter and lighter until we literally vanished to third-dimensional eyes and ascended. As the Christ said, "I go to prepare a place for you," he disappeared through the upper chamber opening, still in the belly of the sacred feathered serpent. Those of us who ascended at that time followed him out through the opening, joining him inside the belly of Quetzalcoatl.

The next scene took place in the halls of the fifth-dimensional City of Light where the 144,000 plus the Christ were gathered, each appearing as we would in our next incarnation. We were reviewing and planning the events to come in preparation for them. We were told that a similar appearance by Pleiadian Archangels and the Christ took place in power spots all over the world: Machu Picchu, Glastonbury, Hawaii, Greece, Egypt, Africa, and Tibet. The "chosen ones" had been gathered from all of these cultures and brought together prior to being reborn into our lives with the Christ. The event and its timing had been preplanned long before. (During a channeling once, the Christ said that the term the "chosen ones" is a misinterpretation. It should be "the ones who chose," because this group consists of beings who chose long ago to give their service to Earth and her people by incarnating, forgetting who they were until certain points in their evolution, and then becoming enlightened and Christed. This set the pattern of spiritual evolution for others to follow.)

The day on Mt. Shasta, approximately one and one half years prior to the hypnosis session, when I was first told about the Pleiadian Lightwork Intensives I would be teaching, the Christ was so strongly present with the Pleiadians, and Ra specifically, that I realized there was a connection between them. Strangely enough, I had never made the association between them in my mind prior to that time. I had recently noticed that when the Pleiadians were present, so was the Christ, but I had not realized that this was anything more than coincidence.

I had been told previously that the Dolphin Brain Repatterning and Dolphin Star-Linking work were vital in the healing and preparation of our nervous systems for the ever-increasing frequencies of the Pleiadian Lightwork. And I was aware that the Pleiadian Lightwork, especially the Ka Channels aspect of the work, was needed to help in the divine alignment with and embodiment of the Higher Self. But now the link with the Christ was unmistakable, as well. If we as the human population are to make the quantum leap into Christ consciousness, many people will need very specific healings and openings to prepare for it. And that is the sole purpose of Pleiadian Lightwork: to clear the way for the Second Coming of Christ en masse. Mayan, Egyptian, and Hopi prophecies—and perhaps other spiritual sources of which I am unaware—have foretold of this time when we are to be awakened to states of mastery, enlightenment, and then Christ consciousness while still on Earth in human bodies.

This great and massive awakening is precisely what Jesus Christ came to prepare us for almost 2000 years ago. Many avatars and enlightened masters throughout the ages and from many different cultures have attained the same level of consciousness as he did. However, this book focuses on Christ-consciousness and the Pleiadian Lightwork connection because they are specifically relevant to our times as previously mentioned. In order to understand the purpose of the Christ, we must also realize that orthodox religions and the censoring of the Bible, which occurred around 150 years after his death, all but destroyed his true message. Yet we can still find glimpses of it even in the King James version of the Bible. "Be ye as perfect as I am" and "You shall do even greater things than I have done" are unmistakable invitations to choose spiritual evolution, enlightenment, and ascension, and to let go of limitation on all levels. These messages are invitations to let go of the idea of a chosen *few* and to realize that we all are chosen; it is up to each of us to choose whether our answer is "Yes" or "No."

The Christ's murder was a result of his defiance of governmental and religious rule over the common people. He taught the masses that they were equal in God's eyes to all those who pretended to be their superiors—whether they were statesmen or kings, priests or tax collectors. He taught them to respect themselves and to be willing to question authority in order to find truth.

The Christ walked Earth showing the commoners that miracles happen, and that miracles are natural phenomena when people are in direct alignment with their God Presences. He healed the sick and raised the dead, all the while encouraging the onlookers to believe they could do the same things. When he said he was the "son of God," he was also telling the people that they were the sons and daughters of God. He told people God loved them and wanted them to be well and happy, and he brought that about in his followers and listeners in order to demonstrate it.

His disciples, who were both men and women, by the way, were from all walks of life: common people, wealthy people, and members of the Goddess temples, like Mary Magdalene, who was also his wife. There were thousands of disciples by the time of the crucifixion in addition to the twelve spoken of in the Bible. All of these disciples opened spiritually to gifts of healing, prophecy, and visioning. They proved that what Jesus said was true. One after another, the disciples performed miracles, and even initiated others into spiritual awakening as the Christ did.

Much of the Christ's empowerment came through awakened women. For the first twelve years of his life, he was taught by the Goddess embodied: Mother Mary, her mother Anna, and others. Then, at age twelve, as was the natural course for males, he went to the learned men for sharing and teaching. He traveled to Egypt and India and was initiated in the pyramids. He learned ancient healing-temple practices and mystery-school initiatic teachings. He learned dominion over the body functions from old yogic practices, and secrets of longevity and conscious death. He taught these things, as well as what he learned naturally through communication with God/Goddess/All That Is, the angels, and Melchizedek. He shared them with his disciples, who practiced the disciplines and gradually awakened as well.

The governments and churches at that time were very threatened by all of this. A population of self-mastered sovereign beings would soon outgrow the need for those who proclaimed to be authorities. When humans open to their full sensory awareness and spiritual heritage, they easily perceive deceit, unkindness, and injustice in others. The so-called authorities can then no longer hide behind high offices and intimidation; they are dethroned or simply never put into high positions in the first place. The threat of these possible changes led to the crucifixion, with the hopes that the populace would take to heart this frightening example of what would face them if they continued pursuing such radical ways.

Today, the corruption in our worldwide governments and churches is no secret. We even have movies and books about it, and yet it continues to worsen every day. So here we are nearly 2000 years A.D., still living on a planet where the masses are controlled by the few and are too scared, numbed out, or lazy to do anything about it. Spiritual awakening is the only cure to this vastly spread social disease, for the magnetic pull on Earth at this time to remain powerless and socially conformist is stronger than ever. Spiritual awakening is what the Christ, with much help, began to prepare us for during his time on Earth.

Now we are coming to the Age of Light—a time of reawakening. In order for us to evolve as a species, we must become one world. We must bring together the purity of the ancient sacred spiritual teachings of the major eight cultures and their ancient Pleiadian teachers. All people must drop their differences now and choose divine love and harmony with all things and all beings—whether they be human, animal, or sentient. All must win from this new Harmonic Convergence. So, as the Pleiadians and the Christ have said to me in numerous situations, "It's time now."

The Pleiadian Emissaries of Light and many other extraterrestrial groups from this galaxy and far beyond are very excited about what is happening on Earth at this time. Have you ever wondered why so many extraterrestrials, angels, and Ascended Masters are much more available than they used to be? Or why we are being watched and guided so carefully now? According to the Pleiadians, it is because we are at the point in our evolution here on Earth when we have an opportunity to make a tremendous paradigm shift. If accomplished, this shift would be so great that not only would it eradicate all karma for the entire solar system, but it would set free planets and star systems throughout our entire galaxy and several galaxies beyond.

What is so unique about us and this time? In order to answer that question, the next chapter presents information channeled to me by Ra, who is the spokesperson for the Pleiadian Emissaries of Light and the Archangelic Tribes. Ra's cosmological overview of Earth's current and future role in this galaxy will help you understand why "It's time *now*."

Chapter 4

RA SPEAKS

Since I channeled this chapter and most of the processes in the workbook section, I want to clarify what I mean when I say I channel information or Light Beings. I *never* bring other entities into my body, nor do I intend to. Doing so is extremely hard on the body, sometimes even dangerous, except in rare cases. Most entities or disincarnate beings who come into a human body do not know how to take care of the body so that it remains unharmed by the experience. Besides, bringing an entity into the body is just simply unnecessary.

I am extremely clairaudient as well as clairvoyant, clairsentient, and intuitive. (Respectively, I have full sensory hearing, vision, feeling, and knowing.) I channel by first going into a full multidimensional Higher Self alignment similar to what is described in chapter 13. After that, one of two things happens. An etheric being may stand in front of or above me, presenting itself to my clairvoyant vision and talking to me. If I am teaching a class or giving a private session, I then repeat its message word for word. If I am alone, I merely listen and assimilate, or write the message down.

Alternatively, with the Pleiadians more than with the Ascended Masters, I may receive words through my Higher Self channel and spontaneously voice them or type them into my computer. When this happens, I do not know what is to be said prior to my speaking or typing the message. I do, however, hear the words inside my head as they are transmitted to me, since I always remain in my body. Afterward I can usually remember the essence of what was said, but not the details. This is because I am in a trance, or altered state, during such a transmission. Even though I am in my body, my consciousness is operating from a deeper state; this state is of a higher frequency than the one in which I have normal conversations with my eyes open. The following material was channeled in this manner.

Ra is the spokesperson for the collective Pleiadians Emissaries of Light and Pleiadian Archangels assigned to communicate with and teach me. The following is a message from Ra:

You and your planet are undergoing a unique and wondrous transition in your spiritual evolution at this time. You are preparing for a quantum leap unlike any that has ever occurred before. In order to help you understand this more fully, I must first tell you about the orbit of the entire galaxy around the Great Central Sun of All That Is. Just like your "solar ring"—our term for "solar system"—orbits around the Galactic Center, the galaxy itself moves through space in the form of continual, connecting circles, like a great cosmic spiral. At the completion point of a multibillion-year single circular orbit around the Great Central Sun, our galaxy connects diagonally to the next ring on the great cosmic spiral. When this diagonal move from one ring of the great cosmic spiral to the next takes place, all of the planets, solar systems, and their inhabitants simultaneously take an initiatic step into a new evolutionary cycle. This is occurring now. You are not only at the end of a 26,000-year Earth/Sun/Pleiadian cycle; the entire Pleiadian system, which includes this solar ring, is at the end of a 230,000,000-year orbit around the Galactic Center, and the entire galaxy is at the completion of its infinitely longer orbit around the Great Central Sun. All three cycles are synchronistically completing the last step of the spiral dance-within-a-dance-within-a-dance, making this a very crucial transition time. The objective is to finish the dance and begin the new one without anyone's toes getting stepped on. Then the next, more sophisticated and gracious dance will begin right on time.

What this adds up to in terms of Earth's planetary evolution is this: when the 100,000-year Ice Age ended nearly 150,000 years ago, the galaxy was midway in its diagonal shift to the next ring on the great cosmic spiral—the old dance had ended, and the new one was being prepared for. In order to prepare for the next evolutionary spiral, the entire galaxy entered into a cleanup period of past karmic patterns that will be complete at the end of the year 2012.

Karmic cleanup always happens at the end of a major cycle. Whatever is left unresolved from the previous evolutionary spiral is brought to the surface and acted out one last time for the purpose of transmutation and transcendence. When this housecleaning is completed, a different evolutionary cycle in relationship to God/Goddess/All That Is begins. This housecleaning is being completed now.

Rebirth and initiatic spiritual leaps are experienced during such a transitional time. The consciousnesses birthed are products of new paradigms, and new potentials, and they benefit from all of the learning of the previous spiral, although they do so unconsciously. Metaphorically, it is like you take all of the dance steps you learned in previous lessons, polish up on the rough spots, master them, and then begin to add new steps that are much more exciting and challenging. Even the rhythm of the music speeds up, adding more inspiration.

When the next ring on the great cosmic spiral of the galaxy and Earth's next 26,000-year cycle begin simultaneously in the year 2013, the following will have already taken place: (1) Pole shifts will have repositioned Earth in relationship to the Sun. (2) The Sun will have simultaneously been repositioned with a similar pole shift relative to the Pleiades. (3) The Pleiades will have undergone a spiral completion, which will have repositioned that system relative to Orion. (4) Orion will have undergone a complete upheaval and spiritual housecleaning. The entire Orion system will have been darkened for a period of what on Earth would be twenty-four hours, and there will have been pole shifts of every star and planet in that system. Vaporization of many of the planets in that system, and a reopening and rededication of Orion as a galactic gateway to the Galactic Center of this galaxy and beyond, will have been completed. Sirius has been serving that function for roughly the last 300,000 years, since the Lyrans invaded Orion and interfered with access to the galactic gateway there. (5) Sirius will have been elevated to the position of a *galactic* spiritual mystery school, instead of one operating specifically for this solar ring and regional arm of the galaxy. (6) Instead of the current orbital pattern of your solar ring around Alcyone, central sun of the Pleiades, the entire Pleiadian system will begin to orbit around Sirius. Sirius will be the new central sun for this arm of the galaxy, and the Pleiades will have become part of the Sirius star system.

At the beginning of 2013, when all of these preparations have been completed, the entire Pleiadian system, which includes your Sun as its eighth star, will become a system of higher learning and home to Cities of Light. Cities of Light are places where entire populations are spiritually aware of evolution and the sacredness of all things. All residents of Cities of Light recognize and live for the evolution and growth of themselves as individuals, of the rest of the group, and of all existence. In other words, their lives are dedicated to serving the Divine Plan, and they are, at the very least, at the level of Christ consciousness. Earth and your solar ring are the last in the Pleiadian system to make this shift. All of the rest of the seven Pleiadian solar rings, the Seven Sisters, are presently actualized as mystery schools and homes of Cities of Light; each of these seven solar rings will elevate to its next natural higher-evolutionary function when the new dance called the Age of Light begins in 2013.

Prior to the shift at the end of 2012 and the beginning of 2013, Earth will undergo a spiritual and physical housecleaning corresponding to what have commonly been called "Earth changes." These changes, which have already begun, intensify both externally and internally as your solar ring moves deeper into the photon band, a high-frequency cosmic emanation from the Galactic Center. You have been in and out of the edges of this photon band for a few years now, and, by the year 2000, will be completely immersed in this band for the next 2000 years. Sacred encodings, necessary for your solar ring's spiritual awakening and evolutionary leap, will be transmitted to the Sun, Earth, and all of your solar ring via the Galactic Center, Sirius, Alcyone, and Maya, which is also one of the stars of the Pleiades. Once these initial transmissions are completed, your Sun will continue to transmit the encodings to the entire solar ring. These photonic emanations and encodings will be of such extremely high-vibrational transmissions that they will require that your central nervous systems, emotional bodies, and electrical bodies be well-tuned in order to be capable of withstanding them. [Author's Note: Barbara Hand Clow gives a much more detailed description and story about the photon band and the cosmological changes in dimensional relationships we are undergoing in her latest book, *The Pleiadian Agenda: A New Cosmology for the Age of Light*.]

Many of you are already experiencing an intensification in your own growth and clearing processes as your planet goes in and out of the edges of the photon band. The increase in frequencies will continue to accelerate without letup for the next seventeen years, until the galaxy as a whole is fully anchored in its new orbital pattern, and Earth is initiated as a mystery school and home for the Cities of Light.

Floods, earthquakes, changes in land masses, volcanic eruptions, and finally a complete pole shift will all take place within the remaining years prior to the year 2013, at which time the galactic solar initiation of Earth will take place. You who now live on Earth must choose whether or not you are ready to become spiritually responsible human beings in order to remain on Earth beyond that time. Those who do not wish to remain on Earth will be taken to another planet in a different part of the galaxy where karmic lessons and third-dimensional evolution will continue. Those who do intend to stay must learn the new dance of the Age of Light that requires opening and activation of the Divine Ka. Unless the Ka is fully functional, your bodies simply will not be able to withstand the frequency increases as the ever-intensifying photonic light fills the atmosphere of your planet and the bodies of all who remain. So, the appropriate and only attire that is acceptable for the new dance is your *Ka-stume*.

Harmonic Convergence in 1987 was a planetary wakeup call notifying all planetary citizens to learn the new dance and embrace a "win/win" philosophy in order to make it to the 2013 shift in planetary focus. It was indeed a message to learn about cocreation for the mutual benefit of all affected, and to understand mind-linking with higher collective consciousness. This event was not actually limited to the two-day experience that occurred at that time. There is an ongoing twenty-five-year Harmonic Convergence, with many activation days for renewing your commitment to the spiritualization of Earth and her people.

[Author's Note: Once, in a hypnosis session, I was taken to a place outside Earth's atmosphere where the higher collective consciousness of all of Earth's people exists. In this place, I saw billions of smiling, loving faces without bodies, encircling the planet from just outside a clear bubble surrounding Earth. This higher collective consciousness was exclusively made up of loving, sweet, intelligent, innocent Light Beings: all of us living on Earth. These beautiful ones were observing and sending love and encouragement through the bubble to their counterparts on the planet's surface. They also watched from a perspective of facilitating the greatest good for the whole. At the time, I was only allowed to observe. As a whole, they were planning a large earthquake; I later realized it was the quake that occurred in Japan in early 1995. Observations were being made about the robotlike behavior of the people, their absorption in materialism, and their lack of deep loving connections. The consensus decision within the higher collective consciousness to ask for an earthquake in Japan was not by any stretch of the imagination a punishment. The beings were emanating love and goodwill to that part of the planet in a concentrated way, hoping the quake would awaken the people from their spiritual sleep and help them rearrange their priorities in life and become more loving and cooperative with one another. In fact, there was a feeling of delight and joy among the beings of the higher collective consciousness because they had found a way to help their human counterparts evolve.

In response to their decision, a message was sent to Sirian ships at the edge of Earth's atmosphere to begin the process of creating an earthquake. I was shown later the process that was used to accomplish this task. Throughout the layers of what we call Earth's atmosphere there are many circular rings of plates that correspond to the tectonic plates of Earth's surface. These multiple layers of plates are geometric in nature and continue beneath Earth's surface to approximately the inner core of the planet, which is about a half mile in diameter. When an Earth change is to be brought about, the Sirians shift the atmospheric plates in the farthest outer layer from Earth first. All of the atmospheric plates are then realigned layer by layer to match the exact proposed position of the tectonic plates in order to effect the desired change. When the outer layers are completed, the inner subterranean plates are shifted to correspond to the outer ones. Finally, the earthquake happens, realigning the tectonic plates with the new positions of the atmospheric and subterranean plates. Volcanic eruptions, floods, and other planetary changes are brought about in much the same manner.

There are also planetary changes that occur naturally when the inner and outer plates shift on their own in response to pressure buildups, contamination by pollution and psychic energy, holes in the ozone layer, reduction in rain forests (which changes the atmospheric balance), excessive mining, geothermal tapping, and government-engineered underground explosions and experiments. At times, natural "disasters" are lessened by the Sirians in response to requests from the higher collective consciousness. People on Earth can assist in this process by aligning with higher consciousness through meditation and living rightly. I am aware of several earthquakes and volcanic eruptions that have been lessened or prevented in this way since 1990, mainly due to the alignment of human consciousness with higher collective consciousness.

One volcanic eruption was prevented in Mt. Shasta in 1991, for example. Early that year, I was given a clear vision and message that Mt. Shasta would erupt in November. Within one week of that prophetic experience, I ran into a local astrologer who told me he was predicting a volcanic eruption in November as well. He told me about his prediction without first knowing of my own. The same week, word came to me that a local Native American medicine woman had received identical information about the predicted event and timing. In late August that year, I stood outside in the rain and watched the most amazing electrical storm I had ever seen. Unusually wide bolts of extremely sharp and bright lightning poured from the mountain and dissipated high up in the atmosphere. There were several such storms over a three-day period after which a deep calm coming from Earth, and Mt. Shasta in particular, could be felt by sensitive people. I was told that enough people had cleared and transmuted the buildup of emotional and lower astral negativity that the hierarchies had intervened and assisted in dissipating the built-up charge in the mountain that would otherwise have been released as a volcanic eruption. As myself and others who were consciously involved in spiritual growth, meditation, and alignment with higher consciousness were clearing the atmosphere on the surface of Earth, the Sirians shifted atmospheric plates to match the shift in the tectonic and subterranean plates that had been occurring. When the plates in the atmosphere were realigned, and the built-up electrical charge was released through lightning, there was no longer a need for a volcanic eruption.]

Ra speaks again:

When a person has reached a certain point in the evolution of consciousness, he or she may be living in an area where a massive earthquake or flood kills everyone, yet he or she simply ascends to the next dimensional level vibrationally and experiences a spiritual elevation instead of death. This person may even assist others who are ready to embrace the Light in making the vibrational shift. In areas of large quakes, floods, fires, and other Earth changes where fear, denial, hate, greed, and anger have created dense, lower-astral, amorphous energy planes, souls can become entrapped in these illusionary realities at death. However, Light Beings are always there to assist those who are willing to free themselves. Beings who ascend, instead of experiencing physical death at those times, can elevate the entire area around them to a light field where those who wish to evolve and enter the light may take refuge and make the transition smoothly. Those who perform this service chose to do so prior to entering this lifetime, and generally have past-life experience working with souls going through the death transition.

There is nothing to be feared. Those who are genuinely committed to the Light and are living in it will simply move to their next higher alternative. Others will be given choices every step of the way; they can choose to progress spiritually through their experiences, or remain in fear and illusion. It is vital that all judgment be suspended with regard to those whose bodies are killed in these Earth changes. Some people will choose natural "disasters" as ways of leaving because their higher consciousnesses realize that their human selves have gone too far into illusion to change in this life-time. Others will exit Earth in this way in order to assist beings move into the Light during the death transition and to set the pattern of ascension, as mentioned previously. Yet others will choose this way of dying because they are ready to leave Earth and go to the next planet of their evolutionary choice. Still others will die physically because their body genetics and cellular mutations are too extreme to be transmuted in the remaining time for transformational process on this planet. Regardless of why a person's body dies, or, in the case of ascension, appears to die, the collective higher consciousness has a significant enough influence to see to it that there are no accidents. Those who leave the physical world are intended to leave. Those who remain on Earth will have the responsibility of assisting one another both in physical survival and in spiritual evolution.

By the year 2013, everyone who remains on Earth must under-stand the following four evolutionary principles: (1) The human purpose on Earth is to evolve physically, emotionally, mentally, and spiritually. (2) Every human being has a Divine Essence made of light and love whose nature is goodness. (3) Free will is an absolute uni-versal right; impeccability calls on the self to surrender its free will to divine will in faith and trust. (4) All of natural existence is sacred beyond how it serves or meets the needs of the individual self.

At this time, every human alive is being presented with these four spiritual principles in subtle or direct ways. It is a planetary law that before the end of a major time cycle, such as the one occurring at this time, every single living person must be reminded of the four evolutionary principles they are expected to embrace. Some people will receive these messages through books such as this one, *Return of the Bird Tribes*, *The Celestine Prophecy*, *The Fifth Sacred Thing*, *Mutant Message Down Under*, and *The Pleiadian Agenda: A New Cosmology for the Age of Light*, as well as others. Others will receive these messages through movies such as *Dances with Wolves*, *Little Buddha*, *Star Trek IV: The Return to Earth*, and *The Emerald Forest*. [Titles provided by author, not by Ra.] Others will have death experiences and return to their physical bodies changed and able to affect change in their loved ones. Many people will have visitations from angels, Ascended Masters, or Mother Mary; such visitations have already been reported often in this century. The message of evolutionary consciousness and sacredness will also be given subconsciously to all who see, wear, or hold certain objects such as crystals and gemstone jewelry. These are only examples of ways in which the planetary movement to impart the four spiritual truths takes place.

Your part in all of this is to live right, learn about and practice impeccability, pray to know the Divine Plan and your part in it, and heal and clear yourself on all levels as much as possible. On a collective level, there are seven primary karmic patterns that need to be cleared and transcended at this time. The patterns that are currently being exaggerated in order to bring them into your awareness so that you can transform them are: arrogance, addiction, prejudice, hatred, violence, victimhood, and shame. These seven sources of pain, illusion, and separation are listed in the order they developed in this solar ring—beginning on Venus and expanding on Mars, Maldek, and finally Earth. How they have culminated on Earth is so obvious that it seems pointless to elaborate very much.

Whether the United States has an attitude of supremacy in the world or a New Ager has an attitude of being superior to less aware, nonspiritual people, the attitude is still called arrogance. Whether an alcoholic lies in the gutter in Los Angeles or a person obsesses about his/her physical appearance or the body of his/her mate, this pattern is still called addiction. Whether the KKK burn crosses in black people's yards or a spiritual person looks down on a "redneck," it is still called prejudice. Whether capitalists hate communists or the "politically correct" person hates the loggers and builders, the attitude is still called hatred. Whether the United States creates war in Vietnam or Central America or a parent spanks and degrades a child, the activity is still called violence. Whether Native Americans, Aborigines, or other indigenous people are killed and have their land destroyed by white people or squirrels and deer are killed by unaware people driving too fast, the problem is still victimhood. Whether Germany bears the scars of Hitler or poor people feel unworthy because of their poverty, the feeling is still called shame. From the most obvious to the most subtle, each person individually must do his/her part to recognize and heal these patterns. The variations of individual expression of these seven main karmic issues are many. However, if you look closely enough, you can see that the source of every problem on Earth today is one or more of these seven solar-ring karmic patterns. These patterns are accompanied by the absence of awareness of the four evolutionary principles, which must now be learned.

[Author's Note: The seven karmic patterns listed above are general to this solar ring, although their resolution is being worked out on Earth. There are also seven primary vices, or ego allurements, that are specific to the Incan mystery school teachings and to planet Earth. They are: lust, laziness, gluttony, pride, anger, envy, and greed. In the Incan teachings, humans must overcome these ego allurements prior to attaining spiritual power.]

For those of you who have mastered the behavioral and attitudinal levels of these patterns, or are sincerely working on them, your next step is conscious alignment with your Higher Self, higher collective consciousness, and Divine Oneness. This is the purpose of this workbook. It is the desire of the Pleiadian Emissaries of Light to assist those of you who wish to prepare for Earth changes, evolve, and ascend to do just that. We [the Pleiadians] have always made ourselves consciously available to beings of this solar ring during times of evolutionary cycle changes, and now is no exception. You see, when we began to interact with individuals and groups on Earth in the early part of this century, 100 years prior to the end of the current 26,000-year cycle, the people of Earth had asked for a chance to wake up on their own before any large-scale direct communications were made by the hierarchies: namely, the Pleiadians, Light Beings from Sirius, Andromedan Emissaries of Light, the Supreme Being, the Higher Council of Twelve, the Great White Brotherhood, and other, smaller spiritual groups. We [the Pleiadians] are among you both in bodies and etherically. Amorah Quan-Yin, Barbara Hand Clow, and numerous others are carrying the messages now as they and other Pleiadians have always done at the end of other major evolutionary cycles on this planet.

At the end of the last 26,000-year cycle on Earth, there were less than 1,500,000 humans left on the planet after the destruction brought on by the pole shifts and Earth changes at that time. This may sound like a lot, but when you consider that those people were spread out all over the planet, and that prior to that time the population of Earth had been close to 2,000,000,000 people, those humans remaining were few in number.

The collective higher consciousness was not as developed at that time, but it did exist, and this consciousness requested that mystery schools be established in every cultural group on the planet. All of the people on Earth were to have equal opportunity to learn and grow. As the younger souls whose bodies had died in the Earth changes were reborn onto Earth and the population began to increase again, the spiritual practices and teachings were to be well established, and the life styles commensurate with spiritual evolution and awareness. Even today, there are Native American and Mayan groups whose histories of spiritual practice are estimated to be roughly 25,000 years old. This is no coincidence. Pleiadian, Sirian, and Andromedan teachers precipitated bodies and helped organize various civilizations such as those in Machu Picchu, Egypt, and even Atlantis. Lemuria had lost most of its land mass and population, but the initiatic temples and teachings were preserved on what territory still remained in Hawaii and Mt. Shasta, California.

Different mystery schools were begun at each location, although the information and practices often overlapped. The Order of Melchizedek and the Temples of Alorah were established in Atlantis. Although the use of crystals had been developed extensively and then lost in previous times, the use of crystals for healing and multi-dimensional communications reemerged. Thoth brought solar initiations and consciousness to Egypt, along with advanced spiritual trainings such as teleportation, telekinesis, and merkabah travel through dimensions and beyond time and space. The Great Pyramid was also constructed during this time period for the purpose of receiving and transmitting solar encodings and initiations for the people of Egypt and the whole planet. Sacred dreaming was taught in every culture and evolved into shamanic practices, dream healing, and other means of multidimensional travel and communications.

The Pleiadians, Sirians, and Andromedans who taught the people and helped establish the mystery schools often traveled back and forth between dimensions. Many of them specialized in materializing and dematerializing their light bodies and served as go-betweens for Earth beings, subterranean civilizations, and the many lightships that were located around the planet at that time. As the young, less-evolved souls began to reincarnate around 25,000 years ago, the higher-dimensional teachers continued their relationships with humans for another 250 years in order to assist with the transition into civilizations consisting of many different levels of soul evolution and galactic origins. Some humans were still barely evolved beyond instinctual behavior and survival consciousness. Their next evolutionary step was to be born to more evolved parents, intermarry with more evolved beings, and thereby expand their level of awareness. Many of the Pleiadians accepted assignments as permanent guides for these young souls as the intermixing began; some of the Pleiadians even took on human lives and mated with humans in order to help clear the genetic patterns and awaken the urge for spiritual evolution. This process is sometimes referred to as "starseeding."

Everything was done in response to requests from, or agreements with, the higher collective consciousness of Earth dwellers. Earth beings had asked to form their own mystery schools and higher-dimensional initiatic schools by evolving, becoming enlightened, and remaining in the higher dimensions around Earth in order to assist their fellow humans. The Great White Brotherhood had previously existed for nearly 15,000 years, at which time there had been a simultaneous group awakening of over 1000 humans from various cultures on Earth. These 1000 unanimously had agreed to establish the Great White Brotherhood, which at that time was called the Order of the Great White Light, to set a precedent for spiritual enlightenment and transcendence on Earth.

Some of the members of this bodhisattva order chose to reincarnate from time to time as Ascended Master teachers. They experienced physical birth to spiritual parents and generally became enlightened again by age twenty-one. At that time, they remembered their own past lives, ascension, and spiritual purpose. These reincarnated bodhisattvas were wonderful and powerful teachers due to the fact that they had a more natural camaraderie with Earth people than those who had not been human before. At times, these Ascended Masters were—and still are today—born into younger-soul families with varying degrees of genetic damage and karmic patterning. These bodhisattvas took on the responsibility of transformation, transmutation, and transcendence of the lower energies in order to create etheric and consciousness "maps" for others to follow; they have been, and are, evolutionary forerunners.

The hierarchies agreed to expand the Order of the Great White Light to include enlightened and ascended humans for such roles as: the Office of the Christ; Buddha; the Order of Merlins; Goddess positions, such as that of the Holy Mother now held by Quan Yin and Mother Mary; kachinas; and regional teachers and guides. Prior to the beginning of the current 26,000-year cycle, higher-dimensional offices, guides, teachers, and planetary spiritual leaders had been mostly Light Beings from the Pleiades, Sirius, and Andromeda. Now the people were developing enough of their own enlightened and ascended beings to establish their own guides and mystery schools.

At the beginning of this 26,000-year cycle, it was also requested that, except at crucial cyclical and evolutionary turning points, higher teachings and guidance come from those enlightened ones who had experienced human incarnations. The people of Earth had to evolve to the point that they were capable of communicating with the higher dimensions and star systems themselves. This is where the Ka teachings came in. The people needed to understand how they could hope to accomplish their spiritual goals and become a race of masters on Earth. The Pleiadians taught them about their Higher Selves, the Ka through which they could permanently connect with their Higher Selves, the higher dimensions, and the star systems. By living right, evolving, meditating, praying, and mastering their consciousnesses, they could align with their Higher Selves. By awakening the Divine Ka, they could merge their Higher Selves with their physical bodies and embody their Divine Master Presences, or Christ Selves. There would be a period of time preceding their full enlightenment during which their genetic transmutations would be completed as a result of the flow of Ka energy through their Ka channels and minute circuitry into their astral bodies and physical bodies' nervous systems, glandular systems, and electrical meridian systems, such as those used in acupuncture and Shiatsu.

Over the following 5200 years, several thousand people who were initiated in the Ka Temples in Egypt and Atlantis became enlightened, and many of these people attained the next level, Christ consciousness, as well. Some chose to remain on Earth and were capable of living up to 2000 years in the same body by maintaining their Ka Channels and spiritual practices. That same 5200-year period also birthed other paths to enlightenment that were successful for the more evolved humans on the planet who were ready.

At the end of that 5200 years, there was a massive earthquake that destroyed most of the remaining temples of Lemuria and half of the land mass of Atlantis. Those members of the Lemurian race who remained on Earth chose to recolonize as a subterranean culture under Mt. Shasta. A few of the Lemurians integrated into Native American, Hawaian, and Tibetan tribes, later becoming Maya, Inca, and Buddhists. These former Lemurians served as spiritual leaders and teachers in those cultures. The Atlanteans who remained were still numerous enough to continue their culture. As a group consciousness, they asked for the being whose Earth name was Thoth to incarnate among their people and reestablish the ancient teachings that had been lost to them in the quakes. Thoth, who was a Ra member of the Pleiadian Archangelic Tribes, responded to their requests by precipitating a physical body. He became the spiritual leader of Atlantis.

Shortly after Thoth's arrival in Atlantis, there was a major breach in Earth's atmospheric time-space continuum during which a group of beings who had originally invaded Orion from the Lyran system arrived on Earth. Lucifer was leading them and helped them both create the breach and penetrate it afterward. This was accomplished by intense, high-frequency transmissions into Earth's atmosphere from outside the solar ring, followed by immediate transport of a ship through the breach it had created. The Orion beings, or Lyrans, with Lucifer's help, had mastered "no-time-and-space" travel, enabling them to project through the breach within seconds of its creation, before they could be stopped. Their interaction with Earth was inevitable at some point in time due to karmic connections between the Lyrans, Lucifer, and some of the humans on Earth. They landed in Atlantis as preplanned, because it was the place most conducive to their purpose. Immediately, they began to indoctrinate the Atlanteans with their "superior" knowledge of technology. The Atlanteans had taken pride in being the most evolved race on Earth at that time, and they were always searching for new areas of mastery. The Lyrans manipulated them with promises of unlimited power, technology, influence, and with demonstrations of Lyran "superiority" via technology, psychic control, and intelligence. The Atlanteans were promised that they could have those abilities, too, if they welcomed the Lyrans and allowed them to infiltrate their culture. Many Atlanteans were immediately distrustful of the Lyrans and discerned the spiritual trap that was being set. Others were more gullible and hungry for power and supremacy and welcomed the Lyrans wholeheartedly.

For the following 10,000 years, Atlantis was divided into two distinct population segments: one that included the Lyrans and excelled technologically, and one that remained spiritually pure and devoted. The Temples of Melchizedek were badly infiltrated by the controlling and manipulative invaders and their influence. A group called the Gray Robes, and later the Black Robes, was formed. Their focus was on the development of psychic power and black magic. Some of the Melchizedek priests remained pure, but more did not. There were Temples of Alorah in Atlantis at that time that housed Goddess-priestess orders whose teachings came from the ninth dimension through a hierarchical order called the Council of Nine. These teachings remained untainted by the Lyrans and Lucifer, and the priestesses openly defied and discouraged involvement with the Dark Brothers, as they were also called. Originally those Atlanteans who wished to practice the arts of magic and alchemy were first trained spiritually to ensure that they learned the right use of the powers. But eventually the spiritual protocol broke down, and training in psychic power and black magic became widespread. Lucifer was always invisible to the people but nonetheless was a major subconscious influence. He controlled the Lyran Dark Brotherhood and could possess the bodies of members of the Dark Brotherhood at any time in order to communicate with them or through them to other Atlanteans. Lucifer used this means of reaching the people often. His purpose was to break down the Atlanteans' trust in the forces of Light that ruled the planet and solar ring; eventually, he hoped to take control as Supreme Being on Earth.

Lucifer and the Dark Brothers penetrated the consciousnesses of many males on Earth who were vulnerable to psychic control due to their own shadow desire for control and domination, especially over females. A subterranean astral plane, as well as subterranean ceremonial grounds and dwellings, was created where the lower collective consciousness of the Dark Brotherhood established territory and sent energy waves and subliminal messages through Earth to the people on the surface. This collective consciousness was, and still is, what you call "Satan." It was created by a fusion of the lower consciousnesses of all members of the Dark Brotherhood. This Satanic force has the ability to operate as a single large entity. The bigger this collective consciousness grew, with its control and imposed supremacy over the Goddess, Earth, your solar ring, and Divinity, the more power this dark force had to generate its own continued growth. The polarization of Dark and Light intensified quickly on Earth as the subconscious minds of humans were bombarded with negative thoughts and images about distrust in God and the Divine Plan, the inferiority of females, and the superiority of the mental realm over the emotional and spiritual realms.

Technology and black magic grew to proportions never before experienced on Earth. The temples of Light became more and more the realm of females, and the temples of Darkness became more and more the realm of males. Of course, this division was not absolute, but it was true for the most part. By the end of the Atlantean era— 10,000 years after the arrival of Lucifer and the Lyrans—chaos and fear were rampant in that civilization. Competition for control and supremacy was the general attitude in Atlantis, and even in the Temples of Alorah, fear and hiding were prevalent.

Before the end of Atlantis, the leaders of the orders and temples that still held the Light were warned, and advised to disperse their teachings around the globe. It would be a long time before all of the higher knowledge could remain in any one place due to the Satanic influence upon the people of Earth. Therefore, people trained in all areas of spiritual development left Atlantis in small groups. They took with them many crystals containing Akashic Record information that had been channeled and programmed into them by the Council of Truth. One of the crystals that was removed and taken by the high priestesses of the Temples of Alorah to Greece was shaped like the skull of Thoth, who had left Atlantis almost 9000 years before. The crystal skull was buried beneath the Temple of the Oracle at Delphi—which this group of priestesses created—and served to protect the temple from the dark subliminal messages and energy waves sent from beneath Earth's surface. Since this temple could not be psychically polluted, the Dark Brotherhood, under the name of the "Warriors of Zeus," eventually imprisoned and killed the priestesses and claimed the temple for their patriarchal god.

Other groups took crystals and teachings to Central America, Western Europe, the Himalayas, South Africa, Eastern Asia, Australia, South America, and Egypt. (Indigenous tribes of North America were in their own unique evolutionary phase at that time, and therefore infiltration by the Atlanteans was inappropriate.) The largest group, consisting of both men and women, went to Egypt, as per the instructions from the Council of Nine. The people in all the groups were very dedicated to the preservation of divine truth, which is Light, and spent the rest of their lives establishing initiatic temples and teachings in the various countries. The reason the largest settlement was in Egypt was chiefly due to the existence of the Great Pyramid there; it had always held, and still holds today, the vibrations of divine truth and solar evolutionary encoding.

Many pyramids were to be constructed in Egypt as well as in other locations. They were to be built over large Akashic Record crystals placed in varying grid formations that would hold the light and prevent lower-density vibrations from entering. Several pyramids had been built in Atlantis by the Lyrans and their slaves for the purposes of distorting and controlling the encodings from the Sun. But all of these sank beneath the Atlantic Ocean or blew up when Atlantis was destroyed.

The final destruction of Atlantis was primarily caused by an underground transmission of sonic waves so intense that it created a sonic boom beneath Earth's surface. It was intended to break up the higher-frequency patterns of light in the still-existing sacred temples, and to infiltrate these temples with the black-magic and Satanic-control energies of the Dark Brotherhood. Instead, the sonic boom was so powerful that it echoed back on its own source, reverberating within the nuclear and crystal energy centers that powered the sound generator. This caused a large explosion that created a chain reaction in other subterranean power generators and resulted in earthquakes the likes of which had never before happened on Earth. [And have never happened since.] Many of the pyramids were literally blown into pieces, while others remained intact. The major Earth changes continued for over two months until the last of Atlantis was laid to rest at the bottom of the ocean.

By then, the people who had left to reestablish spiritual order in other locations were mostly well out of the way of danger and were able to reach their destinations. A few of the groups who had attempted to leave were not far enough away and were swept away by giant tidal waves resulting from the explosions. This final destruction of Atlantis took place roughly 10,400 years ago.

Lucifer collected the Lyrans on the astral planes and began a plan for his next step. The Lyrans chose to remain on the astral planes in both Earth's atmosphere and in the subterranean Satanic realms to intensify their influence on the subconscious minds of the people of Earth. As a result, tribal warring and feuding began to occur more frequently all over your planet. Many Native American, African, European, Central and South American indigenous peoples split apart into separate tribes, whereas in the past they had all been part of a vast brotherhood. Territorial competitions, disputes over mineral and water rights, spiritual differences, and unexplainable distrust became reasons for the segregation movement. In other areas, the arrival of the spiritual Atlanteans pulled the people together, and the evolution of these various cultures accelerated. The subliminal messages of patriarchal supremacy infiltrated the subconscious realms more and more, but some groups were able, with the help of the Atlanteans or their own evolved spiritual leaders, to withstand the pressures and lies presented by the negative psychic thoughtforms.

Grids, such as the one at Stonehenge, and medicine wheels were created to stop the destructive astral energies and create safe spaces in which people could hold ceremonies and other gatherings.

For nearly 5000 years, the temples of the Goddess were strong in many of the new Atlantean lands. Male and female temples alike presented and held the sacred teachings of Melchizedek, Thoth, and Alorah; they also expanded their teachings to include the local archetypal deities and spiritual practices. Teachings about male and female roles, spiritual initiation, Ka temples and healing practices, and spiritual evolution soared in Egypt, Greece, and parts of Central and South America. Not all of the tribes in other locations were affected by the astral pollution; some remained pure and humble. But a polarization of Light and Dark was definitely building.

Around 5000 years ago, the Lyrans and their colleagues who had been converted to the Dark Brotherhood began to reincarnate in various spots around the world. Their main objective was to infiltrate the areas of the more spiritually advanced cultures and to incite war and destruction against them. Though this took place gradually over time, the planet experienced many shifts in the ruling forces of the people. Cycles of Light and Dark occurred in Egypt, Greece, Europe, and Central America. The Dark Brotherhood killed, destroyed, raped, and established their rule; then the forces of Light rebelled and overthrew them. This cycle happened repeatedly.

Earth as a whole has always maintained alignment with the Light, the Supreme Being—also called Spirit of Oneness—and the Higher Council of Twelve. However, Earth's population has undergone many changes with respect to the balance of power. Interestingly enough, the majority of people on Earth have always believed in love and goodness, but they have remained weak and ineffectual against the intimidation of governmental and religious forces who operate for the purpose of control. The population of Earth has, for the most part, felt powerless to affect the ruling classes for a long time; this is the greatest paradox on Earth. One reason for this fear and powerlessness is the fourth- and fifth-dimensional astral control by Lucifer, the Lyrans, and the Nibiruans, or Anunnaki. [Author's Note: This is explained in depth in Barbara Hand Clow's book, *The Pleiadian Agenda*.] What is important for you to know at this time is that you do have the power and ability to break free of the psychic control of these astral beings. The information and processes in the rest of this workbook will guide and assist you in doing just that.

When certain groups first came to inhabit Earth about 150,000 years ago, a large meeting of the collective consciousness, including the Pleiadians, Andromedans, etheric guides, and devic kingdoms, was held. It was decided that a hierarchical structure would be created that would allow as much room for trust and security as possible. This was due to past experiences among the new Earth arrivals with betrayal by members of the higher realms, and deep-seated self-doubt. The self-doubt was the main impetus for the group to demand rulership. The new Earth dwellers simply did not trust themselves to make important decisions and be sovereign. Their request was met by the hierarchies who agreed that when the time came for a Supreme Being to be appointed for your planet, there would be a structure of descending spiritual authority with the power to override any decision made by the Supreme Being. The most immediate structure under the Supreme Being would be the Higher Council of Twelve. Its membership would consist of four delegates each from the Pleiades, Sirius, and the neighboring galaxy of Andromeda. All of the members would be highly evolved Light Beings. Unless the Higher Council of Twelve agreed by consensus with an order from the Supreme Being, the decision in question would be overridden. This way, the people of Earth would know, at least subconsciously, that they were free of the possibility of corruption in the spiritual hierarchy. There would even be a double safeguard within the structure of the Higher Council: at least two members of different origins would be responsible for each area of authority in the next lower realm. For example, in the area of giving instructions to and overseeing the work of the healing angels, one Pleiadian and one Andromedan would overlap in their responsibilities, and neither could do anything about which the other disagreed. This type of structure still exists throughout all of the higher-dimensional offices and groups.

The planetary belief in the need for *authorities* to rule and make important decisions for you must now be cleared. You are ready to become fully responsible sovereign beings. The existence of so much corruption in government is a product of the lack of trust and self-trust still on Earth. As the Age of Light, also called the Age of Enlightenment, unfolds, it will become increasingly important to end patriarchal systems of government and to return true power to the people. Those who are not capable of handling this responsibility without bringing harm to others can be kept from posing a threat with a group decision-making process. No elected officials will preside. Roles such as meeting facilitator, reporter, and any others required will rotate among the members who are willing to serve in that capacity. In this way, one person or a small contingent can never assume authority over others. [Author's Note: In *The Fifth Sacred Thing* by Starhawk, a wonderful utopian model is given for this type of rule, which is truly "of the people, by the people, and for the people."]

What is needed at this time is for the people of Earth to find the spiritual courage to demand what they want. Of course, many of the well-meaning citizens of Earth have become enmeshed in the struggle for survival and have forgotten about spiritual ideals. However, most humans understand basic morality and desire love. This gives Earth a tremendous opportunity for a spiritual quantum leap at this time. The higher collective consciousness of all human beings on Earth has asked for a chance to create something that has never happened before: a planetary ascension. If this occurs, Earth and all of her people will move together into fourth- and fifth-dimensional consciousness and separate their consciousnesses completely from the Satanic and controlling astral planes. The present, ongoing control by destructive forces is based on, and held in place by, two things: (1) the illusion of the supremacy of hate and fear over love, and (2) the belief that the Dark is more powerful than the Light. If by 2013 the entire remaining population of Earth can eliminate these two beliefs and recognize and accept the four spiritual principles mentioned earlier, this planet will be the first ever to accomplish such a spiritual jump.

In order for there to be any hope of this great event taking place, between now and 2013 a minimum of—but not limited to—144,000 humans must become enlightened and embody Christ consciousness. When this critical mass of awakened beings is reached, it will be the "Second Coming of Christ en masse." At that time, a "hundredth monkey effect" will occur: a vibrational wave of enlightenment energy will move through the entire planet and its population, eradicating the lower-astral thoughtforms and realms, and dissolving the veils that separate humans from their own inner experience of divine essence and truth. The entire population of Earth will feel this enlightenment wave as it penetrates all of existence on the planet. Planetary enlightenment and the inherent soul purpose of spiritual evolution will be activated at that time. If the Lyrans, Annunaki, Lucifer, members of the Dark Brotherhood, and humans who have aligned with darkness choose spiritual surrender at that time, they will simply join the planetary ascension and be released from the past. Those who do not choose the Light will experience the destruction of the planet and will find themselves in a galactic recovery center, so to speak. They will be given opportunities for evolution and divine alignment, but not forced. If they request freedom to explore darkness after a certain amount of time, they will be sent to another galaxy in which that option still exists.

Even if something as extreme as a planetary explosion were to occur at that point, the 144,000 or more Christed Beings would simply move into their ascension bodies and take the rest of Earth's newly awakened people with them. When the critical mass of 144,000 is reached, the impact of these Christed Beings on the rest of the people will be so powerful that each of them will have the ability to pull 144,000 other humans into the higher planes of consciousness. In other words, 144,000 Christed ones will create a quantum leap for 20,736,000,000 humans. The dark veil, or "net," as it has been called, that surrounds the outer atmosphere of Earth will dissolve. This will allow the full galactic encodings to impulse Earth through the Sun. No lower astral planes will be left, and all of the people will have a "white light," or *shaktiput*, experience, after which they will find themselves on a new Earth that is more beautiful and clear than the one left behind. They will be on Earth but in the fourth dimension. Those who have ascended in previous lifetimes will move straight to the fifth dimension, or even higher.

Training schools will have been prepared in advance for these new spiritual beings who become fourth dimensional. These beings will learn about their own creations of the past, their souls' origins and purposes, and all of the spiritual teachings appropriate to that level of evolution. A grace period of 1000 years will envelop Earth, during which time peace and a spiritual evolutionary focus will be prevalent. In other words, the mystery schools will be the center of all activity for the entire 1000 years. At the end of that time, Earth will officially step into the galactic role of home of the Cities of Light and mystery school for other third-dimensional planets.

You will become the guardians and teachers for third-dimensional lifeforms as we, the Pleiadians, have been for you. If you are successful, which we believe you will be, a giant wave of love and joy from the union of higher collective consciousness with third- and fourth-dimensional consciousness will emanate throughout the entire galaxy. This enlightenment wave will instantaneously transmute all remaining karma and lower astral energies in your solar ring into pure light, just as the planetary enlightenment wave will do for Earth and her people. The power of this wave will be felt and have impact on the entire galaxy and all of existence. Why?

The position of this galaxy in relationship to the Great Central Sun of All That Is has just undergone a cycle change, as mentioned previously. The evolutionary name for this new galactic cycle is "The Evolutionary Spiral of Mastery." Each solar ring of this galaxy must step up into its next highest evolutionary paradigm. For Earth and your solar ring, that step is to become home of the Cities of Light comprised of Light Beings who have specifically gone through physical incarnations and achieved enlightenment. At the end of the 1000 years of peace, you will have become exclusively a race of Christed Beings.

The Pleiadian Lightwork, and especially the Ka aspect of Pleiadian Lightwork, is one of the avenues of healing and awakening that we, the Pleiadians, are bringing to you at this time. It is essential that your Ka Channels and Ka Template be cleared of karmic residue and blocked energies in order to enable your Christ Selves to anchor into the physical realm through your physical bodies. You are among the 144,000 or more who will bring about the Age of Enlightenment,

Age of Light, Golden Age, or New Age on Earth. The materials presented in this workbook will assist you in making that transition and becoming available for and conducive to the higher frequencies of the Ka, and therefore the Christ body, or Master Presence.

We have faith in you and your planet's higher consciousness. Although the future looks good, you must not allow any laziness, resistance, or arrogance to stop your progress toward ascension. As long as you do your part and are willing to become the best you are capable of being, we will be there assisting you in any way that is appropriate for us. We will never, however, usurp your own learning and growth. You are here to become Masters, not invalids who need to be rescued. Let no one tell you that they will do your work for you, or save you. It is time for you to save yourselves through persistent and dedicated healing, growth, and continual spiritual awakening. With willingness and determination, all things divine are possible.

"So-la-re-en-lo,"
(With great love and devotion),

Ra,

spokesperson for the Pleiadian Archangelic Tribes of the Light,
members of the Pleiadian Emissaries of Light,
who are guardians of this solar ring
and members of the Galactic Federation of Light
of the Great Central Sun.

Section 2

PLEIADIAN LIGHTWORK
Spiritual Transformation by Awakening Your Divine Ka

Introduction to
SECTION II

I am extremely grateful for the opportunity to introduce the Pleiadian Emissaries of Light as healers and spiritual guides for individuals as well as for the planet. The purpose of this section of the book is to teach you how to invoke the Pleiadian Emissaries of Light to do energy work on you personally. Along with the Christ and other Ascended Masters, guides, and angels, they can facilitate your evolution and spiritual healing in very specific ways as will be explained throughout this workbook section. The Pleiadian fields of expertise can prepare you for full-body enlightenment and ascension.

My own past few years of consciously working with the Pleiadians have been a gift, to say the least. Their devotion to me as a human being has been, and is, ever present. Their integrity has been impeccable. And the energy work itself has ranged from extremely subtle to miraculous with obvious results. From my personal experiences with this healing and spiritual practice, I would like to give you a few general pointers.

Although I will mention this again, I would like to recommend that when working with any nonphysical beings it is always good to invoke only those who are "of the Light and serving the Divine Plan." What this implies is that the beings themselves must be at a certain level of consciousness and evolution in order to provide you with genuine assistance. If an etheric being simply comes without your conscious invitation, then ask the question three times, "Are you of the Light and serving the Divine Plan?" It is Universal Law that when this question is asked three times, it must be answered truthfully. Even dark beings must answer it truthfully. It is also Universal Law that if a being answers no to this question and you ask it to leave, it must do so, thus honoring your free will. I have always found this method to work. If you are in this situation and a being is evasive in answering you, simply ask it to leave at once.

Many authors and channels pull in disincarnate human beings, astral entities, power-hungry extraterrestrials, and even dark beings in the name of spiritual pursuit. Some people believe that any disincarnate human or entity is automatically superior to those of us who live in bodies. These people give an enormous amount of undeserved seniority and trust to the entities they channel. Just because a being is not in a body does not mean that it is at a level of evolution whereby it can assist you—or that it is even harmless, for that matter. You are responsible for using discernment and discriminating wisdom. So please, follow the criteria for invoking higher beings and channeling messages outlined in this section of the book—unless you have learned other ways that you prefer.

Chapters 5 and 6, "Preparing for Pleiadian Lightwork, I and II," are especially given for those of you who are novices at healing and spiritual work, or who have problems with boundaries and grounding. What this means is this: If you have a cluttered aura or clogged chakras, or tend to be a psychic sponge for other people's emotions and pain, the Pleiadian Lightwork may be too deep to begin with. As the higher-frequency energies of the Ka work and other aspects of Pleiadian Lightwork begin to come into your aura and body, the release of emotions, blocked energies, and karma is greatly accelerated. I feel a responsibility to tell you that *if you have not done much meditation, worked with light for self-healing, or cleared etherically, mentally, and emotionally, you definitely need to work with these two chapters for at least one month before you proceed with the rest of this book.* If the techniques given in these chapters are still vague or erratic in their effectiveness after one month, continue working daily with them until they start to become second nature. This will assist you in doing some initial clearing to prepare you for the deeper work to come.

These guidelines may even apply to some of you who have been into spirituality and lightwork for many years. I meet many New Agers, healers, and even workshop facilitators who still take on other people's emotions and pain, or dump theirs indiscriminately in other people's energy fields. Some of these people may have had spiritual awakenings, but skipped learning the basics of grounding, aura clearing, boundaries, and so on. Others have jokingly called these ungrounded spiritual types "airy-fairy" or "space cadets." However, the truth is that most of those who have been so labeled are simply uninformed about the need or methods for grounding and boundaries. Therefore, the information and processes in the two chapters on "Preparing for Pleiadian Lightwork" are essential.

You will most likely need to utilize these self-healing and clearing techniques during the Pleiadian Lightwork sessions as well. So, even if you have been around the spiritual and metaphysical arenas for a long time, at least scan the techniques in the first two chapters of this section to be sure you are ready for the Pleiadian Lightwork sessions in the rest of the book. *If you know you get scattered easily, still take on other people's energy and problems, or are ever aware of feeling dark presences around you, please do these two chapters thoroughly before proceeding.*

The guided processes throughout this section of the book are available for purchase separately on audio tapes for those who want them. Certainly not everyone needs the extra help of taped guidance for the meditations and healing sessions. If you do, instructions for ordering the tape set are given in the back of the book. Directions for coordinating the tapes with the text are on a separate sheet accompanying the tapes; please note the icon ⌸ following various exercises in the text, which tells you to turn on your tape. You could also make your own tapes by recording the processes yourself; if you do so be sure to allow time for the completion of each step before going on to the next one.

Much of the information and many of the techniques in this workbook section may seem to stray from the subject of awakening your Divine Ka. Though only two chapters deal very specifically with the Ka, this entire section on Pleiadian Lightwork is designed to augment, expand, and facilitate the deepening of the Ka work. When the Ka is awakened and activated, deep clearing is directly proportional to the influx of the rarefied, high-frequency Ka energy. Unless a person is living in spiritual alignment, consciousness, and integrity, the Ka will never open fully; instead it will gradually shut down completely. As Ra said, "You are encouraged to do the workbook thoroughly since even the processes that are not directly related to the Ka will assist you in integrating the Ka work emotionally, mentally, physically, and spiritually." The healing processes, boundary information, and meditations throughout the workbook section are presented for the purpose of assisting your own healing and spiritual growth, as well as that of beloved planet Earth. They create the best possible inner atmosphere in which the Ka can be fully awakened and continue to expand.

Earth cannot be healed until we as a species evolve spiritually. Evolution must include everything from basic ethics to higher morality and Ka awakening; from not polluting physically to clearing our negative thoughts and feelings, which pollute psychically and spiritually. Earth cannot afford for us to continue as a race that is spiritually irresponsible. Only through developing a conscience, awakening to the sacredness of *all* life, and choosing to honor these awarenesses will we become inhabitants of this planet in a nonharmful and restorative way.

It is obvious we must make that choice in order to survive, as well as embrace the four evolutionary principles:

1. Our purpose here is to evolve physically, emotionally, mentally, and spiritually.

2. Every human being is Divine Essence made of light and love whose nature is goodness.

3. Free will is an absolute universal right; impeccability calls on the self to surrender its free will to divine will in faith and trust.

4. All of natural existence is sacred beyond how it serves or meets the needs of the individual self.

There is enough knowledge of the threats to our planet's future that we must choose to evolve *now*. Any one of the following, only to mention a few, could bring about the end of life on Earth very soon if we do not change: the ozone layer holes, the greenhouse effect from planetary warming, the destruction of the rainforests and old-growth forests, the death of our oceans, underground nuclear waste, nuclear explosions . . . the list could go on and on. It is no longer a safe option to remain ignorant, uncaring, unconscious, and irresponsible.

We must examine our own psyches, beliefs, and feelings and start cleaning them up; they are the real cause of all the planetary harm that has been done.

Our thoughts, beliefs, feelings, and attitudes toward ourselves and others are behind every destructive and unconscious act—or behind the circumstances through which our planet and we ourselves can heal. It is our choice. These energies are constantly contributing to the cocreation of our world on every level. Thoughts are measurable energy, and movement of energy impacts everything around it. A thought was the beginning of Creation, and our thoughts are constantly recreating—or destroying—everything. The phrase "think globally, act locally" really means that we must start by examining and changing ourselves; then our attitudes and actions will naturally spread to our loved ones, communities, and beyond.

Once we are clear on the basics of being "good" people, higher evolution continues. There is always a next step toward truly being the best we can be. It is this for which we are all ultimately responsible. Hopefully, the longing for—and anticipation of—becoming the best we are capable of being fills every day of our lives. This longing can motivate us to keep going and never become so satisfied that we become stagnant. Of course, acceptance of ourselves wherever we are, each moment of each day, is also vital to our growth. Without it, we languish in low self-esteem and self-punishment. Still, our spiritual longing for God, enlightenment, divine love, and an end to separation is the source of our achievements. It is our souls' only inspiration.

Since the Christ set the example for what we are to become, we have had almost twenty centuries to play out the control dramas, karmic patterns, and planetary thoughtforms made manifest. We have seen and experienced all of the addictions and obsessions that have kept us disempowered and in low self-esteem. They are the seven solar ring karmic patterns listed in chapter 4 that have kept us hooked since the colonization of this solar system began: arrogance, addiction, prejudice, hatred, violence, victimhood, and shame.

The only thing left to us now is to seek the higher truth and power that will put an end to this madness and help us become a world of sovereign, self-respecting, Christed Beings. Pleiadian

Lightwork is certainly not the only way this can happen. Any spiritual group or healing practice that makes such claims and believes itself to be the *only way* is definitely one to be avoided. However, those who are attracted to this work are the ones for whom it is intended, and for them it is important. I once asked the Pleiadians, "Why, if this work is key to anchoring the Christed Presence in the body, is it necessary for it to be done hands-on to achieve maximum results? Doesn't that create an exclusiveness? Christ didn't need hands-on healing sessions to anchor in the body. Why do we?"

Ra replied, "Christ was born to awakened parents. He was never damaged and mutated the way people today were. If you were born to awakened parents and were never abused and damaged, and if your DNA with its genetic coding was clear the way his was, this work would not be needed. You would be born with the Ka Channels and axis alignment to the multidimensional aspects of the Higher Self intact. What's more, your DNA and Ka Channels would not become damaged through life experience. Spiritual growth and attainment would be accelerated and much more directly accessible. However, Earth has been spiritually in the dark ages for so long that all of its major civilizations have spent centuries focused on greed, guilt, control for power, and destruction of the indigenous peoples. Due to these and other karmic patterns, as well as your modern society with its chemical additives, pesticides, noise pollution, radar, electricity, microwaves, television, and computers, you have become a mutant race. Besides that, your generation chose to come in with genetic addictions and mutations, as well as societal and parental programming, for the purpose of transforming them. You are the bridge generation—the bridge between the old world and the new one being birthed in the twenty-first century.

"Not everyone will need the Pleiadian Lightwork in person. It will be made available to as many people as request it and are ready for this work, both during sleep and waking states. This workbook will help bring Pleiadian Lightwork to the awareness of many people who would never have heard about it otherwise. Just as we have been working with you [Amorah], we will work with others also. Until you had students trained who could finish the Pleiadian Lightwork through hands-on healing, you benefited greatly from the etheric work we provided. Once students were trained and activated your Ka Channels with hands-on healing, the work deepened in your body/spirit relationship quickly. In general, the results usually range from 40 to 80 percent effective when done etherically by the Pleiadians and Christ only. Those who have been less damaged in this lifetime will have a greater percentage of effectiveness. For them, etheric work will be enough. Those who are to receive Pleiadian Lightwork hands-on will recognize the need for it, as will those who are to be practitioners; and the results will be increased to 100 percent, as yours have been.

"At least 50 percent of the practitioners will have done this type of healing and spiritual work in other lives. They will also have been enlightened at other times on Earth. Their experiences will be reawakenings with much life experience and wisdom gained in the process. You see, your generation took on the genetic mutations and programming because you knew you were capable of transmuting them. Many of you are very old souls and have been serving Earth and learning about humanness for a very long time.

"Most of you will not be returning here after this lifetime. There is a new group of master souls being born on the planet now. They began to arrive here in the mid-1970s and will continue to arrive in ever increasing numbers for the next two decades. These new ones will take up where you leave off, so to speak. By doing your own clearing work and spiritual practice, you are paving the way for them to be born with much less to transmute. There is an added grace: as their parents continue to heal and grow, these new Light Beings will automatically receive the benefits as well. Some of them have been human a few times to anchor their awareness of karmic and genetic patterns, and they may bring some karma in with them. However, this will be relatively minimal.

"You must nurture these children and help them be aware from the moment they are born that they are welcomed here on Earth, that they are loved, and that they are holy spirits made of light. As they grow, they need to hear these things over and over again. You must look at them with the intent of seeing the beauty of their essences and loving them. They must be communicated with as if they are intelligent, aware beings from the very beginning—because they are.

It is a rare gift to have the opportunity to birth these wise Light Beings and include them in your lives. Always honor that gift.

"Many couples who wish to have children will want to receive Pleiadian Lightwork and genetic clearing before conceiving. This will enable the children to be born without blockages in their Ka Channels. Even if they only receive etheric work from the Pleiadians, this will help tremendously.

"So you see, dear one, you are being reminded of this work again because *it's time now.* As there is need for more, you will be contacted. Has it not always been so? Trust us to keep our promise to you before you came here: *To be with you all the way to the end. That you will never be lost or forgotten. That when the time is right, you will be reunited with us again.* This promise is still so. We love you, for you are a part of us. We are grateful to you for the courage and loving dedication it has taken to be here. And remember, it is almost done now. You will be home again soon."

After this discourse Ra proceeded to give me details about the Pleiadian Lightwork Intensives and the healing work in general. Of course, it all made sense: I needed Dolphin Brain Repatterning and Dolphin Star-Linking for my own body, and to practice it for a few years before relearning and personally receiving the Ka work. My own nervous system is extremely sensitive and had been badly damaged. I needed time to heal it and release the holding patterns in my own skeletal system in order to be ready for the higher-frequency work to come.

In addition, over the years I had brought through a lot of Higher Self connection techniques that had prepared the way for me. Most of the information in this workbook section I channeled. Chapters 5, 6, and 11, however, consist primarily of techniques I picked up from other teachers along the way. I am very grateful that the right person or etheric Light Being has always shown up at the right time. My experiences with the Pleiadians have certainly been no exception to that general rule.

As you go through this workbook section, the higher purpose for each technique will be revealed. For now, what is important to realize is that the awakening and enlightenment of humans and the planet as a whole are the long-range—and only—purposes for this presentation. As your spiritual awakening deepens and gets closer and closer to full enlightenment, your experiences of psychic (full sensory perception) phenomena may also increase in frequency. It is very important, when this happens, that you do not succumb to fascination with phenomenal power. To do so would be an immature distraction from the true purpose of finding your God/Goddess Self again and returning to Oneness with All That Is.

I have created the term *full sensory perception* to replace the terms *psychic* and *extrasensory perception*. This new term more accurately describes what such an experience truly is. I believe that we all have the inherent ability to use our senses at expanded levels beyond physical stimuli. This full sensory perception would automatically occur if we lived in a natural environment. People in indigenous cultures all over the world have been able to *feel* or *know* what herbs or natural substances have been needed to balance illnesses in loved ones or animals. It is how they have *felt* or *seen* their cultures' spirit helpers, devas, and fairies, and have known how to build their pyramids precisely to higher specifications.

Once, when I was driving down an on-ramp to the freeway in San Diego, a Native American spirit about twenty feet tall appeared beside my car. He floated along beside me as he observed, "No wonder your people have forgotten how to listen to and feel Earth. You go too fast. You have to slow down and be still if you want to be sensitive to these things." I knew he was right. The blocks today to full sensory perception are electricity, chemicals, noise pollution, job and life-style–related stress, and simply going too fast. We need to get out in nature and sit still under trees or by streams where only natural sounds occur. We need to sit there until our thoughts, emotions, and nervous systems slow down, and we can feel inner peace all the way to the core of our bodies and souls again. Then we will be able to hear the trees and streams and nature spirits when they talk to us. Then we will begin to remember what Oneness is again.

Until we re-find this natural and open way of being, it is easy to let our egos get carried away with feeling special or spiritually superior when full sensory perception returns. As our third eyes open or we begin to receive teachings through channeled sources or the Higher Self, it is easy to take on an elitist attitude or try to create a following. These are traps to avoid. They will take us nowhere that is worth going. We must begin to relate to those experiences by celebrating that we are becoming normal again, not extrasensory or psychic. We are recovering what is a natural and healthy way of communing with our environment and other people.

Once I was at the home of an elderly woman who suffered constantly with the aches and pains of arthritis. Her daughter had met me and arranged for a private reading and healing appointment with her mother. About twenty minutes or so into the session, the woman suddenly exclaimed, "Why, honey, I just realized the pain in my back is gone! This is the first time in twenty-five years I haven't felt that back pain. How could you know those things about my childhood?"

I replied simply, "It was easy. It was right there in your aura and your back. So how could I miss it?" My attitude was that it was more natural to see what was there than to not see it. My reply to her was followed by a very soft voice inside my chest saying, "Now you are ready to prepare for doing healing work fulltime. It needed to become simply a natural phenomenon first." I began a plan at that time for selling my crystal and gemstone jewelry company. There was a deep and calm feeling of rightness in all that happened.

Beware of teachers and healers who purport to being "gifted" in ways you are not or cannot become—people who have all the answers and try to make you dependent on them. There are stages at which you may need to trust people who have attained knowledge or abilities before you. You may need to take a class, training, or workshop occasionally, or go for a healing session. Make sure that the experience is set up for you to complete at some point in time and that it enables you to take care of yourself better than before. You should always be given tools and awarenesses to use on your own when the exchange is complete. I do not intend to negate in any way the grace of going to a true healer when the time is right. Sometimes we all need a jump start or a tune up. There have always been those with spiritual healing gifts here on Earth: the shamans, medicine men and women, seers, and hands-on healers. When you meet true healers, they are gifts. Yet it is important not to create dependencies on these people. They are here in the name of grace and are not intended to take the place of your own inner work. They are most certainly not intended to supersede your awakening to your own gifts and abilities. The genuine ones can help, however, when you are "stuck" and need assistance.

As the recipient of healing work, spiritual assistance, and teaching, you have a responsibility. I have had the unfortunate experience of having to cut off clients because they did not do their part. Every time a painful emotion or unclarity would arise, they would be on the phone for me to do an emergency fix-it. I had to say, "I feel I am becoming a crutch for you, and I really want you to walk on your own. I am here to enable you, not disable you. Therefore, my integrity tells me our relationship must end."

This is different than when clients who have suffered extreme sexual or physical abuse come for healing. In these situations, the healer has a responsibility to stay with the healing process until the clients are through the trauma. These clients must be able to trust that, once the doors to the old trauma are opened, they will not be abandoned by their practitioner until a natural completion is reached. Yet, even in these situations, the practitioner needs to clarify in the very beginning that there are times when the clients will need to do homework or make life changes in order to augment the work or get stronger. If clients cannot commit to this beforehand, then the healing sessions should not begin. Whether you are the client or the practitioner, a preliminary establishment of boundaries and expectations is a good prerequisite to healing.

If you are the client, ask healers and therapists about their purpose in doing their work. It is also appropriate to ask these persons if they have a spiritual life and how it interfaces with their work. I would personally never go to healers who are not working toward their own enlightenment and using their healing practices as ways of assisting others on this journey. This is not due to a prejudice or elitism on my part; it is simply discernment based on my own choice to live in Divine Truth in every way I can. Even herbologists, naturopaths, acupuncturists, and chiropractors can consciously use their healing modalities in this way if they are so inclined. So use your discernment. Go for the best—that which will serve you as a whole being on a spiritual path—even if the work is primarily geared to your physical body. All aspects of yourself need to be clear, healthy, and functional for the best holistic results.

The above guidelines are included because the purpose of this book is to assist you in your spiritual awakening, and to make you aware of available assistance from Light Beings with very high integrity. The workbook section of this book gives you techniques to use on your own if you find them helpful. Keep and use what works for you and leave the rest behind.

Even in Pleiadian Lightwork, Christ and the Pleiadians will cease to work with us if we become too dependent on them to *fix it*. We must always do our part: change our behaviors; expose our denials and judgments; express and release our emotions; be truthful with ourselves and others; live virtuously and become impeccable; observe and transform our thoughts. In other words, we are each ultimately responsible for our own integrity, evolution, spiritual enlightenment, and ascension. To become our Christ Selves, we must first master ourselves. Christ, Mother Mary, Buddha, Quan Yin, Pacal Votan, and many other Ascended Masters have achieved self-mastery while in human form, and thus have shown us the way. Christ and the Pleiadians are here to guide and assist us in self-mastery without usurping our own authority and responsibility. They care too much to do otherwise.

Chapter 5

PREPARING FOR PLEIADIAN LIGHTWORK
PART I: HEALTHY BOUNDARIES

A s the name of this chapter indicates, it will prepare you for the Pleiadian Lightwork that comprises the rest of this book. Because the Pleiadian Lightwork works on subtle-energy bodies and clears a lot of old energy blockages, emotions, and other people's energies you have taken on, it is essential that you first learn some basic psychic self-care tools. So let go of any expectations you may have about moving through this workbook section quickly. You may find it helpful to read the processes before actually doing them. It will sometimes be necessary for you to work with a new process for a few days before going on to the next one. And after particularly intense clearings, you may need integration time.

The information in this chapter may be familiar to some of you. If so, scan each section until you find parts of it that are new or different from what you have learned before. Compare the processes to your existing ones and see which work best for you. It is important that, by the time you go to the next chapter, you are able to quickly and easily use the techniques in this chapter, or their equivalents.

Grounding

Grounding is a term used quite frequently in healing and spiritual groups, and yet it means many things to many people. To some of you it may mean being aware of feeling your feet on the floor; or you may relate it to the way you feel being in nature. Essentially, being grounded means being in your body, conscious of your surroundings, and present and available for whatever happens. The technique used for grounding in this chapter is a visualization that results in bringing your consciousness and spiritual presence more into your body. A lot of spiritual people who meditate regularly, as well as others who have not developed much awareness yet, have not learned grounding and may tend to "hang out" in the ethers above the body. If you are one of those people, you can be left very susceptible to taking on foreign energy—energy from other people, or even entities. At best, even if you are not being a psychic sponge, you cannot move your emotions or karma out of your body very well without first being in your body.

The Pleiadian approach to spirituality involves full-body, cellular enlightenment and/or ascension. In other words, the goal is not to leave your body and transcend the physical; the goal is to transcend your belief in and fear of the limitations of the physical plane. You accomplish this by spiritually descending into matter fully for the purpose of clearing lower-frequency energies such as repressed emotions, belief systems, judgments, control, and other contracted energies that are the source of limitation in the third dimension. As this is done, you make way for your Higher Self to completely blend with you, as the Christ, Quan Yin, and Buddha did. This results in full-chakra, cellular enlightenment or ascension instead of escape.

This spiritual goal requires you to be in your body, and thus there is a need for grounding. The technique used for grounding is as follows:

1. Sit in a comfortable chair with your back relatively straight, your feet on the floor, your feet and hands uncrossed, and your eyes closed.

2. Use your breath to bring as much of your conscious presence to the center of your head as possible. Let go of any stray thoughts inhibiting this process until you feel centered.

3. Now take a couple of deep breaths. Notice how much of your body expands with your breath. What parts do not expand?

4. Consciously expand more of your body with your breath until you are inhaling as far down your spine as possible without strain or discomfort. Do this two to four times until you feel more alive and present in your body.

5. Feel your feet on the floor. Use your breath to bring more aliveness into your feet.

6. MEN ONLY: Bring your awareness to your first chakra, at the base of your tailbone. Visualize a tube or spiraling cord of light about four to six inches in diameter attaching itself to your first chakra. (See illustration 1a on page 78.)

WOMEN ONLY: Bring your awareness to your second chakra, about halfway between your navel and the base of your spine. Visualize a tube or spiraling cord of light about four to six inches in diameter attaching itself to your second chakra. (See illustration 1b on page 79.)

BOTH MEN AND WOMEN: Follow this *grounding cord* visually and see it extending into Earth while your consciousness remains in the center of your head. See the cord move through all the layers of Earth until it reaches the center of the planet, where the magnetic core or gravity center is located. You may feel or see the grounding cord simply anchoring and be unable to go any further.

7. Take about half a minute to a minute to breathe gently and feel the changes happening in your body and consciousness. Occasionally, some of my students and private clients have experienced parts of the body aching or throbbing as they ground for the first time. Some have even experienced buried emotions coming to the surface. If this happens to you, just be aware that these pains, whether physical or emotional, are probably at least in part why you were not grounded in the first place, since the natural tendency of humans is to avoid unpleasantness of any kind. However, since awareness of a problem is the first step in healing it, allow yourself to explore the feelings with your breath and curiosity instead of contracting or pulling away from them. Let go of judgments or fear of feeling and attempt to assume an attitude of gladness at being made aware of the need for attention in this area of your body or emotions.

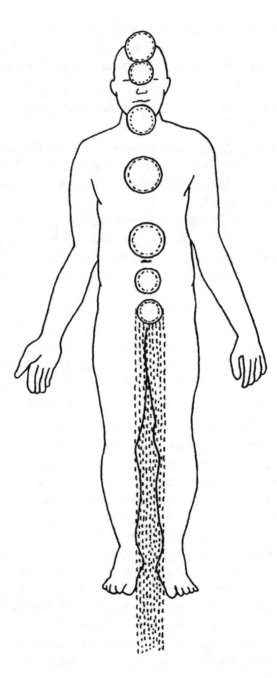

1a. Male grounding cord extends from the first chakra to the center of Earth

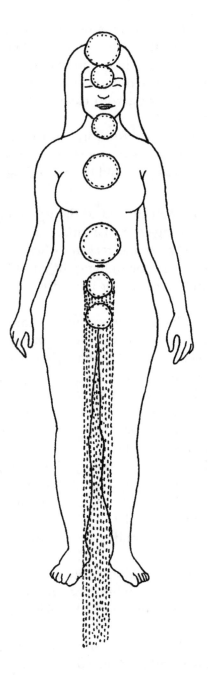

1b. Female grounding cord extends from the second chakra to the center of Earth

Keep breathing into your area of discomfort. Usually this will bring ease fairly quickly. If it does not, it could be an indication of a more chronic problem with which you may need assistance in healing unless you are well versed in dealing with such things yourself. More techniques for working with clearing yourself will be given later in the chapter as well.

If you experience no discomfort, you may notice a sense of becoming more present and real. You may feel relaxation and a slight heaviness in your body as you hold the grounding cord in focus for a while.

8. After becoming accustomed to the grounding cord, visualize the color of the grounding cord changing. See a full spectrum of colors and use varying shades and textures of each color. Make it fun. Stay with each color long enough to feel its effects on you. Explore as many colors as you can think of in addition to the ones named below:

Start with blues. Change your grounding cord color to pale baby blue, then royal blue, navy blue, teal blue, and finally cobalt blue.

Add a little green to the blue, and visualize the cord as deep turquoise, then pale aquamarine.

Experiment with greens: soft baby green, emerald green, forest green, olive green, grass green, and peridot or light yellow green.

Next visualize yellows: pale soft yellow, bright sunny yellow, golden yellow, and mustard yellow.

Then see shades of orange: pale yellow orange, peach, bright orange like the fruit, salmon, rust orange, then red orange.

Visualize reds: pale pink, carnation pink, hot pink, bright red, blood red, maroon, and red violet.

Now see the purples: lavender, royal purple, grape purple, and blue violet.

Then try whites: pure white, white with sparkles of sunlight, mother of pearl or pearlescent white, and cream.

Next see brown tones: tan, camel, chocolate, caramel brown, tree-trunk grayish brown.

Do metallic colors last: metallic silver, metallic gold, copper, platinum, and finally silver and gold mixed.

You will find that some colors are soothing and calming while others help you feel stronger and more confident. Some colors help you feel more in your body, while others are extremely unpleasant and ungrounding. Find the ones you like and either write them down, along with how they make you feel, or, if you have a good memory, make a mental note of them.

9. When you have completed scanning the colors, determine the one you want for now. Remove your original grounding cord by pulling it down and releasing it into Earth. Now give yourself a new grounding cord of the chosen color and send it to the center of Earth.

10. Open your eyes.

In the future, if you wake up feeling tired and grumpy, you can use the grounding cord color that helps you feel lighter and more energetic. Or, if you are experiencing lack of certainty and confidence in your life, you can use the grounding cord color that gives you more of those positive qualities.

Grounding will not solve all your problems or take away every unpleasant emotional state, but it can help you get through them more quickly and easily. Knowing the best color for a given situation can help keep you grounded and able to cope at times you might normally tend to check out.

For about a week, begin each morning by removing the old grounding cord and giving yourself a new one. The color may be the same as the previous one or different, based on your current need. As often throughout the day as you think about it, repeat this process. Even if it is fifty times a day at first, and even if it is while walking down the street or doing your work, give yourself a new grounding cord. The more thought-energy you put into creating anything, the more real and long lasting it becomes. You will become so proficient at grounding yourself that you can quickly do it with your eyes open while at work, or while walking or moving in a car. You need not take a lot of time to do it, even if you do it fifty times a day in the beginning.

After about a week, you will be able to ground yourself in the morning and have it last longer. Once a day may be all you need.

You will be familiar enough with the difference in being grounded and ungrounded by then that you will know when you need to replace your old grounding cord with a new one.

Through personal experience and teaching many students, I have not found that this one-week focus on grounding is optional—though some people have a tendency to skip over it. Those who do this one-week exercise consistently feel more grounded, present, and available for life and healing than those who are less persistent. Those who bypass this step may find that their healing processes take longer, that their emotional disturbances are lengthier in duration, and that their full sensory perception is not as accessible or useful. So I highly encourage you to follow through until grounding becomes second nature.

After doing the full grounding meditation as outlined in steps one through nine, it is unnecessary to repeat the full sequence of colors unless you have a personal reason for doing so. That part of the process is only for the purpose of identifying your best grounding colors.

My favorite story about grounding comes from a children's meditation class I taught a few years ago. After taking the young students through the grounding meditation, which was much abbreviated by necessity, I asked each child to tell the group how it felt to be grounded. The first to reply was a little boy, three and a half years old, who said, "It feels like my mommy feels."

The next child, also a boy the same age, responded, "It feels kind of like a health food store. Like it's good for you." After pausing and wiggling he added, "I don't know if I like it or not."

The rest of the children gave their renditions on grounding until we came to the last one, a seven-year-old girl, who would not speak. Her head was tucked down as low as she could get it, and she looked as if she might cry. I knew that her parents were going through a separation and preparing for divorce. I also knew that she was having a rough time with this change in her life.

I looked away from her and began to explain to the group that sometimes when you ground yourself, you discover that you have feelings inside you that you were unaware of before. I went on to say,

"Sometimes these feelings are loving and warm, as Elizabeth described. But other times these feelings hurt, such as when you feel sadness or anger. The trick is, instead of trying to make them go away, stay with them. Breathe really deeply and try to feel the feelings even more than you already do. Then something really magical happens. After a few minutes of feeling, suddenly the painful feelings will just be gone and you won't even know when they left. You'll feel better again. But, if you don't stay with them and feel them until they go away, they'll just sit there in your body waiting for you. So it's better to feel them now instead of having to dread them coming back."

The sad little girl still said nothing. However, about ten minutes later, while in the middle of a new project, she sat upright and exclaimed, "They're gone!" Then she sheepishly tucked her head, realizing she had cried out. I asked her what was gone. She answered, "The feelings—just like you said. I was very sad, but I did what you told us, and now the feelings are gone! Just like you said." Her eyes were full of amazement and even a little awe—like maybe the technique, or even the teacher, did have magic.

A few days later, the girl's mother called to tell me her daughter came home from school looking very upset. When her mother asked her what was happening, the child replied, "I'm having feelings, so I'm going to my room to feel them." Twenty minutes later she sprang from her room in play clothes, ready to go outside. When asked what was going on, she told her mom about the class and how she had learned this magic way to get bad feelings to go away and stay gone. That child's innocent willingness was a great example to us all.

You need not wait to go on to the next step unless it is your preference. There is a natural flow and complementary relationship between grounding and aura clearing.

Healing Your Aura and Keeping It Clear

The aura is the energy field that radiates around the body. It is created by the production of energy in the chakras, and each chakra contributes to the building and sustaining of the auric field. When your chakras are minimally open and/or damaged, your aura may appear dull and weak. Whereas, when you are in good health and reasonably open emotionally, you will have more open and active chakras and a stronger, more vibrant, and resilient aura.

If your aura is rather contracted, it may extend only a foot away from your body. If you have an overextended aura, it may expand anywhere from five feet to a dissipated half-mile radius from your body. Neither of these aura types is ideal. A contracted aura tends to make a person feel more uptight, fearful, and separate. This type of aura can also be caused by those types of feelings. An overextended aura can result in spaciness, escapism, and the tendency to feel and take on everyone else's emotions, thoughts, and even pain in the entire area your aura covers. An overextended aura can also be the result of these same feelings and situations that it tends to cause. In other words, the cause of unhealthy aura conditions also tends to regenerate more of the same conditions that caused them.

What you are aiming for is an aura that is egg-shaped and equally distributed above, below, behind, in front of, and to the sides of your body. By experimenting, I have come to believe that an aura radius of no more than two to three feet in every direction is the most manageable and desirable size, especially in public situations. When I go into a natural setting, I consciously allow my aura to expand into the forest, lakes, and streams surrounding me. It deepens my feeling of connectedness with God/Goddess/All That Is through Creation. I feel a communion with the plants, water, and nature spirits, and I receive a lot of nervous system healing and calming. However, when I go straight from nature into town or other public areas, I always pull my aura back to within two to three feet around me again. When I forget, I really feel it. I become unnecessarily aware of other people's life agendas and sometimes even feel their pain. So I tend to remember quickly.

In my own home, unless I am entertaining or seeing clients, I let my energy field expand to wherever it is comfortable within my house. I also keep my house very psychically clear, so it feels good to be in it.

The following is a process for clearing and healing your aura:

1. Ground yourself, using the previous technique.

2. With your eyes closed, feel the area around your body. At first, just extend your breath about one foot into your auric field by using your intent. As you breathe into that area, get a general sense of whether your aura feels contracted and thick, weak and dissipated, or vibrant and soft.

3. With your breath and visualization (or using your intuition or listening for a message) observe how far your aura extends from your body in front of you.

4. Observe the width of your aura on either side of your body.

5. Now see and feel your aura above your head and below your feet. Compare the two areas.

6. Use your breath, feelings, vision, and any other means natural to you to identify the space your aura covers behind your back. How does this compare to the front area?

7. Now that you know more about the nature of your own aura, adjust your aura to exactly fill a two-to-three-foot-radius egg shape around you. Use your breath, vision, and clear intent to accomplish this. In the beginning, you may find it useful to use your hands to physically reach out around your body and pull or push the aura where you want it to go. For most of you, adjusting your aura involves pulling it in and making its edges more defined. For the rest of you, it requires pushing your aura out to fill the space. If you are a beginner, you may have a problem getting your aura to go beneath your feet at all. Persistence and practice are the best antidotes in this case.

8. Observe any changes in your feelings, physical sensations, and awareness with the adjustment of the energy field around you.

9. Now visualize a rain shower made of golden liquid light pouring down on and through your aura. Let it rain at least two to five minutes the first time. Notice how wonderful this feels. (See illustration 2 on page 86.)

10. Next, visualize a giant, violet-colored fire the size of your aura. Bring it around your entire aura, including beneath your feet. It will not destroy anything. Violet flame simply transmutes lower

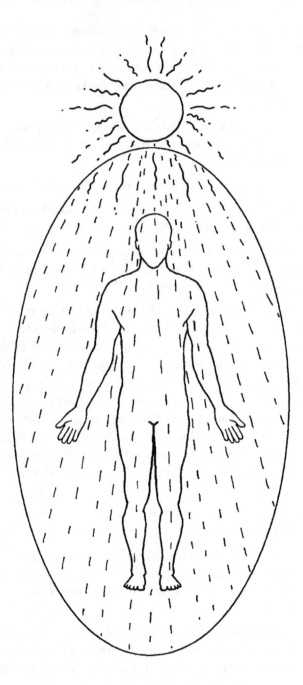

2. Golden rain shower of light cleansing the aura

frequency energies into higher frequency ones that constitute a more natural state of being. Remain inside the flame for only one to two minutes if this is your first experience with violet flame. You may feel warmer and more energized by this technique. If you overdo the use of violet flame, you may experience a state of overwhelm from the etheric burning away of old energies. So take the moderate approach at first; then build to your own level of usage by experimenting over time.

11. When you are complete, remove the violet flame and open your eyes.

Most meditators visualizing the rain shower for the first time report feeling lighter, fresher, and psychically cleaner and shinier. It is a simple yet effective way to clear out any extraneous junky or foreign energies you have picked up. It also works well to remove energies you have released from your body during healing or meditation.

When I first began using these techniques, I used breath, feeling, vision, and intent so I could make it as real and effective as possible. You may wish to experiment to find the methods that work best for you. [cassette icon]

Next, I will discuss *aura protection*. However, before going further, I want to make it clear that in no way are the following techniques intended to create a sense of being allergic to or afraid of people or the world. They certainly are not intended to discourage intimacy. They are quite simply designed to help you choose what you do let into your auric field and what you do not. If you have a problem with indiscriminately taking on any energy that is floating around, you can literally spend most of your life in overwhelm, being emotionally imbalanced, in turmoil, and feeling ineffectual. I know, because I was formerly one of the worst psychic sponges I have ever known. If I came near someone with an aching back, you could be sure I would have one, too. When I did hands-on healing, or even just hugged a friend, the other person consistently felt better and I usually felt worse. You might call it the "human dumpster syndrome." Learning boundaries was literally life-changing for me.

As a reward for learning boundaries, I have found healthy intimacy and sharing with friends and loved ones. I can now go into a restaurant without fear of becoming ill or paranoid. In fact, I don't even have to think about it most of the time any more, because it has finally become natural for me to repel lower vibrational energies and accept divine ones. However, getting to this point took a few years and a lot of meditation, Higher Self work, and dedication to my own spiritual wholeness. Occasionally, I still have to deal with karmic exchanges with people who are close to me; but I do not waste any energy and time at all on the processing of denied problems and pain belonging to John Doe on the street.

The following techniques are intended to help you learn healthy boundaries and discriminately choose what you allow into your body and auric field. One of the best ways I have found is to pull your aura to two to three feet around you. Then surround your aura with different colors of light based on what you need in the way of protection at that moment.

After pulling in your aura and showering it with golden rain, surround its entire surface with a one-to-two-inch-thick layer of golden sunlight. This assists in the ongoing healing and strengthening of your aura, as the gold fills in any holes in your aura and, by its nature, tends to encourage self-healing.

The next depends on how you are feeling. If you are feeling vulnerable or more insecure than usual, you can coat the outside of the golden light with a royal blue light. The nickname of the particular shade you want is "certainty blue" or "true blue." This color actually radiates a quality of confidence and certainty, which naturally tends to repel psychic "glommers on." It also helps you feel more sure of yourself to look out at the world through that color at the edge of your aura.

When you are leaving your house or having people in—especially if you work with clients—it is good to keep a layer of violet light on the extreme outside of your aura. There are several reasons for this. First, as mentioned before, violet light transmutes energies to their natural higher frequencies. If you are working with a client who suddenly releases a lot of pent-up anger, the violet light will transmute the anger and prevent it from entering your field in a harmful way. Second, violet light repels parasitic astral entities. These are etheric entities that feed on repressed emotion and pain. Until you clear your energy field of any feeding and breeding grounds for these parasites, it is wise to keep them out.

Once you clear your subtle-energy bodies to a certain extent and begin to radiate light from your soul, your chakras, and your Higher Self, these entities and lower frequency energies will simply be repelled naturally. Until then, these boundary tools are extremely helpful. Why waste your meditation time, and life in general, processing and clearing what does not even belong to you? Using boundary tools is an example of grace in action.

It is recommended that in your morning meditation, you always include the grounding technique, create your aura egg, and visualize aura boundary colors just discussed. If you do not have time for, or do not feel a need for, the rain shower or violet flame steps, then skip them. The other three steps are the basic essentials for beginning boundaries, and they take very little time once you are accustomed to doing them.

Owning Your Spinal Pathway

The process for owning your spinal pathway actually accomplishes several things. First of all, it clears foreign energies from your spine area as well as blocked energies of your own. This enables your being to inhabit that part of your body more completely. Equally important, it opens the way for cosmic energies and life force to flow freely into and through your body's central pathways, which in turn spins the chakras. This facilitates both the clearing and opening of the chakras.

Another effect of this technique is to balance the downward and upward flows of energy. If you are an etherically healthy person, cosmic energy and life force are constantly flowing in through your crown in the form of a ray of colored light. You have a particular color ray you "run" your entire lifetime. This ray is determined by your soul's purpose for incarnation and the particular types of lessons it intends to learn. (*The Seven Rays Made Visual* by Helen Burmeister is an excellent book on the subject.)

As the ray energy enters your aura and reaches your out-of-body chakra above your crown, it is spun around a series of rings and brought into affinity with your current needs. It then enters your crown, or seventh chakra, reaching a prismatic formation just inside the top of your head. There it is refracted into other colors and sent further down to the center point of your sixth chakra, or third eye. Some of the energy is spun again, this time into the sixth chakra, while the rest goes through the spinal pathway between your chakras and moves down to your throat area. The energy continues spinning into your chakra areas down the spinal pathway all the way down to your root, or first chakra. On the way down, the light is transduced in your heart, or fourth chakra, into a more physically attuned energy that has a firelike quality to it.

At your first chakra, this firelike light swirls around and moves back up your spinal pathway, once again spinning each of your chakras in turn. At your heart chakra it is transduced back into cosmic light and then continues to move upward until it reaches your crown again, at which time it pours into your aura. The downward movement of the ray energy fills the subconscious part of each chakra located in the back of your body. The upward flow rotates and spills over into the conscious aspect of each chakra located in the front of your body.

This entire process is constantly going on day and night. If any one of your chakras completely stopped moving and was unable to continue the flow of ray energy, your body would die within approximately three days. Thus you can see the importance of keeping your spinal pathway clear.

The spinal pathway is one of the most common areas in your body for entity possession and psychic control by other people to occur. Healing and future prevention of this problem are also important benefits of the following technique.

To balance the flow of cosmic energy in your body, Earth energy is brought in through the bottoms of your feet. You have a small chakra located in the center of the bottom of each foot. These chakras are intended to connect you with the planet, and the planet with you, through an ongoing exchange process similar to that of your crown chakra with respect to cosmic energy.

Many people's foot chakras are for all intents and purposes nonfunctional. Due to the amount of pain Earth has taken on through humanity's massacres of indigenous civilizations around the world, her absorption of denied emotions from the human population, the near nonexistence of conscious celebration and ritual gratitude for Earth and all her gifts, not to mention all the blatant abuse of the planet as well, people are mostly cut off from this vital source of nurturing, grounding, and life force. Even the majority of spiritual people I have met and worked with consciously operate primarily upward from the heart chakra. The rest of the chakras are still mostly running on automatic pilot, with little or no Earth connection.

As you open to receive Earth's energy again, it is important to be very specific and clear in your intent. Many people whose foot chakras are functional absorb built-up dark energies from the planet instead of connecting with the planetary being in a mutually nurturing and healthy way. If you are one of those people, following the process for running Earth energy will be very important. You will need to communicate with Earth as the conscious being she is, both giving thanks and asking for exactly what you want from her. Your evolutionary path and health are inseparable from hers. Opening to Earth is more an invocation to Gaia, the sacred Earth Being, than just a technique for the running of energy. Therefore, when Earth energy work is included in the following process, it will be given in a sacred manner, with a suggestion about prayers of gratitude accompanying the technique.

See illustration 3a and 3b on pages 92 and 93 before beginning the next process.

Follow the steps below for keeping your spinal pathway clear and your chakras turning by running cosmic and Earth energy and light:

1. Ground yourself.

2. Pull in your aura to within two to three feet in all directions around your body: above your head, beneath your feet, to both sides of your body, and in front and in back, in the egg shape you learned previously.

3. Check your aura boundary colors and freshen them if necessary.

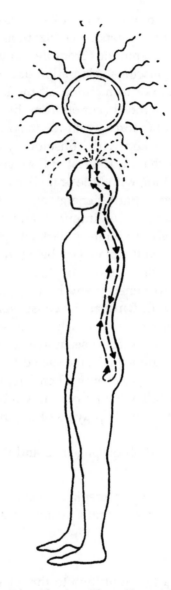

3a. Running energy from the side view: The golden sunlight flows into the crown chakra from just above the aura. From the crown, it flows down the back of the spine, around the tailbone, back up the front of the spine, and back out through the crown.

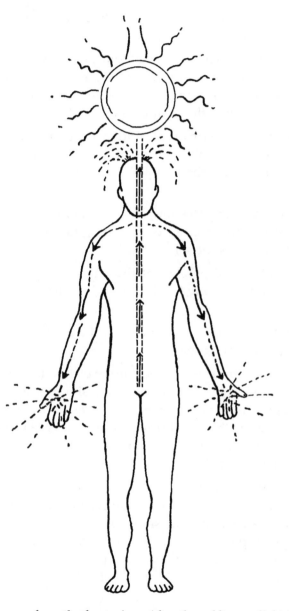

3b. Running energy from the front view: After the golden sunlight has traveled down the back of spine, around the tailbone, and up the front of the spine as far as the throat chakra, the golden energy divides into three equal parts. Two portions flow down the arms and exit through the palms of the hands. The third part flows through the head and exits the body via the crown chakra.

4. Visualize a golden sun about eighteen inches above your head. See it glowing radiantly.

5. Direct a ray, or stream, of sunlight toward your crown chakra in the center of the top of your head. Make it a very small trickling stream at first. This will enable it to move freely down the channel without causing a jam if the channel is clogged.

6. Bring the small stream of golden sunlight inside your head using breath, visualization, and intent. Direct it toward the back of your spine just beneath the occipital ridge at the base of your skull. Go slowly.

7. Continue directing the flow of golden light, still moving slowly, all the way down the back side of your spine to your first chakra, located at the base of your spine.

8. Allow about 10 percent of the energy to pour down your grounding cord, taking any blocked energies with it. This is like cosmic Drano.

9. Direct the remaining 90 percent of the golden sunlight slowly back up the front of your spine.

10. When the light reaches your throat chakra (see illustration 3b on page 93), in the center of your throat, divide it into three equal parts. Then send two parts down your arms and out the palms of your hands, and the third part up and out your crown chakra. There will be a continual inpouring and outflowing of golden light through your crown area as the stream goes down and back up.

11. When you feel the energy flowing smoothly out the palms of your hands and your crown, continue visualizing the downward stream along the back of your spine and the upward stream along the front of your spine. Each time you revisualize this, trace the energy movement with your awareness all the way out your hands and crown. Do this several times until it begins to feel and look natural and easy.

12. Now imagine a gauge with "Manual" and "Automatic" labels superimposed over the Sun. Move the dial to Automatic and allow your mind to be still and quiet.

13. While maintaining the cosmic energy flow on Automatic,

bring your awareness to the bottoms of your feet. Prayerfully say "hello" to Gaia, the Earth Mother, thanking her for all she gives to sustain your life: food, shelter, clothing, cars, warmth from fuel sources in cold weather, water to drink and bathe in, flowers and trees for beauty and the creation of the air we breathe, and anything else that sustains and enhances your physical life and nurtures your spirit. Then tell Mother Earth that you promise to always take care of her and respect her in every way you can; tell her that you will only take what you need from her and give her gratitude and love in return. Find your own sincere way of expressing these things. Then ask the Earth being to fill you with her loving and nurturing light. Open your foot chakras by inhaling through them and using your clear intent to receive what she gives. The energy will flow from your feet up through your legs into your first chakra, where it will blend with the cosmic energy already running upward from that point.

Note: If you have a tendency to take on pain or dark energy from the planet, place a violet-light filter beneath your feet approximately eighteen inches square and six to eight inches thick. This should take care of the problem.

14. *Optional step:* Occasionally you may want to tune in or ask to be shown places on the planet where pain and darkness are held. Visualize filling and surrounding those places with violet flame. Hold the healing vision until you see or sense a release and transmutation of the energies. In chronic areas, it may take several healings to make a big difference.

15. Now put the running of Earth energy on Automatic and use the rest of your meditation time as you normally would. If you have not developed a style of meditation yet, you could simply: observe your breath to create a focus; or repeat an affirmation over and over such as "I am that I am" or "I am filled and overflowing with divine love and Light"; or just gaze into a candle flame, dismissing any thoughts that come to mind.

16. When you are complete, turn both the cosmic and Earth energy gauges back to Manual. Recheck your grounding, then open your eyes and go on with your day. If you feel overenergized, bend over and allow your head and arms to hang, your hands touching the floor, and breathe deeply. You can do this while seated, or you can

stand with your knees bent and feet apart. This is called "bending over and dumping out."

It is recommended that you run energy a minimum of ten minutes at a time for the best results. While it is running, use any meditation technique you like. If you have trouble keeping the golden light and Earth energies flowing when you stop directing them consciously, then make watching them flow through the channels the focus of your meditation. After doing this a few times, you will find yourself able to put the process on Automatic and go on to other meditation techniques or self-healing while the energy continues to run. 📼

Keeping Your Home Psychically Clear and Safe

The last process for creating healthy boundaries and psychic protection is for your home. It can also be used to clear any other place in which you are staying temporarily, such as a motel or someone's home where you are visiting. Although it has not been discussed previously, an important function of healthy boundaries is separation from the lower astral planes. These are the sub–third-, fourth-, and fifth-dimensional planes where dark beings and entities live, as well as negative thoughtform creations of humans. It is the place where nightmares are bred and often experienced.

When you fall asleep at night, you leave your physical body via what is called your "astral body." Your astral body literally travels through and beyond time and space into either the lower astral planes or the higher planes of Light. The latter is much more highly recommended. As you go through an assortment of experiences during this astral travel, you sometimes dream about it. These dreams serve to help you become more aware of and heal your subconscious. Sometimes emotions and past traumas are released through your astral body. At other times you may go into higher dimensions and attend spiritual trainings, or receive healing. You may review past lives for assimilation and growth. These are only a few examples of the possibilities.

Healthy boundaries when you are asleep are essential to healthy boundaries when you are awake. If your astral body is damaged in the lower astral planes, the corresponding parts of your physical and etheric bodies will be left psychically vulnerable to attack or invasion by lower frequency energies. Your astral body, when you are awake, creates a resilient type of protection for your entire energy field. When it becomes damaged, this protective function is in jeopardy. Because of the law of psychic magnetism—"Like frequency is attracted to like frequency"—if you have acquired pain, damage, or fear in your astral body during sleep, you will magnetize those same types of lower-frequency energies into your aura, chakras, or body while awake. You will also be much more vulnerable to psychic attack or invasion by entities vibrating at the same rate who feed off your fear and pain. Their main objective is to keep you in fear, pain, and self-doubt in order to sustain their "feeding ground." Remember, nothing can enter your energy field unless something in you magnetizes it.

In like fashion, if you go into the higher planes during sleep and experience healing, learning, love, or spiritual awakening, those frequencies will be transferred to your physical body space when your astral body returns and you wake up. Can you remember having flying dreams and arising feeling light and full of joy? Perhaps you remember being in spiritual learning situations during sleep and awakening to recall them and apply what you learned in your life. These latter types of experience are the intention of your dream time; another intention is to clear your subconscious.

In order for these healing and learning experiences to happen, it is vital that your home, as well as your aura, be clear of all astral influences. You can accomplish this by using variations on the themes you have already learned for keeping your personal boundaries clear. In addition, there is an invocation that anchors higher-dimensional energies into your home, work place, or other location. For simplification of the following process, the instructions refer only to your home as the space to be cleared. You can adapt the process to your current situation or changing need as appropriate.

Follow the guidelines below for clearing your home:

1. Put a grounding cord of light on your entire house or apartment at the floor level. Extend it to the center of Earth.

2. Visualize a golden sun about two feet in diameter in the center of your home.

3. Expand the golden sun gradually until it fills and surrounds your entire home space.

4. Surround the golden sun with a four-to-eight-foot-thick wall of violet light.

5. Affirm: "This ball of violet light will remain intact until I do this process again. So be it."

6. Next say this invocation: "In the name of the I Am That I Am, I command that this home and grounds be filled with golden light from the City of Light where the Ascended Masters dwell. Only that which is divine may enter. All that is less than divine, which is illusion, must leave now. This will remain so. So be it."

When you use the phrase "I Am That I Am," it is the same as saying, "the Divine God/Goddess Presence," as opposed to the ego "I." So when you use this phrase or affirmation, you are commanding in the name of your own God/Goddess consciousness. It is a very powerful affirmation to call yourself "I Am," and you should do so carefully and in only positive and creative ways. Any time you say, "I am. . .", and then finish the phrase in a definitive manner, even casually, you are identifying your essence as that which you say. For example, you might say, "I am angry," or, "I am a loving person," and the statement literally defines your essence as being that quality.

The second portion of the invocation states,". . . golden light from the City of Light where the Ascended Masters dwell. . . ." This refers to the higher-dimensional "dwelling place" of those beings who were once incarnate upon Earth, became enlightened, and died consciously, or ascended. These Ascended Masters—or Great White Brotherhood, as they are also called—remain in the City of Light to serve other humans on their spiritual journeys toward enlightenment and ascension. They guide and teach you in your dreams and waking state as you are ready, willing, and available. To call upon the light from their dwelling place is to fill your home with the energy equivalent of a sacred temple filled with such a high frequency of light that only divine energies and beings of divine intent can withstand it.

Using this process, in a very short time you can clear your home of astral and negative energies and begin to gradually experience a greater sense of peace and well being in your new temple. This will assist you in experiencing more positive sleep time as well.

You will probably want to repeat this process about twice weekly for a few weeks. As your home becomes consistently clearer, do the house-clearing process whenever you feel a need. I routinely do it about once a week because it feels good.

Before going to sleep at night, do the following steps:

1. Surround your aura with a violet bubble.

2. Ask your Guardian Angel to watch over and keep your body safe all night while you sleep.

3. State this affirmation: "In the name of the I Am That I Am, I command that while my body sleeps, I will travel only to the higher planes of Divine Light. So be it."

Doing this process at bedtime may give you a better night's sleep. It is especially important if you have a tendency to experience night fear and restlessness.

Chapter 6

PREPARING FOR PLEIADIAN LIGHTWORK

PART II: SELF-HEALING AND CLEARING

The techniques given in this chapter are intended to increase your ability to heal and clear yourself easily and efficiently as you move through normal spiritual growth and expansion of consciousness. The Pleiadian Lightwork, which begins in the next chapter, will accelerate not only your spiritual growth and expansion, it will likewise accelerate the surfacing of karmic patterns, thoughts, and beliefs that need clearing, as well as energy blocks from miscellaneous sources. At times, while receiving an energy session from the Pleiadian Emissaries of Light and the Christ, you may find yourself entangled in past images, formerly repressed emotions, or negative thoughts. When these or other would-be problems arise, the self-help tools given here can prove invaluable and enabling.

It is highly recommended, therefore, that you take the time to go through the following training materials as a preparation for handling whatever comes up in your clearing process as graciously and easily as possible. The releases triggered by Pleiadian Lightwork, as well as your ongoing spiritual evolution, not only occur during the sessions but often afterward as well. As you open to higher and higher frequencies of Ka and Higher Self energies, the denser energies held in your body and aura naturally begin to "burn off." The more you raise your vibratory rate, the more "burn off"—or "inner fire"—takes place.

As you mature spiritually, you will begin to recognize these burn offs as releases and transmutations of old energies, and you will identify less and less with them. Issues that surface during or after healing sessions will no longer be so all encompassing. Although they will be intensified at times by the influx of higher vibrational energies, you will find yourself more capable of asking, "What do I need to learn from this?" instead of playing out the dramas in your daily life as if they were real. You will use your self-healing and clearing skills to take care of the issues and move on. This is the natural grace that comes through experience; effective techniques are part of that grace.

Think of the time and energy you invest in learning the techniques in this chapter as investments in a more peaceful and gracious future. You will be properly prepared to receive the more passive light and energy work from the Pleiadians and the Christ in the rest of the book when you know that you can take care of your own stuck energies if or when they need attention.

Clearing with Roses

Visualization and psychic clearing work using etheric images of roses predates contemporary use by at least several centuries. My own past-life memories of myself as a priestess and white witch revealed the use of roses in spiritual practices as far back as the twelfth century A.D. It is certainly possible that clearing with roses goes back further still. The rose, as a healing symbol, is a very effective and useful tool both in your own clearing process and for clearing others.

Just as the lotus has been used for ages as the symbol for enlightenment, the rose has been used to symbolize and bring about the "purity of self-affinity." What this means is that roses have the ability to eliminate energies in your energy field that are unnatural and foreign to your essential and inherent way of being. For example, if you feel congestion in your heart chakra and suspect that it is due to another person's imbalanced energy that you have taken on, you can release the foreign energy with a rose. Simply place the image of a large, fully blooming rose in your heart chakra, and with the person's image inside it, allow the rose to fill up with the foreign energy. Then remove the rose, filled with the other person's energy, from your heart chakra. Send the rose outside your aura, or even outside the building you are in, and visualize it dissolving, vaporizing, or simply going "poof." The other person's energy will dissolve along with the rose. As the rose disappears, the energy being removed from your heart chakra is neutralized and sent back to the person to whom it belongs. This technique is called "blowing roses." Please note that it is always important that you blow roses *outside* your auric field. If you dissolve the rose inside your aura, it will neutralize the energy somewhat, but you will still have the other person's energy in your space.

In other words, if you absorb someone else's fear into your heart chakra and then extract the fear into a rose and send it back, what the person receives back is not fear, but neutralized emotional energy. The person receiving energy back is free to do with the energy as he or she wishes. The person may turn the energy into fear again or choose to use it any other way. You are freed of the energy in such a gentle way that it should not magnetize any karma with the person.

Some psychic or spiritual paths teach techniques like placing mirrors around the energy or around the other person and having the mirror reflect back to the intrusive one whatever has been sent to you, but ten times stronger. Others may teach you to form the energy into a tight ball and hurl it back at the psychic intruder. All these types of practices do is engage you in psychic warfare and create karma. Any practice that can cause harm to the other person involved creates a karmic link between you and that person. There is also a great possibility that you will take on more of the karmic responsibility than the other person will because of your intent to send back harm even greater than the harm that was sent to you, instead of simply protecting yourself.

You are ultimately responsible for not allowing yourself to be "dumped on" or victimized. So if you have a problem with boundaries, you need to learn about healthy boundaries instead of blaming others for dumping on you and then punishing them for it. This in no way negates the other person's responsibility for learning to be harmless. We are all responsible for our impact on one another. That is part of being on a planet where we have agreed to cocreate. What this does mean is that you are responsible for removing yourself from harm without harming anyone else in return, any time this is possible. Using roses can be a very effective way of taking responsibility in this fashion.

Following is the first exercise for using roses:

1. Close your eyes and ground yourself.

2. Check your aura and pull it in or expand it to two to three feet around your body in all directions.

3. Check your boundary colors and make any needed adjustments.

4. Visualize a rose of any color in full bloom in your aura, in front of your eyes. Stay with the visualization until it feels real to you. See or imagine it in as much detail as you can.

5. Then move the rose outside your aura and make it disappear.

6. Now create a rose inside the center of your head. Intend that it take on anyone else's energy that might be there. Hold the vision of the rose inside your head for about thirty seconds.

7. Pull the rose out of your head and outside your aura and then make it disappear.

8. Next create a rose outside your aura in front of you.

9. Think of someone in your life with whom you have had recent conflict or ill feelings. See that person's face in the rose and ask the rose to clear any negative thoughts you have about that person, or any of his or her energy you are holding.

10. Continually watch the rose for about thirty seconds. You may notice it closing up, the way certain flowers, like morning glories, do after dark. This is an indication that the rose is absorbing something.

11. Move the rose outside and above your house, then dissolve it.

12. If this last rose closed up completely, indicating that it removed a lot of energy from or about the chosen person, create a new one outside your aura with the same person's image in it. Keep watching until this rose either fills up completely or stops closing

shut when it is partially full of the person's energy or your negative thoughts about the person, whichever comes first.

13. Once again, place the rose above your house and make it disappear.

14. *Optional:* If the last rose completely filled up, you may want to continue the process of creating and dissolving roses with that person's image in them until a rose remains unaffected for about ten seconds. At that point, you know you have released all you can relative to that person at this time.

15. Open your eyes and continue reading about other uses for roses, if you wish. [🔊]

Roses can also be used for clearing problematic issues in your life. I can give you a practical example of this from a personal life experience concerning my former fear of water. I have had a love/fear relationship with bodies of water my whole life. As a child I loved swimming pools, lakes, rivers, and even the bathtub; but my mother, in her attempts to protect me, was continually gasping and warning of impending drowning unless I was extra careful. She would say, "You can drown in as little as an inch of water if you fall down. So be very careful." I am sure I heard that statement dozens of times by the age of four. This statement, followed by fearful gasps if I walked a little too fast across the eight-inch-deep children's pool, or stood up in the bathtub, implanted an unnatural fear in my body.

In my early thirties, I decided to teach myself to swim since I was too frightened to trust anyone else around water. Slowly, step by step, accompanied by lots of my own gasping in panic, I learned. It became second nature for me to swim in and even jump into swimming pools. Eventually I even felt relatively secure and could enjoy swimming in large bodies of water.

In 1988, I met another challenge. While vacationing in the Caribbean on Isla Mujeres, Mexico, I decided to try snorkeling. I knew by then that I could not sink or even swim underwater because I am a large and very buoyant woman. I planned, therefore, to simply swim and float on my stomach with the snorkeling mask in order to enjoy seeing the coral reef and brightly colored fish that lived there.

Much to my chagrin, when I put the mask on the first time to practice in two feet of water, I came up gasping in complete panic. After trying several more times, only to experience increasingly worse results, I sat down in the water feeling defeated and ready to give up. Then the wee small voice inside me said, "Don't give up. You have tools to use, so use them. Try blowing roses." Though hesitant, I agreed. I began by just putting on the mask and breathing through the mouthpiece while I blew roses. When that became easy I took another step. Still wearing the snorkeling mask and breathing apparatus I placed my face in the water, knelt on all fours, and blew roses as long as I could before I felt panicky. Then I came up for a breather before continuing. It took only about five minutes of this before I felt completely at ease and headed toward the reef. It was unnecessary to stop or even blow roses again as I found myself about 100 feet from shore, all alone, having a wonderful time. I stayed out there for about an hour without any further incident of even momentary fear. I have never taken the use of roses for granted since that time.

The next time you feel nervous or fearful about anything, whether it be a first date or learning to snorkel, try blowing roses. Do so while in the situation itself, ideally while the fear is still occurring. If that is impossible, just imagine the situation at another time and blow roses.

Another way of working on a life issue using roses is to create a symbol or picture for the problem area. For instance, if you have a problem trusting even trustworthy people, you can imagine a symbol or picture that represents distrust. You can even imagine the word *distrust* in big bold letters and use that as your symbol. You will use the symbol to assist you in releasing pictures, emotions, or other blocked energies relative to your distrust issue. Then you can simply sit down and run energy while continually blowing roses with your symbol inside them until the roses cease to fill up with your imbalanced energies any more. Running energy while blowing roses assists you in releasing the blocked energies held in your chakras related to the issue on which you are working.

The following exercise is a way to use roses to clear issues:

1. Close your eyes. Ground yourself, and do any needed aura adjustments.

2. Bring the cosmic gold sun above you and run the golden light along your spinal and arm channels, as described in the previous chapter. When this light is running fully, put it on Automatic.

3. Bring in Earth energy through your feet and legs and allow it to blend with the gold moving up your spine and out your arms and head. When it is flowing smoothly and fully, put it on Automatic as well. Leave the cosmic and Earth energies running for the duration of the clearing session.

4. Think of something you want to work on like a bad habit such as nail biting or chocolate binges. It could also be an attitude or emotional tendency, like lack of confidence, blame, feeling like a victim, distrust, shame, or fear of spiders. Whatever you choose, imagine a symbol for the problem now.

5. Just outside your aura, create whatever color rose comes to mind and put the symbol inside the rose.

6. Breathe deeply to assist in the release while you watch the rose. When it is filled with energy that you have released into it relative to your particular problem area, dissolve the rose.

7. Continue blowing roses with your chosen symbol inside them—creating and dissolving them, outside your aura, until the final rose remains unaffected for at least ten seconds. Then dissolve that rose.

8. Either continue to run energy and meditate, or open your eyes at this time—whichever you prefer. 🗩

One last use for roses is self-protection. Roses can be kept outside your aura with a grounding stem into Earth's surface at all times to discourage unwanted influences and help define your boundaries. They will tend to absorb stray and extraneous foreign energies floating around so that these energies do not enter your aura. Boundary roses will not take care of everything, but they will help greatly.

You may prefer to keep one giant rose rooted into Earth's surface in front of your aura. Or you may prefer to use five roses outside your aura: one in front of you, one behind your back, one on either side of you, and one above you. (See illustration 4 on page 109.)

The grounding cord takes care of protection beneath you. Avoid any tendency to use these roses in a paranoid way. This is not a tool to use because "they" are out to get you, whoever "they" are. This technique is simply a tool to help you take personal responsibility for your boundaries and your choices. It is especially useful if you are very sensitive or have a history of being a psychic sponge.

You may find, during the simple process of placing the roses in the five locations immediately outside your aura, that you have not been owning your backside. In other words, the back part of your aura may be very dissipated, or you may be less aware of it than the rest of your aura. Taking the time to visualize a rose there and to feel the space between your body and the rose naturally strengthens that part of your aura and makes your back less susceptible to invasion, and even physical injury.

The following steps will help you establish boundary roses:

1. After closing your eyes, ground yourself and adjust your aura as needed.

2. Visualize a rose of any size and color that feels good to you, and place it outside your aura in front of you. See it in detail.

3. Imagine that the rose is attached to a stem that is rooted into Earth. Intend that the rose remain there until you consciously dissolve it.

4. Visualize another rose outside your aura on your left side.

5. Also place a rooted stem on this rose, and once again intend that it remain until you dissolve it.

6. Now place a rose with a stem into Earth to your right, outside your aura. Use the same intent that it remain.

7. Above your head and just outside your aura, place another rose. Again see it as having a rooted stem and intend that it stay there until you remove it.

8. Last, visualize a rose with a stem outside your aura behind your back. If necessary, work with your breath and intent to

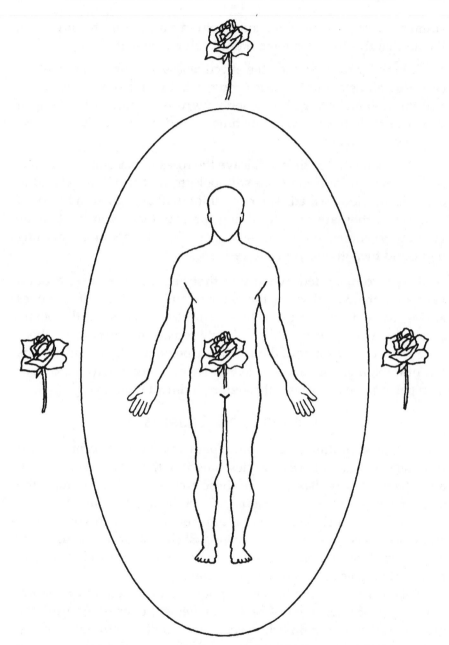

4. Roses are placed around the aura for healthier psychic boundaries: above the head, to either side, in front, and behind. (Not shown: the rose behind, located directly opposite the rose in front of the body.)

strengthen and extend your aura behind you to two to three feet. Intend that this rose also remain until you return to it.

9. In order to strengthen the effectiveness of your intent, dissolve each rose and stem in the order you created them. Then repeat steps two through eight to give yourself new roses in all five locations. If you need to do these steps a few times in order to make the roses feel more real, do so now.

10. When you are finished, leave the roses in place until bedtime. At bedtime, notice if the roses still look fresh, if they have closed at all, or if they look wilted. Their condition will be a good indicator of how much they are actually doing for you. Once you have made your observations, repeat the steps again, first dissolving the existing roses, and then giving yourself fresh ones.

It is recommended, when you first begin to use roses around your aura, that you dissolve the old ones and give yourself new ones at least twice a day for a few days, or until they consistently remain intact when you check on them. I only replace my aura roses about once or twice a week now, though in the beginning they tended to be full of foreign energy and needed replacing at least daily. Find your own personal requirements through experimentation. 𝄢

Clearing Your Chakras

This process utilizes the spinal pathway clearing technique for running cosmic and Earth energies, taught in the previous chapter, in an expanded way. Basically, as these two energies run along the spinal channel, you can consciously direct them to flow into the front and back of each chakra, one at a time, beginning with your crown and working your way down to your first chakra, or root. This flushes your chakras and energizes them much more effectively than just running energies up and down your spine.

This technique may bring up emotions to be felt and released. You may experience a lot of heat or movement of energy during the process. Or you may find the experience deeply soothing, relaxing, and refreshing. Deep breathing into the areas in which you are experiencing intensity or contraction should soon alleviate any discomfort or allow the emotions to be released. If you find the process to be rather intense, go only as far as it feels right to you. For example, if you begin to feel a little burned out or overloaded after clearing only two or three chakras, then stop. You can take up where you left off later in the day or the next day.

In general, it is recommended that you use this technique only once or twice per week unless you are clearly guided to do otherwise. Even if it is pleasant and calming for you, it will accelerate your clearing and healing in an ongoing way after the meditation is done. So find your right pacing and rhythm and enjoy.

1. Ground yourself.

2. Pull in your aura and check your boundary colors.

3. Check and replace your aura boundary roses in front, behind, above, and to the left and right of you.

4. Bring in the golden sun above your head and run energy down the back of your spine and back up again. Remember, 10 percent goes down your grounding cord at the base of your spine and the rest comes back up your front. At your throat, the remaining energy divides into three equal parts and runs down each arm and out the top of your head. After it is running smoothly and fully, put it on Automatic.

5. Now invoke and run Earth energy up to your first chakra through your feet. It will blend with the golden sunlight in your first chakra and run upward in that blended state. Place the Earth energy flow on Automatic.

6. Now place a blanket of roses around your aura to absorb everything that is being released. This will help prevent released energies from hanging around in your auric field.

7. Your crown, or seventh chakra, spins on the top of your head and has no back side. Overflow the gold and Earth-energy blend through this chakra to flush, clear, and strengthen its flow. Doing this for one to two minutes is usually adequate.

8. Turn off the flow to your crown and run the energies through the front and back of your third eye, or sixth chakra. Again, one to two minutes is enough.

9. Shut off the flow to your third eye, and bring the combined energies down to your throat chakra, assuming the same flow pattern out the front and back. After one to two minutes, turn it off.

10. Bring the golden-light and Earth-energy blend to your heart, or fourth chakra, in the center of your chest. Direct the energy out the front and back of this chakra, as you did previously with the others. After one to two minutes, shut off the flow to your heart chakra.

11. Repeat the same process for the front and back of your solar plexus, or third chakra. Shut off the flow after one to two minutes and move on.

12. Now run the blended energies through the front and back of your sacral center, or second chakra. This chakra is located approximately halfway between your navel and pubic mound. After one to two minutes, turn off the energy flow.

13. Now run the Earth and cosmic energies out your first chakra at the base of your tailbone. Like your crown chakra it has no back side. It spins downward between your legs, with its opening pointing toward Earth. After one to two minutes, shut off the flow through this chakra and resume the normal running of energy along your spinal pathway and arm channels only.

14. Remove the blanket of roses surrounding your aura and place them above your house. Then blow them up, or dissolve them.

15. If you wish to continue meditating, use your own judgment about whether to also continue running energy on Automatic or to switch it to Manual, which allows it to turn off.

16. When you are complete, check your grounding cord and reground yourself if necessary. Then open your eyes and "bend over and dump out." ▱

Clearing Pictures

First, I would like to define what I mean by "pictures." Pictures are generally one of three things: (1) other people's pictorial ideas about you, or about an area of life, that you allowed in; (2) your own limited conclusions drawn from life experience; or (3) life experience pictures remaining in your aura or body because of unreleased emotional charge around them. Following are hypothetical examples of each:

1. *Other people's pictures.* Perhaps you were bored in school by the lack of encouragement of individual creativity. As a result, you daydreamed and did not remember your lessons well and were misconstrued as unintelligent or stupid. Your teacher's, your parents', and the other students' pictures about you got into your aura and created self-doubt and low self-esteem. You got *stuck on their pictures* about you. You still carry those pictures even now.

Another example: You got stuck on pictures of your father's repeated monologues about how tough life is. He used the dinner table as his place to expound on the difficulties of trying to make a living, how competitive life is, and how no one gives you a break in this world without you struggling for it. He painted elaborate examples from his life experiences to prove his point, and then projected them out to the family listeners, instilling those pictures in you because you were impressionable enough to take them. These pictures are stuck in your third chakra, reminding you constantly that life is hard. You experience them as tightness and/or pain, even ulcers, when you are faced with normal life challenges. You tend to magnetize a lot of intense challenges and difficulties because you took on your father's pictures and still have them in your aura or chakras.

2. *Your own limited conclusions drawn from life experience.* As an adolescent female, you had several experiences of boys being grabby and projecting lusty pictures of what they would like to do to you. You were looking for validation because of insecurity and were afraid of males because of a negative father. Now you may have pictures stuck in your breasts or female organs about all men looking at women in a lusty, conquering way. This causes fear, relationships in which you are used as a sex object, and an inability to draw respectful males into your life as friends or lovers.

Another example: As a child you excelled in singing and dancing, and it was the only way you ever received any appreciation. You have the pictures of those experiences imprinted in your heart chakra as the way to get love. They are also in your third chakra as the way to create self-esteem, and in your third eye as your only source of positive self-image. This greatly limits your ability to become a well-rounded adult, grounded in a sense of overall self-love and self-appreciation. You are still attempting to earn love and approval in the same old ways. Because of this, you can create problems in the very areas you are so reliant on. As a singer you can create thyroid imbalance or a tight throat. As a dancer, you can dislocate your knee just before that most important audition.

When you rely on any one thing or person for your sense of self-esteem, self-image, and self-worth—whether it be sexual validation, singing, dancing, or any other personal obsession—you internally hold the fear of losing that ability or appearance because it has been elevated beyond normal importance. That fear eventually creates breakdown in some form or other, whether it be physical, mental, or emotional. The answer is to clear the pictures, change the behaviors, and develop a spiritual sense of worth based on acting in integrity and simply living as the beautiful being that you are. Then the singing, dancing, or sexual expression can be a natural outpouring from your healthy and loving sense of self.

3. *Life experience pictures with unreleased emotional charge.* If you were physically or sexually abused as a child, adolescent, or adult, you may still be carrying pictures of those experiences in your energy field. These pictures now cause great fear and trauma to be magnetized into your life. When the original experiences took place, you probably were not safe or able to release your emotions and feelings, thereby trapping them, along with the life pictures, in your body and aura. You may need to be in a safe setting with a trusted therapist or spiritual healer in order to finally express and release these traumas as an adult. Or you may be able to release just by knowing how to help yourself.

It can help greatly to sit down in a safe place and run energy while you breathe deeply and blow up the past pictures in roses until they are gone. If you cannot find them yourself, you may need to seek the help of a good clairvoyant healer.

A less intense example of this category of pictures is exhibited by people who buy only name-brand, advertised products. This actually occurs quite rampantly in today's society. Certain pictures are constantly reinforced in magazine and newspaper ads, as well as in television and radio commercials that claim: "Ours is the best" or "If you want your family to love you, serve them . . ." or "Wash their clothes in . . ." I think you get the picture. Excuse the pun.

As a person with certain chemical sensitivities, such as allergies to commercial detergents, shampoos, soaps, and perfumes, I have learned about the neurotoxins in these products that literally deaden brain tissue and nerve endings. Of course, I have had to make students and friends with whom I spend much time aware of the problem so they can stop using these products if we are to spend time together. Some people are very gracious about making the changes and are even grateful to know about the toxic nature of these substances. Some take it very personally. However, a few have actually looked at me in fear or dread and said things like: "But I have to use Tide. It's the only thing that really gets my clothes clean" or "It's the only shampoo that really works on my hair. Everyone knows it's the best." The first few times I heard such responses, I was so surprised that people actually believed them that I was speechless. Then I began to tell them about the cleanliness of my own clothes, washed only in baking soda and occasional chemical-free stain remover, and the shininess and strength of my hair, cleaned in Earth Science Unscented Shampoo and Conditioner. I also turned people on to unscented, biodegradable laundry detergents, cleansers, and soaps. Gradually they started to blow their pictures by hearing about, using, and seeing the results of nontoxic alternatives. Many thanked me later for their healthier hair and skin, fewer sinus problems, and less brain fuzziness after changing detergents or switching from perfumes to high quality essential oils.

Of course, these are only a few examples of the pictures you can get stuck on, but they are enough to give you an idea of what to look for in yourself. Now you need to know what to do about these pictures. Once you identify the pictures you feel stuck on, it is fairly easy to clear them. Basically, you run energy while blowing the pictures up in roses over and over again until they disappear. If the pictures have a lot of charge on them, you may need to do the clearing process frequently for awhile, until you feel a consistent new feeling and/or behavioral response in related areas of your life. Deeper core issues with extreme trauma or ingrained beliefs and thoughtforms may still require outside help, but this process works incredibly well for most stuck pictures.

Use the following format for clearing pictures:

1. Close your eyes and ground yourself.

2. Check your aura size, colors, and roses and make any needed adjustments.

3. Run the cosmic gold and Earth energies through your body channels and put them both on Automatic.

4. Determine a picture you feel stuck on from an example given above or a different one of your own.

5. Work with the pictures in your mind's eye. If you do not automatically see or remember the pictorial scenes as you think about an issue, ask for a picture to represent it.

6. Place the picture outside your aura and put it inside a large rose of whatever color you automatically create.

7. Dissolve this first rose and create a new one in its place around the remaining picture.

8. Continue creating and blowing roses around the picture as quickly as you can, without feeling rushed, until the picture finally disappears. If emotions arise during this process, breathe deeply to assist yourself in releasing them completely. If you begin to cry or tremble, tell yourself that you are safe and you are simply reexperiencing old emotions as they leave your body. Then proceed to feel the emotions as fully as you can while you create and dissolve roses. If you need to scream, beat pillows, jump up and down, or simply observe the feelings, trust your inherent knowing about what is needed. The correct expression will end contraction, help you feel more emotionally honest, and bring you relief even while it is going on.

9. Now visualize another picture associated with the same issue and blow it up in roses over and over until it is also gone. Repeat this process until you come up with no more related pictures.

10. Continue to run energy and breathe fully to assist the ongoing release of emotions and energies that are attached to the pictures.

When you feel complete with the energy and/or emotional release and are filled with light again, you are through.

11. Next, create an affirmation to replace the old pictures. Make sure it is worded in a positive "I am..." type of statement such as: "I am safe and free to express myself now" or "I am a beautiful and radiant Light Being and deeply worthy of respect and love both when I sing and when I do not" or "I am supported by life and people effortlessly and joyously." The affirmation will help anchor an alternative reality more in alignment with who you truly are and what you want to create in life.

12. Open your eyes and thank yourself for the gift you have just given yourself.

13. Bend over and dump out. [cassette icon]

Clearing Beliefs, Judgments, Perfect Pictures, and Thoughtforms

"There are no limits, just beliefs" is a favorite expression of mine. It says a lot. What it says is that you create your own reality, and that whatever you believe will manifest in your life whether you consciously intend it to or not. It is useful, therefore, to examine some of the beliefs you may not wish to have controlling your life. If you find yourself faced with being taken for granted all the time, you may have a combination of self-esteem issues that need healing, along with lots of accompanying beliefs. Your beliefs might be: "People don't like me because I'm not very likable" or "I'm not a very good conversationalist. I'm boring" or "I'm everybody's doormat. Everybody just walks all over me and there's nothing I can do about it." As long as you hold beliefs such as these as your *truths,* you will continue to manifest situations and people who will prove you are right. Likewise, as you change these beliefs, the world is free to give you new and different kinds of situations and people more in alignment with a higher truth.

I have had conversations with many friends and clients about the validity or invalidity of their beliefs. One client had a belief in his third chakra to the effect of: "No one likes me or ever gives me a chance." When I pointed it out as a belief that needed to be changed, he became very defensive saying, "It's true. It's not my fault. I didn't make it that way. It's just the way my life is, and I can prove it over and over because of what keeps happening to me." He was so protective of his belief and his own victimhood that I had a hard time talking to him.

I tried to explain to this client that life kept proving his belief to be true due to the law of magnetism. What he held inside, he drew to him. I went on to say that the deeper source of the problem was his own anger and hurt with people in his past who had treated him unfairly, and that what he needed to do was clear the belief, release the old emotions, and eventually come to a place of forgiveness. The most he would ever concede during that session was, "Well, I'll burn the belief, but a hell of a lot of good it'll do!" When I tried to work with him on the emotions holding the belief in place, he was so resistant and attached to proving that his former wife had wronged him that he felt justified in holding on to the blame, hurt, and anger until she admitted she was wrong. There was nothing more I could do except honor his free will to choose.

You have to be willing to let go of the past if you really want to heal and create a more positive future. There was a great song that was popular a few years ago with the line, "And I think it's about forgiveness, forgiveness, even if . . . you don't love me anymore." Not all beliefs require forgiveness in order to be released; but some, like the one my client was holding, certainly do.

The main things required in order to clear a belief are:

1. awareness of the belief

2. willingness to acknowledge your belief as a belief and not the truth

3. willingness to let go of the belief

4. willingness to feel and release associated emotions

5. acceptance of the responsibility for creating your own reality and not being a victim

6. the ability to imagine an unlimited healthy alternative to the belief

7. a method for releasing the old belief

The method I use to clear beliefs is fairly simple. After identifying a belief you would like to clear, such as "I'm not attractive enough for a person to ever love me," you close your eyes and imagine a picture or a symbol to represent your belief. For example, you might see yourself looking in a hand mirror and the glass breaking in response to your image. Then you hold the image of you looking into the broken mirror in your mind's eye, while thinking about the belief and breathing deeply in your body to find out where your body contracts and what emotions you feel. You might notice that your chest is caved in a little and your heart chakra is tightened in grief and shame. Perhaps your head is tucked, your eyes are tense, and your lower back and rectum are contracted. Next, you breathe into those areas one at a time, talking to them and telling them that the broken mirror image and the idea of not being attractive enough to be loved are false; they are only reactions to a belief structure. Then you tell your body to relax and let go of the contraction and the emotions. When your body begins to relax and the emotions soften, imagine the picture or symbol as a photograph. Stamp it vehemently several times with a red rubber stamp that says, "**CANCELED!**" Then rip it up and burn it in a violet flame until it is completely gone. The violet flame transmutes the energy to a higher vibrational frequency, or enlightens it. If you still feel a charge or more contraction, get another image for the belief and repeat the steps.

Now that you have an understanding of what a belief is and what is needed to clear it, try the following:

1. There is a planetary belief, or lie, that says, "If you are born, you must die." This widespread belief negates all possibility of ascension and spiritual evolution from the third to fourth dimensions. In this exercise, you will use this as your belief to be canceled.

2. Close your eyes, ground yourself, pull your aura in, and check your aura boundary colors and roses.

3. *Optional*: Run cosmic gold and Earth energies to help you release more deeply if you want to take the time, but this is not crucial.

4. Ask internally for a picture or symbol to represent the belief,

"If you are born, you must die." Any image that comes to you is okay. It could be a coffin, a skull and crossbones, your own funeral scene, or whatever you come up with.

5. While holding the image, think about the belief a few times while breathing deeply and observing where your body responds and how your emotions react to the belief. Your responses may vary from very subtle to very intense.

6. After identifying the body areas and/or emotions, talk to your physical and emotional bodies. Tell them to accept the deep breath and let go of the holding and contraction. Tell them the holding is due to a lie, a false belief that you are ready to let go of now.

7. When your body and emotions have relaxed, imagine a photograph of the belief symbol.

8. Use a red rubber stamp that says, "**CANCELED!**" and stamp the photograph of the belief symbol emphatically as many times as you need to in order to feel that it has been canceled in your conscious mind as well as in your subconscious.

9. Now tear the canceled photo into two or four pieces and burn them in a violet flame until they disappear completely.

10. If you still feel a charge on this belief, repeat the process with new symbols or pictures until you feel clear. If this is a core belief (one with a lot of charge), you may need to repeat this process for several days or even weeks until you feel it is truly gone. This is due to the layering, or onion effect, of your holographic nature.

11. Think of an affirmation to replace these beliefs, such as: "I am ready to transcend death and ascend in this life" or "Ascension is the final evolutionary step for human beings." Make up your own if you prefer. Say it silently or out loud a few times until your body responds to the affirmation by relaxing, feeling freer and lighter, or more expanded and filled with light.

12. Open your eyes.

13. Now go back to step 1. This time think of a belief you know you have that is limiting your life or your relationships to others, God/Goddess, or yourself. Put it into a phrase. Then repeat all the above steps to clear your belief.

Judgments are cleared the same way as beliefs. The only differ-ence is the nature and source of the energy being cleared. I would like to describe the difference between judgment, opinion, prefer-ence, and discernment. There seems to be a lot of confusion and con-troversy about these areas among today's spiritual seekers.

A *judgment* is a thought projection onto or about another person or yourself that negates the value of the person's essence. It identifies the other person or yourself as that which you dislike and see as hav-ing no value. For example, if you say or think, "He's just a stubborn, pig-headed jerk," you identify the person as that which you have called him. You dismiss the value of the person's essence and label the whole person based on his attitude or behavior. This is a judgment.

Alternatively, if you say or think, "I feel really unsafe, frustrated, and angry when he behaves so stubbornly, and I don't like it," you express your feelings and state an *opinion* about what you perceive in the person's behavior. If you further say or think, "I don't feel safe around or respected by this person, and I choose not to spend time with him anymore," you state a *preference* based on life experience. This is using *discernment*.

Remember: You are spiritually responsible for not judging your-self and others, no matter what. Every spirit or ensouled being is on its own evolutionary journey, and you have no right to condemn, judge, and therefore dismiss his/her—or your—own inherent value. However, you are simultaneously responsible for making discerning choices in life, taking care of yourself, and not being a victim. If you know someone has consistently behaved in a distrustful, disrespect-ful, or harmful manner, you must use discernment and choose what degree of relationship, if any, is appropriate for you to maintain. This is not negating the person's ability to grow, it is simply choosing how you need to or prefer to relate to them in the meantime.

Once, while I was meditating in a hot-springs pool in California about nine years ago, a rather loud and gruff-acting man entered the large pool. Keeping my eyes closed, I began to bicker silently about why they let such obnoxious, unspiritual people into the pools. Why not limit access to sensitive, spiritually appropriate people like me? The louder and more obnoxious his behavior became, the more judgmentally and arrogantly I reacted. Then I clairaudiently heard a loud male voice say, "If you judge it, you shall become it!" Needless to say, this got my attention and humbled me very quickly. Silently I replied, "Help me see him differently. What must I do?"

The member of the Great White Brotherhood who was speaking to me explained it like this: "Imagine a circle with 360 degrees. Every aspect of your character, personality identification, and behavior undergoes an evolutionary process that begins at 0 degrees and eventually finishes at 360 degrees. For example, in the area of sensitivity to others and to your surroundings, you are currently at about 280 degrees and the man you are judging so harshly is at about 40 degrees. And yet, the only thing that creates the illusion of difference between the two of you is that you are in a time-and-space-reality-based consciousness. On a being and spirit level outside of time and space, you both identically occupy all 360 degrees simultaneously, which makes you equals. You probably won't be drawn to create a friendship with each other here on Earth in time and space because in this lifetime your evolutionary levels are incompatible. But you must see him as an equal in truth and acknowledge his spiritual value even as you make a discerning choice not to spend time with him."

I sincerely thanked the Brother with tears in my eyes for the much-needed and cherished lesson. I do not think I will ever forget that lesson, though I still find myself needing to apply it at times.

Basically, you must make discerning choices about whom you associate closely with and to what degree of intimacy. Vibrationally, there are people you resonate with and people you just do not relate to at all. It is natural to have preferences based on resonance and compatibility. It is important to realize that your evolutionary level of compatibility may be very different from your soul attraction to someone. You may be drawn to someone by soul attraction and karmic magnetism only to find that day-to-day life with that person is painful, unpleasant, or incompatible, at best.

One partner of mine accused me of blaming him, judging him, and not treating him as an equal because I pointed out that he never kept his promises to me, and I gave him examples of specifics. I also explained that I felt hurt by this particular behavior. Every time I expressed hurt feelings or wanted to discuss something that was not working for me in the relationship, I received the same message from him, and I responded by crying, feeling guilty, and working really hard to be more understanding and loving. But I also continued to feel wronged.

One day, when the same scenario had just played out between us, Archangel Michael said to me softly, "Amorah, you are being manipulated and controlled by his withholding of love, and his guilt- and shame-based accusations. You have a right to point out what is not working for you. When a person is treating you badly, you are responsible for standing up for yourself and not allowing it to continue. To speak out in that way is not blaming; it is using discernment. You may know that he is an equal on a soul level, but on a day-to-day personality level, he is a rebellious and punishing little boy most of the time, and you are a mature woman. You are simply not at equal levels of growth and maturity here on Earth. It is important that you guiltlessly acknowledge that and stop feeling so ashamed for noticing his actions and attitudes."

Lessons like this one are incredibly valuable on the spiritual journey. To make sensible and loving choices in partnerships and friendships, you must not only take into consideration your soul connection with other people and their spiritual intent. You must also examine their day-to-day actions and behavioral responses to life situations. If people are not putting into daily practice what their spiritual ideals portray, are unable or unwilling to keep promises and treat you respectfully and with integrity, you must make discerning choices about the nature of the relationships you want or do not want with them.

Now that I have demonstrated what judgments are versus discernments, preferences, and opinions, you are ready to clear a judgment. Think of someone you hold a judgment about. Think about what the judgment is. Then go back to the process for clearing a belief and follow the same procedures for clearing the judgment. At step 12 simply affirm: "I acknowledge that _____ (name of the person) is a divine holy spirit of light whose life has value." You may still choose not to be in close association with that person, and that is your right to choose.

Now repeat the same steps for clearing a belief, but this time clear a judgment about yourself. Create your own affirmation at step 12, similar to the one above that you used for releasing judgment about another person.

When you catch yourself having a judgmental thought about anyone, including yourself, stop immediately and say, "I command that this thought be canceled now." Then affirm your higher truth in its place. If everyone on the planet did this, we would soon have peace.

"Perfect pictures" can also be cleared using the same process you used for clearing beliefs and judgments. Perfect pictures are created when you take an ideal or a goal for something you want or want to be and make it into an absolute. Generally, when you do not live up to your ideal or goal, you trash yourself for it. For example, you may have a spiritual ideal of being compassionate and understanding. However, if you blame yourself and feel ashamed of every shortcoming on your path along the way to becoming compassionate and under-standing, you may never get there. When you are feeling angry or judgmental instead of compassionate and understanding, you may feel like such a failure that you get depressed, feel ashamed, and punish yourself. The more appropriate attitude would be one of awareness of the imperfect attitude or behavior, followed by trans-forming it nonjudgmentally.

Once I went for a reading and healing session with my teacher because I was feeling depressed and suicidal. I knew I was not actu-ally going to commit suicide, but I felt overrun with negative emo-tions. When she went into trance she said, "No wonder you're feeling suicidal. You have so many perfect pictures—of your own and from other people—lit up in every chakra, that you decided you could never live up to them all and you gave up." The entire hour and a half was spent identifying perfect pictures and clearing the ones from other people. I was also given a list of perfect pictures of my own cre-ation to take home and clear. I actually walked out of my teacher's house that day laughing and feeling happy again.

Think about areas of your life in which you feel inadequate, ashamed, or like a failure. Then identify the perfect pictures about who you think you should be. Use the above process for clearing beliefs and judgments to clear these perfect pictures. At step 12, create an affirmation such as: "I am a compassionate and understanding person who is still growing. I love and accept myself exactly as I am right now." If you find perfect pictures that originate from other people, you can remove them in roses.

Clearing thoughtforms is done using the same technique you have used for beliefs, judgments, and perfect pictures. The only difference is that a thoughtform is a composite structure made up of many past and/or present life pictures, beliefs, judgments, and/or perfect pictures all amassed around a central theme. When I see a thoughtform clairvoyantly, it reminds me of a spindle around which thoughts, beliefs, and/or highly charged life-experience pictures about a common theme are wound. One after another they join, wrapping themselves like video tape around a spool. A thoughtform has the capacity to actually become so charged that it grows to be what I call "a thoughtform entity." This type of entity gradually begins to control aspects of your life and inhibit your growth.

One client I worked with had a thoughtform of this magnitude that made him feel like he had to control women or he would die. Of course, he was at the mercy of his own creation and lived both in fear of loss and in resistance to intimacy. This thoughtform was comprised of many beliefs and judgments. Some of these are listed here to give you an idea of the makeup of a thoughtform. They were:

1. If I do not have a woman's love and light to drain for my own use, I'll die, because I have none of my own.

2. I am incapable of saving myself.

3. Whatever I have to do to save myself is justified, even if it harms or drains others.

4. The only way I will ever be happy is to have control over a woman sexually by making her want me and then withholding from her.

5. I must keep the woman feeling inadequate, unwanted, and unfulfilled so she will need me.

6. The only power that ever satisfies is absolute power.

7. I must hide who I really am at all costs and be cunning and manipulative to get my needs met.

8. If I use self-pity to get the woman to feel sorry for me and try to save me, then I'll have her.

9. No one will ever make me surrender. I am more powerful than love and I'll prove it.

The core, originating picture that started the whole thoughtform was from a past life in which this man was hurt by a wife whom he loved deeply who ran away with another man. He swore at that time to never allow himself to love or trust anyone again. He also vowed to punish every woman he could for what this one had done to him. He further convinced himself that hate was stronger and more powerful than love and that he would choose hate from then on.

These oaths—made in anger, hurt, and revenge—stuck with him through many lives, creating a thoughtform that got bigger and bigger in each lifetime. By the time I met him, this thoughtform controlled his entire lower body, just as possession by a demonic being would do. The thoughtform had a voice and a will of its own and was bigger than this man's light self in his body and "twice as ugly," as the saying goes.

Believe it or not, there was a lot more to this thoughtform, but I think you get the idea. Luckily, not many thoughtforms grow to such proportions, but you need to be aware of their potential if they are not dealt with in time.

I cannot really tell you how to identify thoughtforms in yourself unless you are clairvoyant or clairaudient and can see them or receive messages about them. But as you grow and progress, whether through guidance, dreams, or sudden realizations, you may at some time become aware of a thoughtform that is controlling some aspect of your life. If that happens, simply use the procedure for clearing beliefs given earlier in this section and clear all the pictures and beliefs that make up the thoughtform one at a time, until it is completely gone. If you have good dream memory, ask before you go to bed that the last dream of the night portray the theme of a thoughtform you need to clear. When you awaken remembering the dream, go into a meditative state and simply ask to see or hear what its components are. You can take it from there, using the process for clearing beliefs given previously.

Psychic Agreements (Contracts)

In your daily life, you are constantly making psychic agreements, or contracts, with people. Some correspond to conscious agreements such as luncheon dates, or telling your housemate you will do the laundry if he or she will cook dinner. When the activity is completed, the contract dissolves and no hooks are left over. However, there are many types of contracts you make with others that are totally unconscious or subconscious. For instance, you may have a friend who has a strong tendency to blame others. You, on the other hand, may be afraid to disagree with people for fear of making them mad at you and losing their friendship. So you and this friend have created a subconscious agreement: you will always side with him or her against others, no matter what, and your friend will never get angry at you.

This type of contract is very codependent. You assist this friend in remaining blaming and negative, and he or she helps you stay afraid of anger and rejection. Neither person has much freedom to grow and evolve in these areas of life. Therefore, when you discover or even suspect that you may have unhealthy contracts with others, it is important to clear them.

Some contracts need to be released because they usurp your free will in inappropriate ways. For example, I have had numerous clients who, after ending relationships, cannot seem to let go completely and make way for new relationships in their lives. Often I find clients holding such contracts as: "If you ever change, I'll get back together with you" or "I'll wait forever for you" or "I won't ever allow myself another relationship because I left you and you were hurt and angry about it." I have also found contracts between ex-lovers to have children together even though they do not intend to get involved again. These types of agreements literally paralyze you in the particular area of your life they rule; they do not allow you to change your mind, forgive, or do whatever is needed in order to move on.

If you tend to take on other people's emotions and problems, you probably did that for one or both of your parents when you were very young. Most families have at least one member who functions as the emotional dumpster for the parents and/or other children. People's contracts for this arrangement vary with respect to specifics, but they have similarities. The following are examples:

1. You take on your mother's fear so she will be more capable of meeting your physical needs.

2. You absorb all the anger between your parents so they do not hurt each other or you, but you never have permission to express anger.

3. As the oldest child, you take care of the younger children's physical and emotional needs, and put your own needs last.

4. Since Mom has stopped nurturing and being sexual with Dad, you become surrogate wife, absorbing his excess emotions and sexual energies, and letting him take your second chakra energy whenever he feels the need.

5. Mother can drain your life force any time she wants because she gave you life, therefore, you owe it to her.

6. You feel guilty for being a burden to Mom or Dad, so you volunteer to take on their emotions and pain and give them your energy.

This list is not intended to make anyone look like a bad guy; it is meant to awaken you to the nature of psychic agreements in a society that tends to encourage emotional repression, codependency, and denial. Following are other common types of agreements:

1. Family members never ever acknowledge a parent's drinking problem, violence, bad temper, financial lack, or whatever else there might be family shame about.

2. You take on another person's fear to prove you will not hurt him or her like others have in the past.

3. You exchange sex for financial support.

4. You never disagree with the boss, so he will not fire you.

5. You will never marry until after your mother dies, nor will you

live far away from her. Therefore, you will always be available if she needs you or is lonely.

The list could go on and on and on. Hopefully, by now you have a sense of the nature of personal contracts. There are also societal and planetary contracts. Examples of societal contracts are:

1. We who live on the east side of town do not associate with the other race or general lowlife on the north side, and we agree that the west-side residents are snobs.

2. People in our social group do not wear bright colors.

3. We support each other's victimization by playing "poor me" games and agreeing with one another that we do not have a chance in this world. "Misery loves company" is another way to say it.

4. We will only associate with members of our church because we are the only good people in town.

Some of the planetary contracts I have found and cleared in myself and/or clients are:

1. We agree that everyone on the planet must be under the rule of and answerable to an organized government. If that government has dark entities running and possessing its leaders, we must submit to them as well.

2. We are the only living beings in existence. There is no life beyond Earth.

3. Women shall be held in oppression with the "Adam and Eve" lie that women brought down darkness upon the planet.

There are many, many more. By now, at least one example of a contract probably has a familiar ring to it for you personally, and you probably have ideas about ones not specified. You can clear these agreements using the following process. Begin with one of the planetary contracts mentioned above, then do a personal one of your own.

1. Close your eyes, ground yourself, pull your aura in, and check your boundary colors and roses.

2. *Optional:* Run cosmic gold and Earth energies and put them on Automatic.

3. Visualize a legal document that says "CONTRACT" at the top.

4. At the bottom of the contract, on one side, see your own name.

5. On the opposite side see the person's or group's name with whom you have made the agreement. The first time you go through these steps, see "All citizens of planet Earth" on the side opposite your own name.

6. Now, simply tell yourself what the contract is about, or visualize the words on the contract, if you prefer. The first time, imagine that the contract says, "All human beings on this planet must be under the rule of an official government and the government's controlling entities."

7. Write "VOID" across the contract in your own handwriting in large red letters.

8. Rip the contract in two and burn it in a normal-colored fire.

9. Repeat the process from step 3 on, this time using a contract you have with a person or group.

10. When complete, open your eyes.

Next, I would like to take you through a process for clearing your chakra system of all extraneous contracts with significant others in your life. Your intent is to clear only those contracts that do not serve your highest good and about which you do not directly need to know in order to learn and grow. The following example assists you in clearing contracts with your mother:

1. Close your eyes, ground yourself, and check your aura size and boundary colors.

2. Run cosmic gold and Earth energies and turn them on Automatic. This step is not optional this time.

3. Focus your attention on running the cosmic gold and Earth energies through your crown chakra. Hold out your hands in front of you and ask for all extraneous contracts with your mother, or surrogate mother figures, that exist in this chakra and that need to be burned.

4. When you sense the contracts in your hands, or imagine them

being there, simply tear them in two and burn them in a normal-looking fire.

5. Run the mixed energies through your sixth chakra, or third eye. Ask for all of the contracts with your mother that are ready to be released from this chakra.

6. Tear them in two and burn them.

7. Run the Earth and cosmic gold energies through your fifth chakra, or throat. Ask for contracts with Mom that are held in this chakra and rip them in two and burn them.

8. Run the energy mixture through your fourth chakra, or heart. Now tear and burn your mother contracts in this chakra.

9. Run the mixed energies through your third chakra, or solar plexus. Rip and burn all contracts with your mother from this chakra.

10. Run the mixed energies through your second, or sacral chakra. Tear and burn contracts with your mother that are held in this chakra.

11. Last, run the mixed energies through your first chakra, at the base of your spine. Ask for all of your agreements with your mother from this chakra, and rip and burn them.

12. Run energy through the spinal pathway and arm channels at least two more minutes to assist in the ongoing clearing. If you are feeling emotional about this process, keep running energy, breathe deeply, and allow yourself to express the feelings in whatever way you need to until they are released. If a chakra area feels tight or painful, flush it out with the cosmic gold/Earth energy blend while breathing in and out through the local area until it relaxes and the emotions have eased.

13. Reground yourself if necessary. Open your eyes.

14. Bend over and dump out.

It is recommended that you wait a few days to a week before going through this process to clear contracts with your father, siblings, ex-lovers, spouses, or anyone else you feel is appropriate. 🖭

Decording

Psychic cords are condensed, tubelike energy forms with which you bond or exchange energy with another person. There are both healthy and unhealthy uses of cords. I will give three examples of healthy cords. First, when babies are born, they ideally have cords in their heart and root chakras with their mothers. The heart-chakra cords allow infants to bond with their mothers on a soul level. Root-chakra cords help the infants to feel grounded and safe. By the time children are between five and seven years old, optimally they dissolve these cords, creating more autonomy and self-confidence.

The second example of healthy cording is in sexual relationships. Lovers generally have cords between their heart and sacral chakras for exchanging love, sexual energy, and soul bonding.

The third example is one that is generally more fleeting. There may be occasions with friends or loved ones during which you will choose to share love through heart-chakra cords. However, the rest of the time most cords are not only not needed in order to relate but can tend to create codependence and overmerging.

A good alternative to creating cords is simply allowing your aura to blend, or overlap with the aura of the person with whom you want to have a more intimate connection. Then when you part, you are not as likely to be left with their pictures or emotions in your chakras and aura, nor are they likely to be left with yours. Learning about decording allows you to choose what level of connection you desire.

Unhealthy cords can: drain your energy; dump other people's pain, pictures, or emotions into your body for you to process; control you in any number of ways—such as through guilt or subconscious messages, intimidation, or fear-of-loss pictures; create overdependency of you on other people, or of them on you; usurp your free will; keep you stuck on old pictures such as low self-worth or having to earn love through sacrifice. The variations are as endless as the number of people and their individual problems and imbalances.

You may be completely unaware of cords you have received from or given to others. Most people are. Luckily, once you get clear of cords, you gradually begin to feel new ones as they come into you, which makes them easier to keep up with and make choices about. If you have a parent or someone else in whose presence you always feel drained or whose emotions you always feel inside yourself, it is a good indication that you have an unhealthy cord with that person.

Removing a cord is done very gently in order to elicit minimal reaction in the other person and to eliminate chances of chakra damage. (See illustration 5a on page 134.) Pulling or jerking a cord out can in some cases actually create scar tissue or tears in your etheric body. It can also cause the other person to retaliate psychically. Therefore, when you remove a cord, always pull it away gently all around its perimeter, a little at a time, where it attaches to your body. Then, place the end of the cord that you have loosened from your body in a rose. Gently push the rose with the cord in it outside your aura and blow it up in a rose, as shown in illustration 5b on page 135.

Fill the hole in your aura with golden sunlight in order to seal your aura and create an atmosphere of self-healing. This is shown in illustration 5c on page 136. During this process run gold energy through your "healing channels," which extend from your crown chakra down to your throat chakra, then down your shoulders and arms, and out through the palm chakras in both your hands. Running this energy helps you *feel* the cord more easily. After a few seconds, or minutes for long-term cords, you will no longer see gold in your aura where you filled in the hole left after removing the cord. The hole will fill in with your own energy and appear normal again.

Following is a guided process for finding and removing cords:

1. Close your eyes, ground yourself, pull in your aura, check your boundary colors and roses, and make any needed adjustments.

2. Imagine a gold sun above your head and direct the golden light into your healing channels: see it move from your crown chakra to the top of your throat chakra, then out the little channels that go down through the top of your shoulders, down through your arms, and finally out through your palm chakras. Use the gold light, visualization, and your breath to open the healing channels and flush them for about thirty seconds before continuing. You will actually feel the energy moving out through your palms.

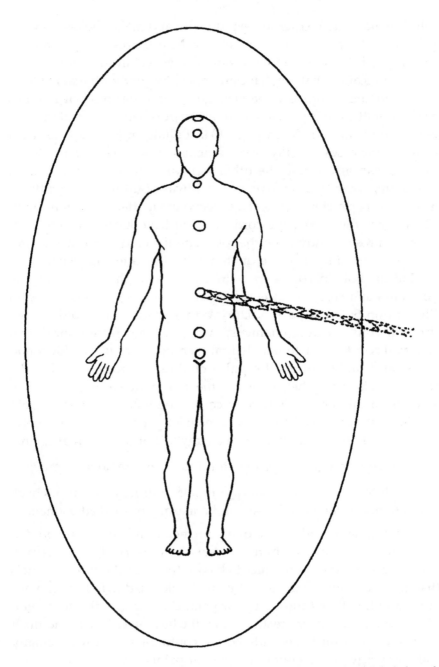

5a. A psychic cord with energy flowing through it is shown in the third chakra of the person.

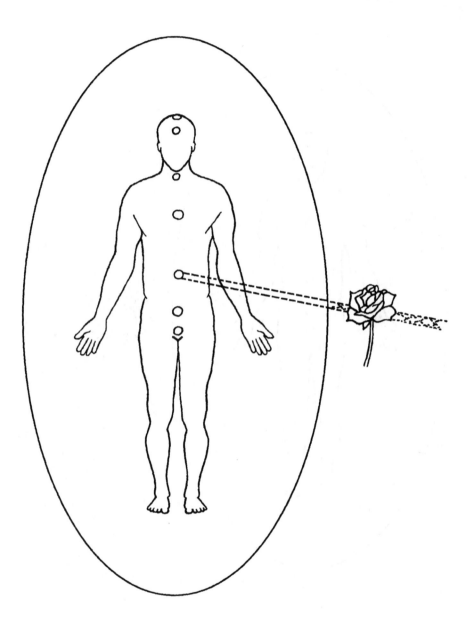

5b. The cord has been loosened from its attachment to the body, placed in a rose, and pushed to the outside of the person's aura. The rose is now ready to be blown up, which will dissolve the cord, but leave a hole in the person's aura.

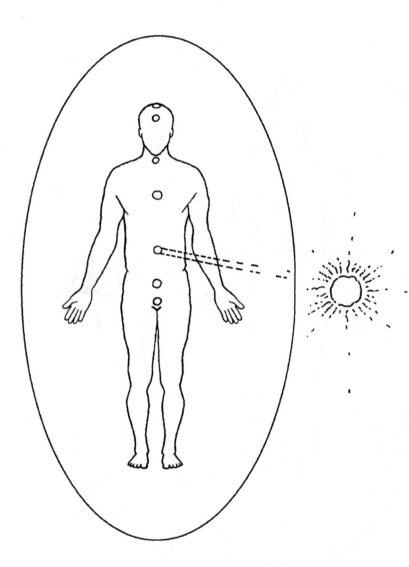

5c. After the cord is blown up in the rose, a golden sun is used to fill the hole in the person's aura with golden sunlight, which stimulates self-healing and protects that spot in the aura from further invasion.

3. Very slowly move either hand through your aura, keeping it close to the front of your body. Begin at your head and face, then move to your chest, solar plexus, and all the way down in front of your groin area. Move your hand slowly enough that you feel the subtle changes in your energy field. If this is too subtle for you, practice on a friend first and then try it again on yourself.

Sense places where the energy feels more intense and concentrated. The cords may feel "buzzy" or "tingly" to your touch. Or you may experience them as thick and heavy feeling, or harder and more solid than the rest of your aura. When you find something, slowly move your hand forward toward the front of your aura. If the sensation disappears a short distance away from the original spot, it means the energy is not a cord. In that case, use roses to collect the denser energy and remove it from your aura. You will perceive a cord all the way out to the edge of your aura. So if what you are feeling has well-defined borders and continues out to arm's length, it is most likely a cord.

4. Once you have located a cord, you may want to attempt identifying the person with whom you are corded. Sometimes the identity is obvious by the feeling of the cord. If not, there is a little trick you can use. Say out loud the name of the person with whom you believe you have the cord, while keeping your hand on the cord. If you are correct, the cord will respond to the name by changing in some way: vibrating, getting stronger, or feeling hotter, for example. If it does not change, keep trying names until you find the correct one. It may even be with someone you have not seen or talked to for awhile. I have cleared parental and ex-spousal cords for myself and clients who have not seen or talked to the people in years.

5. Now that you have identified a cord you wish to remove, bring your hands to the place on your body where the cord connects. While continuing to run the cosmic gold light through your palms, gently pry the cord loose around the edges, a little at a time, until it is freed from your body.

6. Place the end of the cord you have just freed from your body in a rose, and push it to the outside of your aura. Blow up the rose with the cord in it.

7. Fill in the hole left from the cord removal, all the way from your body to the outer edge of your aura, with the gold light running through your hands, or from a small sun outside your aura.

8. Now try removing a cord another way. First, visualize a movie screen outside your aura.

9. Touch the screen with both hands, clearing it with the gold healing energy.

10. See the image of your own backside on the screen.

11. Take a ball of purple light and throw it at the image of your back on the screen. Intend that the purple energy stick to and illuminate any cord in your back that needs to be removed. (I remove all cords in the back as they tend to be more covert, subconscious, and controlling than cords in the front.)

12. After locating a cord, repeat steps 4 to 7 to remove it. Simply feel the cord and fill in the hole on the screen instead of in your own aura. Come back to step 13 when you complete step 7.

13. When you are through decording for this sitting, put the screen in a rose and blow it up.

14. Seal your aura in whatever color you are using.

15. Reground yourself if necessary.

16. Open your eyes.

If you find a cord in the same spot over and over again, or if it pops back in as soon as you try to push it outside your aura, it means that you either have a belief about or a contract with the person cording you. You can identify this belief or contract fairly easily by simply feeling the energy and identifying the person. After doing so, simply clear the belief or contract as described earlier in this chapter, and then remove the cord again. It should stay out. If the person is still very psychically persistent, place a rose outside your aura with his or her face in it and a "No Trespassing" sign. Replace this rose daily until you no longer feel a need for it. 🖭

Being in Present Time

Present-time, or "be-here-now," consciousness is the most creative, effective state of being in which to meet your goals and heal. If your consciousness is out of present time, meaning pieces of your energy are in the future or reliving the past, it is almost impossible to create that future or let go of that past. On the other hand, when you are in your body, alert and in present time, you are in charge of your life to the best of your ability at this time.

When you are in the past or future, parts of your chakras or aura are literally in stasis and unavailable to you. It is as if you are spinning your wheels. Your energy is not even in your body. You may have trouble being present with loved ones or at work, and may generally feel scattered and spacy, which is literally true: your energy is scattered and in another space.

The technique to use for coming into present time is as follows:

1. Close your eyes and ground yourself.

2. Pull in your aura, check your aura boundary colors and roses, and make necessary adjustments.

3. *Optional:* Run cosmic gold and Earth energies and put them on Automatic.

4. Imagine a straight line, called a "time line," extending both right and left into infinity. Place the time line in front of your first chakra at the base of your tailbone. In front of your chakra, on top of the line, place a small golden sun. (See illustration below.)

6. *Sun icon. The golden sun sits in the "present time" position on the time line between past and future.*

5. Exhale out through your first chakra with the intention of releasing any past or future energies held in that chakra into the golden sun.

6. Now imagine this sun dividing into two pieces that simultaneously roll out to the right and left, representing the past and future. As the sun divides and rolls in both directions, each part releases the past and future energies from the chakra into their appropriate time frames.

7. When the two parts of the sun have gone as far as they need to go to accomplish their task, they automatically roll back toward the center point. They bring with them any energy that belongs in your body in present time that was in the past and future.

8. When both parts are back at center and are reunited as one sun again, move the time line and sun in front of your second chakra, halfway between your navel and groin. Once again, breathe out through your second chakra with the intention of releasing into the sun any past and future energies in that chakra.

9. Divide the sun into two parts again and simultaneously send them down the time line in both directions as far as they need to go, until they stop on their own. See them roll back to center once again, bringing your present-time energy back with them as they re-form a single sun again.

10. Now move the time line and golden sun in front of your third chakra, located at your diaphragm, or solar plexus. Breathe out through this chakra to release the out-of-present-time energies.

11. Imagine the sun dividing and rolling out and back again, to and from both directions, releasing and retrieving energy as before.

12. Move the time line and golden sun up to your heart chakra in the center of your chest, and repeat the same steps as for the previous chakras.

13. At your throat chakra, repeat the same steps again.

14. At your third eye, located between your eyebrows, once again follow the same procedure.

15. Finally, repeat the same steps for your crown chakra located on top of your head.

16. Now move the time line and sun into your aura, at least a foot in front of your body, and intend that the sun pick up all out-of-

present-time energies from your aura and deposit them in their appropriate time frames in the past and future. As the two halves of the sun roll back to center and become one sun again for the last time, they bring back any energy that belongs in your aura in present time.

17. Place the time line and sun in a rose and dissolve the rose outside your aura.

18. Open your eyes, and bend over and dump out.

Once you have done this process the long way, there is a shorter version you can use. The third chakra handles your social interactions, and your goals in the world and with other people. Distribution of energies from all the other chakras takes place in the third chakra, as it involves the other chakras in social exchanges and the meeting of goals. Because of this unique multichakra focus, the third chakra can be used to bring all the chakras into present time as follows:

1. Place the sun on the time line as before, this time only in front of your solar plexus, or third chakra.

2. With the intention of releasing the past and future energies from all your chakras into the golden sun, inhale into your crown chakra and exhale from your crown down to your solar plexus and out into the sun.

3. Now inhale into your root chakra at the base of your spine and exhale upward into your solar plexus and out through the front of that chakra into the sun.

4. Allow the golden sun to divide into two parts. Simultaneously roll them right and left, depositing the out-of-present-time energies from all the chakras into the past and future.

5. As the sun halves roll back toward the center, they return the energies from the past and future that belong in your body in present time.

6. When the sun is whole and in the center again, place it and the time line in a rose outside of your aura and blow them up.

7. Open your eyes. [cassette icon]

Use the techniques for clearing and self-healing in this chapter as often as you feel a need for them. Suggestions for applications of the techniques are given in other sections of this workbook, so familiarize yourself with them well.

Chapter 7

KA ACTIVATION

K a may be described as the electrical, light-body circuitry that exists identically and simultaneously in the third through sixth dimensions and that ultimately functions in all those dimensions to anchor and contain your Christed Presence in form. In other words, it is the interface between spirit, dimension, and form that affords us the opportunity as humans to become fully en-Christed in the body and to move from the third to the fourth dimension and beyond as we evolve and raise our vibrational frequency. The Ka body might also be described as the vehicle in which the Higher Self descends into matter and in which the Higher Self and the body together ascend into the upper dimensions. Through these processes the higher-dimensional translation of consciousness occurs. In *The Keys of Enoch*, Ka is defined as the "divine double."

In Joan Grant's book *Winged Pharaoh*, there is a lovely passage in which the future pharaoh presents lessons to his royal children. In his story, Ptah is the gatherer and distributor of life who created all living things from pure life force. He describes the function of Ka to the children as follows:

> In the body there are many parts which make use of the things of Earth by which we live; our lungs purify us with the air we breathe; our bowels and stomach and many other organs transform our food and drink into fresh blood, which our heart pumps through us. But we have a greater need, which none of these can give us, and that need is life, that life which is everywhere and which you have heard me call "the life of Ptah." It is too fine to contact the khat, *and so we have a finer replica of ourselves, which is a net-*

work, like thousands of invisible veins; and through these channels flows this life of Ptah, without which we would die. This part of ourselves is called the Ka, which means "gatherer of life." It cannot be seen by earth eyes, yet so important is it, that if these channels are injured and cannot carry life, then the body will die . . .

The Ka is written as two upstretched arms rising from a straight line. The line used to mean "the horizon" and has come to mean "Earth;" the upstretched arms with open hands symbolize one who is reaching upwards and gathering the life of Ptah . . .

Later in the same chapter, Ptah-Kefer, a seer and teacher for the royal families, tells the children:

Now when I am looking at a man's Ka with the eyes of spirit, I cover my eyes with my hand so that the slow light, which we know as colour, is cut off, and then with my trained sight I can look upon the swiftness of the Ka, and yet it seems to be as still as a sleeping man, because my seer's sight travels at the same speed.

Ka energy is rarefied, down-stepped, higher-dimensional energy that vibrates so fast it cannot be seen with normal vision. Experientially, it feels sublime and yet subtle when it flows through the body. During the Pleiadian Lightwork Intensives I teach, students notice a lot of tantric sexual energy flow as the channels open and the Ka body awakens. The Ka energy flows in channels throughout the body, not only in those directly relating to reproductive organs. The reason the opening of Ka Channels tends to trigger tantric release is this: The whole body, including all of its organs, is involved in and must be healthy for true tantric energies to flow. When the Ka energy is brought in from the higher dimensions and fills the channels, release of blocked energies occurs simultaneously. The experience of tantric energy flow is a side effect of this simultaneous influx of high-frequency energy and etheric release. Tantric energy flow is the natural and continual experience of beings from the sixth dimension and up. Therefore, as your body lets go of denser energies, interfaces with your Ka, and links with your higher-dimensional self from the sixth dimension and down, waves of tantra are the result. Tantra has been a source of spiritual study and attainment by many spiritual groups for as long as physical life has existed. Certain Native

American tribes, Tibetan Buddhists, many Hindu sects, and the Maya, to name only a few, have practiced their own forms of tantra for a long time. It is a natural fascination and desire considering it is the frequency we are evolving toward.

Tantric sexual energy runs intercellularly, as well as with the kundalini up the spinal channel and through the chakras. It is pure creation energy. It is the stuff cosmic ecstasy is made of, and one of the energies that has been most damaged and distorted on Earth. Opening and running the Ka energy will not automatically change your sexual patterns or attitudes, but it will make the higher frequencies of those energies more available and able to run in your body. Refining and clearing your sexual energy, behaviors, and attitudes is necessary for spiritual growth anyway. Your sexual organs have a direct link to your soul; what you do with sexual energy directly impacts your relationship to your soul. Running Ka energy and tantric energy together is simply one of the fastest and most natural ways to heal your body/soul relationship and clear out traumatic and negative sexual patterning. [I deal directly with healing the soul and something the Pleiadian Emissaries of Light call "Dolphin Tantra" in my later book, *The Pleiadian Workbook II*.]

The main objective of Pleiadian Lightwork is to activate and awaken the Ka Channels and Ka Template in order to bring about cellular availability for enlightenment and ascension, to make you aware of your spiritual responsibilities, and to introduce you to help available during the process of getting from "here" to "there." These objectives may be reached more easily with assistance from the Pleiadians and Ascended Master Jesus Christ, who are working together to aid humans in achieving these goals.

There are thirteen levels of activation that begin with your first Ka session and end with your ascension. These activation levels directly correspond to the Mayan creation cycle of thirteen. It is no coincidence that the Egyptian and Mayan systems overlap in many areas, since both cultures were taught by the Pleiadians. The creation cycle is used in Mayan timekeeping in continually repeating sequences of thirteen days, much like we have a continually repeating cycle of seven-day weeks. The Mayan calendar is also divided into thirteen moon cycles per year as opposed to the more common twelve-month calendar year. Thirteen is the number of divine manifestation, or white magic, as well.

Regardless of the measure of time, or process of magic, in which the cycle of thirteen is followed, each number always has a specific significance. In the chart below, I will give both the general function of the number, and its specific function relative to Ka activation. *The Mayan Oracle* by Ariel Spilsbury and Michael Bryner and *Dreamspell* by José Argüelles are used as guidelines for this information.

Number	General Function	Ka Activation Level
1	Identify Purpose, Initiate	You recognize your longing for unity with Higher Self and God/Goddess/All That Is followed by initiation of action through which it may come about. Invocation, receptivity, and commitment to the goal occur. You initiate your first Ka session.
2	Polarity, Understanding of Challenge	Recognition of need for, and beginning, action to create balance in your internal and external male/female polarity take place. You clear issues and emotions relative to the illusion of separation, conflict, and duality. Initiation of harmony occurs, although the Ka is still breaking through ego resistance.
3	Rhythmic Flow	A new level of allowing takes place as your ego gives way to your divine

Number	General Function	Ka Activation Level
		intent. Ka energy flows more smoothly and continually.
4	Measure, Define	Lessons of discernment and ability to maintain focus with disciplined determination are learned. You are tested to measure your spiritual dedication to your goal of ascension and Oneness. Christ has said that the spiritual question for this activation is, "What is worth not loving at this moment?" Your priorities are reevaluated, and, as you choose correctly, the Ka breaks through in a more permanent and forceful manner.
5	Centeredness, Divine Power	Ego and past identities are shed as you accept your true identity without denying your humanness. Your Ka energy begins to heal your nervous system more deeply as a result of your letting go and acceptance. A new maturity and quiet wisdom ensue.
6	Balance	Commitment to experiencing life fully on all levels creates equilibrium and freedom from resistance to feeling deeply. Your experience of your

Number	General Function	Ka Activation Level
		Higher Self being continually connected to your body begins. Your Ka and kundalini flow synchronistically, continually, and harmonically. Cellular clearing is accelerated.
7	Channel Higher-Dimensional Energies	Soul healing and renewal are accentuated. You begin to remember your true origins and myth. Ka star-linking triggers more access to multidimensional realities. You understand and forgive yourself more deeply now.
8	Harmonic Resonance	Self-love and unconditional love for others are your reality. Blame is no longer possible. Compassion deepens, without pity, and you actualize detachment. Core issues are unveiled. You feel yourself being impulsed harmonically by yourself as one with your own Creator. It is the sound of one voice in love. Ka resonance beyond time and space creates more instantaneous remembrance of your own divine truth.
9	Realization	Completion of all karma and negative pattern-breaking occur. You *do* from a place of *being*. You stop "efforting" and "trying" and simply

Number	General Function	Ka Activation Level
		realize that "you are that which you seek." You accept the responsibility of being a self-mastered being now. Your Ka Channels and flow are self-sustaining. You are deeply committed to fulfilling your own highest destiny, which is your service to All That Is.
10	Manifestation of Goal	You and your Higher Self become fully merged in your human body. All remaining beliefs in limitation are cleared. Your Ka, body kundalini, and Higher-Self kundalini are synchronized, continual, and harmonic. You are recognized by others, who are willing to see, as your true self, and you are fully living your higher purpose.
11	Dissolution and Absolution	All that is nonessential dissolves. Total surrender to your own enlightenment occurs, as any remaining resistance is released. All goals and remaining attachments are examined and released if not in divine will. Your Ka is merged cellularly and you are becoming lighter and lighter. Your light body is activated.

Number	General Function	Ka Activation Level
12	Universal	Your autonomy relinquishes all control to the divine will of the higher collective consciousness. Service is absolute, automatic, and your only desire. Your Ka has completed its link to the stars and galaxies and come full circle to connect with God/Goddess/All That Is and the Christed, future selves of all beings at lower levels than yourself.
13	Transcendence	You have attained to Christ consciousness and can ascend at will.

To truly attain to the full capacity of your Ka awakening, you must choose to embark upon a path of forgetting and remembering, letting go and letting God/Goddess, and total dedication to purification and transcendence of ego. As you move through level after level of Ka activation, you will begin to recognize that each is an initiation and an opening to the next release: emotionally, mentally, physically, and spiritually. When nothing is left but the surrendered, unconditionally loving, illumined self, your true work begins. This Pleiadian Lightwork workbook is more an invitation to join the sacred mystery schools of the Great White Brotherhood, facilitated by the Pleiadian Emissaries of Light, the Sirian collective Christ consciousness, and God/Goddess/All That Is, than it is a workbook. And yet in this modern day when mystery schools and sacred orders are more difficult to access physically, it serves a purpose. How far you go within this system is up to you.

In this chapter, you will begin the Pleiadian Lightwork by first meeting with the Pleiadians and the Christ, aligning your and their mutual higher purpose, and initiating the actual clearing and activation of your Ka Template and Ka Channels.

Meeting the Pleiadian Emissaries of Light

Although the maximum results of Pleiadian Lightwork are attained through receiving the work hands-on with a practitioner, it is also highly beneficial to connect with the Pleiadians etherically and receive assistance directly from them without a practitioner. That is why the Pleiadians asked me to write this book: to make Pleiadian Lightwork available to the masses. All the aspects of Pleiadian Lightwork that can be attained directly through work with the Pleiadians and the Christ are contained in this book [and in my later books].

When you receive the Ka work hands-on, the practitioner runs high-frequency, cosmic kundalini energy through each activation point on your channels in very specific ways. At times, psychic surgery is required for torn or damaged channels. At other times, segments of your channels may be replaced altogether. These are the main reasons the Ka work has been taught to me as a hands-on practice. The Pleiadians have explained that they require physical hands through which to work when psychic surgery is necessary to repair or replace parts of a channel. This work is usually very subtle and relaxing, although at times it triggers deep emotional releases, depossession, spontaneous physical releases, or even sublime altered states.

Much of Pleiadian Lightwork, including the Ka work, does not require hands-on, however. The part of the work that can be done directly with the Pleiadians and the Christ, in general, ranges from about 40 percent to 80 percent in overall effectiveness, depending on the amount and extent of damage in the channels of the person who is receiving the work. Once you personally initiate contact with the Pleiadians and request that your Ka Template and Ka Channels be opened, the Pleiadian Lightwork will be ongoing for you for a few months. Though only a couple of sessions are given in this chapter, repeated ones will automatically be given to you—usually in your sleep—as you are ready for them, simply because you asked for the channels to be opened.

When Pleiadian Lightwork is done thoroughly by a practitioner opening and activating the Ka Channels and Ka Template, as well as accompanying healings and clearings, approximately sixteen to twenty-five private sessions are required. There are sixteen pairs of channels to be opened, neural pathways in the brain to be cleared, Higher Self connection and meditation techniques to be taught, physical holding patterns to be cleared through Dolphin Brain Repatterning, as well as individuated Dolphin Star-Link sessions, and clairvoyant reading and clearing work. Naturally, all of these things cannot be done if you work directly with the Pleiadians without a practitioner, but the healing and energy that are available etherically are enough for most people.

In most of the session-type work throughout the rest of this workbook section, something called the "Interdimensional Cone of Light" is used. The Interdimensional Cone of Light (shown in illustration 7 on page 153) is located at the top of your aura, the cone pointing away from your body. It is composed of rapidly spinning, high-vibrational light frequencies that assist in bringing you into "vertical alignment" and clearing energies released from your body and aura.

"Vertical alignment" means being in rapport and contact with your Higher Self in a spirit-based reality and in your divine axis alignment. All the way up to the ninth dimension, you have a tubular opening in your energy field that is filled with your light and that extends all the way down around your spine to the bottom of your aura beneath your feet. Metaphorically it is as if your spine itself extends etherically downward to the bottom of your aura and upward beyond your aura, creating an ongoing spine for all of your higher-dimensional aspects. (See illustration 15 on page 273.) This spine, or axis, when in place, helps promote your ongoing spiritual evolution, your alignment with Divine Truth, and a spiritual focus in your life. This vertical alignment is the opposite of "horizontal alignment," which refers to a reality based on personality identification with the illusions, addictions, and attachments of the physical world. In a spiritually healthy and Truth-based reality, all horizontal interactions are stimulated by vertical alignment and are not identified with physical reality as an ultimate reality.

The Interdimensional Cone of Light creates an upward pull on your energy field, including your body, which promotes the clearing

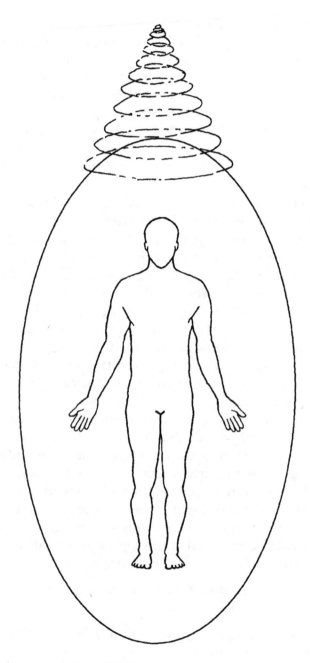

7. *The Interdimensional Cone of Light is located at the top of the aura to assist in clearing and for divine alignment.*

and releasing of energies that are keeping you in horizontal alignment and illusion-based reality. These energies being released may
be from other people, the lower astral planes, entities, or your own
contraction, denial, and repression. The cone literally sucks the
released energies up into and beyond itself into a higher-dimensional
energy field that is so intense that the energies are instantly transmuted, neutralized, and sent back to where they belong. In other
words, the cone vibrationally raises the energies to a new evolutionary state of being and returns them to the person or place from
whence they originated.

I discovered that the cone so greatly accelerated my own growth
process that I found it undesirable to keep it continually above my
aura for nearly the first year and a half of use. To have a constant
strong pull on every out-of-balance thought or energy in your body
can be intense, to say the least. During illness, the Cone of Light can
exacerbate symptoms, thereby speeding up the illness and at times
creating more discomfort and pain. Therefore, it is recommended
that you use it sparingly or not at all when you are ill unless you are
clearly guided to do so, or unless you are doing a chamber session as
introduced in chapter 9. Certainly it can trigger emotional release,
heighten your full-sensory perceptions, and increase your sensitivity
and awareness in general.

You may find when you first work with the Cone of Light for
short and purposeful periods that it works miraculously and feels
wonderful. You might think the cone would be ungrounding, but I
have not found it to be so unless I leave it on for too long. It actually
helps me feel more real, present, and balanced. I invoke the
Interdimensional Cone of Light for meditation, self-healing work,
sessions with the Pleiadians, and when I am doing sessions for
clients or teaching classes and workshops. It is too intense for most
people to use beyond that, at least in the beginning.

In this first exercise, this is how you meet the Pleiadian
Emissaries of Light:

1. Lie down with a pillow under your knees and your feet shoulder-width apart; close your eyes.

2. Ground yourself, and check your aura boundaries.

3. Repeat the following invocation: "In the name of the Holy Presence I Am, I am ready to be fully awakened and enlightened now. I accept responsibility for living in and aligning with Divine Truth, Love, and Will according to the Divine Plan of Light. I am only willing to connect with etheric beings who are likewise of the Light and in alignment with the Divine Plan."

4. Then state: "I now call forth the Ascended Master Jesus Christ of the Light." Wait about ten seconds or until you feel his presence in the room. Repeat the call for his presence if you feel it is necessary. Presences in the room may be extremely subtle to you, if they are noticeable at all. If this is true for you, you may need to simply trust that the beings invoked are with you until your perceptual awareness increases.

5. Next invoke: "I now call forth the Pleiadian Emissaries of Light." Wait about ten seconds or until you sense a change in the room or become aware of their presence. Again, you may feel a need to repeat the invocation to the Pleiadians.

6. Say to the Pleiadians: "I request that the Interdimensional Cone of Light be placed at the top of my aura for clearing and divine axis alignment." Wait about twenty seconds before proceeding, to allow the cone to be put into place and made operational.

7. Tell the Pleiadians and the Christ that you wish to begin the Pleiadian Lightwork and would like them to initiate any preliminary energy balancing, clearing, or healing you need prior to the opening of your Ka Template and Ka Channels. Tell them anything you would like them to know about you and your spiritual intention and needs. You can bring up any blocks or "stuck areas" you are aware of, or vulnerable issues you are working on.

8. Remain receptive, still, and quiet for one hour while the preliminary session takes place.

9. Ask that the Cone of Light be removed. Then go on with your day. You may wish to do this first session at bedtime and simply allow yourself to drift off to sleep afterward. If so, before going to sleep, ask the Pleiadians to remove the Cone of Light at the appropriate time. 🔲

Clearing and Activating Your Ka Template

Your Ka Template is located on top of your head at the back of and slightly behind your crown chakra. It is rectangular in shape and encoded with symbols from a sacred language. (See illustration 8 below.) The symbols closely resemble a combination of Egyptian hieroglyphics and ancient Aramaic. They are, however, more universal than either of these languages alone. The selection and arrangement of symbols are different for each individual; those used on the illustration are totally hypothetical and given as an example only.

As the Ka energies enter your aura from your fourth-dimensional self, they are first received into your Ka Template, passing over and through the encoding that delineates your soul's and body's blueprint for the use of your Ka in this lifetime. If you have a goal to ascend, that goal is encoded on your template and is activated as your template is cleared and opened. Likewise, if your being has chosen to experience physical death through cancer or any other disease, that information is also encoded on your Ka Template. The Pleiadians never interfere with your chosen goals, but they will work with you to attain whatever is in your highest good.

You may have planned, prior to your birth in this lifetime, to take on genetic illness and limitation for the purpose of transmuting and transcending it. This, too, is shown on your template, and the transmutation and transcendental processes are accelerated when your Ka Template is cleared and activated.

When your Ka Template is initially cleared and activated, the Ka

8. The Ka Template

energies will flow from your template to your pineal gland in the center of your head. (See illustration #16a on page 281.) Your pineal gland distributes light throughout your body and tells your brain how to run your body systems, mind, emotions, and physical movements. It also regulates the flow of light and energy to the meridian systems through your Ka Channels and is vital to your spiritual awakening and enlightenment. Impulses for regeneration or degeneration are a direct function of the relationship between your pineal gland and the Ka Template. So you can see that this template is not only important to your spiritual opening to your Higher Self, but it is equally vital to the health and well-being of your body in preparation for housing your spirit and your Christed Self.

You need only fifteen minutes for the initial opening and clearing of your Ka Template, which can be done by following the instructions below:

1. Sit or lie down with pillows under your knees. Place your feet shoulder-width apart and close your eyes.

2. Ground yourself. Pull in your aura and check your aura boundaries.

3. Invoke your Higher Self to come and be in the room with you.

4. Invoke Ascended Master Jesus Christ of the Light.

5. Invoke the Pleiadian Emissaries of Light to join you.

6. Ask the Pleiadians to bring in the Interdimensional Cone of Light for clearing and divine axis alignment.

7. Tell the Pleiadians, the Christ, and your Higher Self that you wish to have the Ka Template cleared and activated as much as possible at this time.

8. Receive and be still for fifteen minutes or fall asleep if you like.

9. If you are not going to sleep, you may need to ground yourself again before going on with your day.

Later in the book there is a process for deeper clearing and activation of your Ka Template. However, the above exercise is all that is required to begin the process at this time. You may go immediately to the next section if you wish.

Opening Your Ka Channels

Your Ka Channels are a group of meridianlike pathways through which your Ka energy flows. Each channel is actually a pair of energy lines with corresponding physical pathways on the right and left sides of your body. This channel system is not the same as any other meridian system, although some of the activation points along the channels overlap with acupuncture, Shiatsu, acupressure, and Jen Shen Do meridian points. These overlapping points actually serve as interfaces through which the Ka energy is fed into the meridian systems for the physical body.

The Ka energy is the key to the revitalization and maintenance of all your meridian systems on the etheric level. This energy is brought by your own Higher Self from the sixth dimension down to the third dimension and is constantly being "down-stepped" along the way. The energy is very refined and pure, as it retains the integrity of your Higher Self's electrical light nature during this process of lowering its frequency, or down-stepping, for the desired dimensional compatibility. When this Ka energy enters your Ka Channels in your physical body, it not only fills and activates these channels, but it also overflows into your physical meridian systems through the overlapping activation points.

The Pleiadians have told me that when your Ka energy is flowing fully in your body all the time, your acupuncture and other meridian systems should remain vitalized and balanced. This does not imply that it is the only source of health for these meridian systems; certainly, you must be aware of eating healthily, thinking clearly and positively, maintaining spiritual connectedness, and living with emotional spontaneity and honesty. All these things affect the quality of your existence and are necessary to integral holistic health. When these areas are in balance and right alignment in your life, your Ka can operate at a maximum efficiency level, moving you toward and maintaining maximum vitality and equilibrium.

As a result of this holistic balance, you eventually reach the state of being in which your higher consciousness can exist simultaneously in all the dimensions without compromising its essential nature. This is accomplished when your daily life is in balance, and your human consciousness and Ka Channels are fully awakened and operable in your physical body.

As mentioned earlier in this chapter, there are sixteen pairs of Ka Channels, or thirty-two energy lines with activation points. Each of these pairs has a specific function relative to your emotional, mental, spiritual, and physical health in addition to its primary function of creating the vehicle in which your Christed Presence will incarnate on Earth. The Pleiadians have instructed me not to show the diagrams of the channels to those who will not be receiving hands-on work with a practitioner because when they are brought to your attention, they tend to "light up." This could cause you to experience unnecessary pain and trauma by activating, or lighting up, your channels with tears, leaks, or extreme damage that cannot be healed by the Pleiadians without human assistance. Therefore, once you have asked that the Ka Channels be opened, you will not know specifically which channels and activation points are being worked on at any given time unless the Pleiadians communicate with you otherwise.

You may experience the surfacing of emotions, beliefs, or other people's energies and thoughts while the Ka Channels are being opened. If so, use the tools you learned in the chapters on "Preparing for Pleiadian Lightwork" as they are appropriate for you.

The Pleiadians and the Christ will work with you in such a way that you will not feel a sense of unresolution, or exposed and unhealed trauma. Their work is always done very conscientiously and in alignment with your overall highest good.

Use the following process to open your Ka Channels:

1. Lie down with a pillow under your knees, and your feet shoulder-width apart.

2. Ground yourself. Pull in your aura, and check your boundary colors and roses.

3. Call on your Higher Self to join you.

4. Invoke the Pleiadian Emissaries of Light to come forth.

5. Invoke Ascended Master Jesus Christ to come forth.

6. Ask the Pleiadians to bring the Interdimensional Cone of Light above your aura for clearing and divine axis alignment.

7. Tell your Higher Self, the Pleiadians, and the Christ that you are ready to have your Ka Channels opened in order to make way for your Master Presence to dwell on the Earth in your body. Ask them to assist you in your ongoing spiritual growth and healing and in the process of opening your Ka Channels in whatever way would truly serve your highest good. Give them permission to work on your Ka Channels while you are sleeping as well as while you are awake from this point forth unless you ever consciously tell them otherwise. My experience has been that most of the Ka work occurs during sleep.

8. Lie still and be receptive for one hour. It is okay if you fall asleep. You may even prefer to do this process at bedtime.

9. If you are not doing this at bedtime, you may need to reground yourself before getting up and going on with your day.

You do not need to set aside special times for Ka Channel work after this first session. The Pleiadians and the Christ will monitor your needs and time the ongoing Ka work accordingly.

Chapter 8

DOLPHIN BRAIN REPATTERNING

Dolphin Brain Repatterning was originally called Neuro-Muscular-Cortical Repatterning. It is an aspect of Pleiadian Lightwork that was founded in the principles and techniques of Moshe Feldenkrais, and greatly expanded by the Pleiadians. *Neuro* refers to anything related to the neurological, or nervous system. *Muscular*, of course, refers to the musculature of the body. *Cortical* implies the motor cortex of the brain, which rules motor function, or physical movement. These three body systems are in constant communication with one another, and the health of their relationship determines the body's structural health and suppleness. The objective of Dolphin Brain Repatterning is to free the skeletal system of holding patterns that inhibit you from being spontaneous and free, and that block the flow of cerebrospinal fluid.

Cerebrospinal fluid is produced in the brain. The cranial bones are constantly expanding and contracting gently and subtly, as are the sacral bones. This process of expansion and contraction pumps the cerebrospinal fluid throughout the central nervous system, keeping it lubricated, supple, and able to conduct electrical currents. Electrical stimuli in the brain cause perceptions of physical sensation and impulses to move. Every movement, whether it be kicking a football or slightly raising an eyebrow, begins with an electrical impulse in the brain that is sent via the cerebral spinal fluid in the central nervous system to the appropriate nerves, which then trigger the body to produce movement.

Dolphins operate from both sides of their brains at the same time, whereas most humans at this time act from one or the other side of their brains, but rarely from both sides together. It has been said that dolphins see humans as being asleep. This is because dolphins sleep by turning off first one side of their brains, then the other, keeping one side functional at all times. It is also fairly commonly understood that average human beings only utilize about 5 to 10 percent of their brain capacity. This is an evolutionary factor and not a normal condition in humans. You are intended to become a "whole brain" being like the dolphins who are "elder brothers and sisters" to the human race.

Dolphins were sent to Earth prior to human colonization to prepare the evolutionary frequencies and patterns. They are highly evolved Light Beings who are lovingly dedicated to the fulfillment of human spiritual evolutionary goals. So, why do you need to become a "whole brain" being? Without whole brain function, you remain split off from your own spiritual wholeness, your connection through oneness with God/Goddess/All That Is. In order to attain whole brain function, you must both spiritually evolve and physically heal the electrical system in your brain and body. This electrical system is literally the communication link through which your spirit speaks and creates in the physical world. Any blockage in your electrical system inhibits your spirit and Master Presence from fully embodying.

Your electrical network is also the most direct interface between your Ka Channels, your physical body, and your Higher Self. Since Ka energy is fundamentally electrical in nature, your electrical conducting system must be in good condition in order for Ka energy to circulate and flow fully and freely. Therefore, your nervous system and skeletal health are vital to full, unimpeded Ka flow. Think about the way dolphins move in the water: they have no kinks in their spines or sluggishness in their neurological response time. They live in spontaneous harmony with themselves and their surroundings, their bodies fluidly responding to every need and situation. When they move their fins, the movements flow like gentle waves through their bodies via their nervous systems, devoid of kinks or contractions. This is what the Pleiadians call the Dolphin Wave Effect. It is only possible because dolphins are uninhibited, whole-brain, spiritually evolved beings who are aligned through their bodies and spirits with the Earth, the Sun, the stars, and the collective consciousness that is God/Goddess/All That Is. They are the blueprint for what the human race is destined to become; they hold the vibrational patterns and frequencies for human evolution on Earth. Their very presence on Earth is a vital boon to human spiritual development.

When a dolphin baby is born, it is nuzzled and touched first by its mother, and then one by one by the other dolphins of the pod who are nearby. A call is sent out through the waters for those who wish to welcome the young one and "pod it." The dolphins who respond "pod the baby" by forming a circle around it and the mother. They swim around the circle first in one direction and then in the other, calling out greetings and blessings to the newborn with their sonar. These sounds also serve to create the harmonic tones needed to bring the full consciousness of the dolphin spirit into its body and to activate its Ka Body, which links the newborn energetically to the stars through axiatonal lines, or Ka Channels. The sonar waves create a Dolphin Wave Effect with sound that is similar to what dolphin body movement creates tactilely. It activates the baby's electrical system and body response and enables the dolphin spirit to operate through the baby's brain and electrical system. The adult dolphins then take turns nuzzling and rubbing the baby with their bodies. This is continued until the baby dolphin's soul is fully anchored and looking out from behind the newborn's eyes.

Moshe Feldenkrais had a theory that when a human being is born, the initial touch from another human to each part of the newborn's body anchors the neurological information of this person into the baby's body. In other words, if your sacrum was first touched by your mother, who held contraction in that part of her body out of fear or shame about her sexuality, then that same holding pattern was transferred electrically through your mother's touch to the motor cortex of your brain via the nerve endings in your sacrum. From the motor cortex of your brain, an electrical impulse was sent through your nervous system to your sacral area muscles and bones, telling them to contract and not allow that part of your body to move freely. This initiated the propensity for fear or shame to be held emo tionally in this area of your body, corresponding to the physical contraction. The results were the prevention of feeling, the suppression of sexual energy, and the beginning of fusion of your sacral bones, including your lower spine and hips. Eventually, you would develop lower-back injuries, stiffness, achiness, and pain in your sacrum and hip areas.

For many years the exterior problems remained unnoticed. Later in life, perhaps as early as puberty or as late as middle age, symptoms appeared. Perhaps you experienced extreme cramping and pain before and during your menstrual periods. Then, after awhile, lower-back pain and headaches accompanied the painful periods. Later still, perhaps you slipped and fell going down the steps to your home and hurt your back. X-rays showed that you had a tilted pelvis and that it had been tilted a long time, as indicated by calcium deposits, fusion, and deterioration of your lower vertebrae.

Depending on the level of holistic awareness of your doctor or chiropractor at the time of the accident, the relationship of your menstrual cycle problems, earlier lower-back pains, and headaches may or may not have been connected to the tilted pelvis problem. Perhaps you found a doctor who wanted to operate in order to cure you. Or you became dependent on ongoing costly adjustments at a chiropractor's office and never really solved the problem, as only the symptom was treated. What was really needed was a way to reteach your body how to let go of contraction, fear, and shame and heal itself.

That is the intention behind Feldenkrais work, and it has been expanded in the Dolphin Brain Repatterning aspect of Pleiadian Lightwork. When I took the month-long intensive training with a Feldenkrais practitioner in southern California, the Pleiadians worked with me constantly. They told me that this work would be vital to healing the nervous systems and skeletal systems of those who intended to survive the upcoming Earth changes and increasing frequencies on our planet. The Pleiadians studied the work through my body and the bodies of others in the training who were willing, and they made improvements on what was being taught. The Pleiadians said at that time that they would be working with thousands of people on Earth over the next few years to help free them of holding patterns and heal their nervous systems.

From my own experience as their guinea pig and trainee, I know that this work can be very effective when it is received directly from the Pleiadians or through a Pleiadian Lightwork practitioner. The effectiveness of the Dolphin Brain Repatterning work by the Pleiadians varies from about 65 to 85 percent, higher than the Ka work effectiveness rate. This is because the Pleiadians are able to work with subtle electrical impulses and direct them into the body in the same movement patterns as would be done by a hands-on practitioner. Chronic problems may need more than what the Pleiadians alone can provide etherically. However, this work can help alleviate holding patterns and prevent injury and skeletal pain.

I have personally experienced incredible results with clearing skeletal problems through my work with the Pleiadians. Part of the credit goes to Dolphin Brain Repatterning guided movement work, which I am able to channel for myself when needed, and part of it goes to the etheric sessions with the Pleiadians. From the beginning of my month-long training, as well as during my studies with the Pleiadians, I had a natural and deep understanding of Dolphin Brain Repatterning work. Practically from the beginning, I knew inherently how to take it beyond what was being taught and to personalize it for myself or for a client. This gift has freed me from the need for chiropractic help, which had been a recurring necessity in my life prior to that time.

Dolphin Moves

The Dolphin Moves aspect of Dolphin Brain Repatterning is guided floor movement work. Dolphin Moves are intended to teach your body how to unlearn old restrictive patterns by moving in specific ways while monitoring yourself carefully in order to be aware of the subtleties of your movements. When you are aware of what you are doing and can feel the results in your body at the same time, you are freed to learn new ways of moving and being that are more commensurate with who you are now and who you are becoming. In other words, you give your body new choices. Interestingly enough, when your brain learns a way of doing something that requires less energy than a previous way of doing it, it drops the old way and accepts the new, more energy-efficient option. It takes much more energy to hold a part of your body in contraction than it does to let it be free, joyful, and spontaneous, as in the Dolphin Wave Effect. Therefore, once your brain experiences an alternative that allows for freedom, joy, spontaneity, and release of contraction, it adopts that *modus operandi* and tells your body how to operate in the new way. This is why Dolphin Brain Repatterning is a learning process: whether you experience the work hands-on or through Dolphin Moves, your body is taught how to operate more efficiently through your tactile awareness and the presentation of healthier, more energy-efficient alternatives. By placing your full attention on your body in the Dolphin Moves listed below, you isolate the learning experience from other potential neurological input, refining and particularizing what your brain and then your body receive. For instance, in the processes you are told to keep your eyes closed. This is because when your eyes are open, your brain is bombarded with neurological input about shapes, distances, colors, light sources, and whatever else is in your visual range. When you close your eyes, you enable your brain to make new choices about your body and health that are more lasting and precise due to the isolation and precision of the input to your brain.

It is ideal, when you do the Dolphin Moves, to lie on a carpeted floor with your eyes closed the entire time. Allow your breath to be free and open, and listen to the instructions step-by-step. As explained above, if you open your eyes to read the instructions, it interferes with your learning process to some extent. When you open your eyes, or read, these actions continually feed additional neurological information to your brain, making it more difficult to isolate the Dolphin Moves experiences. It is recommended, therefore, that you either tape the instructions yourself—if you do not have the tapes already—or have a friend read them to you, going slowly enough for you to explore each movement before you continue to the next.

Plan on doing the Dolphin Moves when you will have about two hours free time. This will allow up to an hour for the actual movement work and another hour afterward to relax without doing any detail work, reading, exercises, or watching television. It is also important that you not stretch for one hour after the floor movements. Doing them before going to bed is a great idea, as this allows your nervous system to integrate before going on to other activities.

Whether you choose to do the first Dolphin Move by reading it as you go, working with a friend, or listening to a tape, step-by-step directions for the process are given below:

1. Wear loose, stretchy clothing only. Wear no belts, bras, jock straps, or jewelry during this or any Dolphin Brain Repatterning work. Remove your contact lenses or glasses.

2. Find a comfortable place on a carpeted floor with room to spread out so that you do not touch walls, furniture, or items on the floor with any part of your body. Lie down on your back with your arms comfortably at your sides and your feet shoulder-width apart. Close your eyes, and keep them closed until the session is over unless you are reading the instructions as you go.

3. Notice your breathing, without changing it. What parts of your body expand with your breath, and what parts do not?

4. Keeping your eyes closed, feel which foot turns more to the outside than the other.

5. Notice your calves on the floor, then the backs of your knees, and then your thighs. Do they feel relaxed? Does one leg appear to have more contact with the floor than the other? Does one leg feel more solid than the other?

6. Scan your buttocks, lower back, and the small of your back for contact points with the floor. Compare your right and left sides.

7. Observe your back from the waist up, including your shoulder blades. Where are your back's contact points with the floor? Compare your right and left sides.

8. Notice where your arms, wrists, and hands do and do not touch the floor. Are the points the same on both sides?

9. How do your neck and head feel in this position? Is your face parallel to the floor? Does your chin stick up toward the ceiling or down toward your chest?

10. Notice your breathing again. Has it changed? Do you hold

your breath when you scan your body? If so, keep your breathing open and continual.

11. In general, how does the left side of your body compare to the right side?

12. Silently state the following affirmation: "I now establish a reciprocal balance between my pineal gland and the pineal gland of my enlightened future self relative to overall body, mind, spirit, and emotional balance and makeup." This affirmation aligns you with your natural evolution for the purpose of releasing holding patterns and becoming free.

13. Keeping your full attention on your body as it moves, turn your head slowly to the right as far as it turns easily and then back to center two or three times. Notice how far your head turns. Is your movement jerky or smooth? Moving very slowly is important.

14. Now turn your head to the left as far as it rotates comfortably, and then turn it back to center again, two or three times. Observe how far it turns. Is your movement smooth or jerky?

15. Now move your head from right to left as far as it goes in each direction without effort. Do not stop at the center point this time. Move it very slowly to enable yourself to observe the subtleties of the movement.

While continuing to move your head back and forth, notice the impact this movement has on other parts of your body. Observe your right shoulder and shoulder blade as your head moves from right to left and back again. Then observe your left shoulder and shoulder blade as your head continues to move from right to left and back again. Continue the movement while scanning other parts of your body: both sides of your chest, your upper spine, your arms, your ribs, the small of your back, your lower spine and sacrum, both hips. While scanning, think about the Dolphin Wave Effect. The slightest turn of your head translates into an uninhibited wave that flows through the rest of your body—sometimes apparently, and sometimes very subtly. Ask yourself: where in my body is the Dolphin Wave Effect blocked?

16. Rest with your eyes closed for thirty seconds to a minute.

17. Extend your right arm straight out from your shoulder at a right angle to your body while keeping your left arm at your side.

18. Rotate your head from side to side two or three times as before, noticing whether the movement is easier at some points and harder at others than when both arms were at your sides.

19. Bring your right arm back down to your side and extend your left arm straight out from your shoulder at a right angle to your body.

20. Again move your head slowly from side to side two or three times, noticing whether the movement is easier at some points and more difficult at others than when both arms were at your sides. How does the ease of movement compare to when your right arm was extended?

21. With both arms at your sides again, rotate your head slowly from side to side two or three times, comparing the movement to when your right and left arms were each extended.

22. Now extend both arms straight out from your shoulders at right angles to the sides of your body.

23. Rotate your head slowly from right to left and back again three or four times, comparing the movement to when both your arms were at your side; when your right arm was extended; and when your left arm was extended. Keep in the back of your awareness the Dolphin Wave Effect and notice whether your movements catch or are jerky by comparison.

24. Continue the movement with both arms extended and observe various parts of your body: your right shoulder, right shoulder blade, left shoulder, left shoulder blade, neck, arms, the full length of your spine, your sacrum, right chest, left chest, right ribs, left ribs, right hip, and left hip.

25. Rest about one minute.

26. Bend your right knee up toward the ceiling and let your right foot stand flat on the floor.

27. With your arms at your sides, rotate your head from side to side slowly again. How is the movement different with your knee

raised and your foot flat on the floor? Continue the movement while scanning the various parts of your body as before: both shoulders, shoulder blades, spine, sacrum, hips. How are the movement and its impact on other parts of your body different?

28. Lower your right leg to the floor and raise your left knee, placing your left foot flat on the floor. Again, move your head slowly back and forth and scan your body parts, comparing them to how they felt during previous head movements.

29. Without stopping your head movement, bend your right knee so that both your feet are flat on the floor. Again, scan the parts of your body, comparing the impact of the movement on them to when only one leg at a time was raised, and to when both legs were flat on the floor: observe both shoulders, both shoulder blades, spine, both sides of your rib cage, sacrum, and both hips. Remember the Dolphin Wave Effect.

30. Without interrupting your head movement, extend your right arm straight out from your shoulder at a right angle to your right side, and continue scanning your body.

31. Again, without interrupting your head movement, lower your right arm and extend your left arm at a right angle to your left side while continually scanning your body.

32. Continue your head movement while changing your arm and leg positions randomly. Observe the impact of your head movement on the various parts of your body. Make sure you keep breathing and move slowly.

33. When you feel you have explored and compared enough, rest for approximately one minute.

34. With your legs flat on the floor and your arms at your sides, rotate your head to the right and back to center two or three times, comparing the movement to when you first began. Has the range of motion changed? Is the quality of the movement different?

35. Now move your head to the left and back to center two or three times, comparing the movement to when you first began the session. How has it changed?

36. Rotate your head as far to the right and left as it will go with-

out effort or discomfort, moving it back and forth several times. Has this movement changed?

37. Say the following affirmation silently: "I affirm that my body, emotions, mind, and spirit will integrate this movement lesson easily and graciously without replay of any healing trauma. I welcome the Dolphin Wave Effect throughout my entire body and nervous system. So be it."

38. Beginning at your feet and moving toward your head, scan your entire body for contact points with the floor compared to before the Dolphin Move lesson. Observe your breath.

39. Roll to one side and slowly and gently stand up. *Important*: Do not stretch or exercise for one hour.

40. Feel your balance on your feet. Then walk slowly around the room, feeling your feet on the floor. Notice if you feel any differences in yourself compared to before the Dolphin Move.

41. Lie down, soak in a bathtub or hot tub, or sit in a comfortable chair for a few minutes before continuing with your day. Keep your glasses or contact lenses off as long as possible. Engage in no heavy lifting or strenuous exercise for twenty-four hours while your body integrates and continues to change as a result of the Dolphin Move.

It would be ideal to wait a minimum of one hour before doing the next Dolphin Move. As before, wear loose, stretchy clothing. Remove all jewelry, bras, jock straps, belts, contact lenses, and glasses. It is especially good to leave off glasses and contact lenses for a minimum of one hour, or longer if possible, after this Dolphin Move lesson since the movement focus is on the eyes. If you wear glasses or contacts, you may want to do this movement session just before going to bed. ▭

1. Find a comfortable and roomy space on the floor. Lie down on your back with your feet shoulder-width apart and your arms at your sides. Close your eyes. Scan your body for contact points with the floor from your toes to your head. Compare your right and left sides.

2. Silently affirm: "I now establish reciprocal balance between

my pineal gland and the pineal gland of my enlightened future self relative to overall body, mind, spirit, and emotional balance and makeup."

3. Bring your attention to the pupil of your right eye. Keeping your attention on the pupil, *slowly* move your right eye as far to the right as you can with ease, and then move it back to center. Repeat two or three times. Notice whether the movement is smooth or jerky. Your left eye will naturally move, but keep your attention focused on your right pupil only.

4. Now move your right eye as far to the left as it goes easily, and then move it back to center. Do this two or three times. Again keep your attention on your right pupil and notice where your movement is smooth and where it is jerky.

5. Keeping your attention on your right pupil, move your right eye back and forth from far left to far right without stopping in the center, two or three times. Notice what happens in your neck and spine as you move your eyes. How far down your spine can you feel your eye movement affecting your body? How would the Dolphin Wave Effect pertain to this movement and its impact on your body?

6. Rest for approximately thirty seconds to one minute. Compare the feelings of the right and left sides of your face, of your eyes, and of your entire body. Does one side feel more three-dimensional than the other? Is one side more alive than the other?

7. Again following your right pupil with your awareness, move your right eye up and down as far as it goes in each direction easily, three or four times. Notice where your movement is smooth or jerky. Observe the back of your head, neck, and spine, noticing how far down your spine you can feel the impact of your eye movement.

8. Now rotate your right eye in a full clockwise circle, two or three times, very slowly. Observe where your movement is smooth or jerky.

9. Now move your right eye slowly in counterclockwise circles, two or three times. Continue to notice the quality of your movement and where it is not smooth.

10. Continue slowly moving your right eye in circles, alternately

clockwise and counterclockwise, while scanning the following parts of your body to see how far down your body you can feel the impact of your eye motion: back of your head, neck, right shoulder, left shoulder, upper spine, middle spine, lower spine, sacrum, right hip, left hip, right leg all the way down to your toes, and left leg all the way down to your toes. In what parts of your body are you able to feel the effects of your eye movement and in what areas are you unable to feel the effects? What would it feel like if your body were experiencing the Dolphin Wave Effect?

11. Rest for about one minute. While resting, notice any differences in your right and left eyes and in the right and left sides of your body.

12. Bring your attention to the pupil of your right eye again. Move the pupil of your right eye very slowly in figure eights from right to left, two or three times in one direction, and then two or three times in the other direction. Focus solely on observing the quality of your eye movement.

13. Rest for between thirty seconds and one minute.

14. Keeping your attention on your right pupil, move your right eye very slowly in figure eights up and down, or vertically, two or three times in each direction. Focus solely on observing the quality of your movement and the figure-eight pattern.

15. Rest for between thirty seconds and one minute.

16. Focusing on your right pupil, make figure eights slowly with your right eye diagonally from top right to bottom left, two or three times in each direction.

17. Rest for about thirty seconds.

18. Focusing on your right pupil again, make figure eights slowly with your right eye diagonally from top left to bottom right, two or three times in each direction.

19. Rest about one minute while comparing your right and left eyes, the right and left sides of your face, and the right and left sides of your body in general.

20. Now you will transfer the learning experience from the right

side of your body to the left side as follows: Bring your fingertips to your right and left temples. While alternately tapping back and forth gently on your temples, say this affirmation silently: "All parts of my body that have learned now teach their reciprocal parts. Transfer the learning. Transfer the learning."

21. Bring your arms back down to your sides and lie still for about another minute.

22. Compare your right and left eyes, sides of your face, and sides of your body in general to see if they are more balanced now. If not, try transferring the learning again by repeating step 20.

23. When the transfer is complete and you feel more balanced, open your eyes and look around slowly before standing. Notice if your visual perceptions are altered. Are colors brighter, shapes more vivid? How is your depth perception? Your peripheral vision?

24. Silently say: "I affirm that my body, emotions, mind, and spirit will integrate this movement lesson easily and graciously without replay of any healing trauma. I welcome the Dolphin Wave Effect throughout my entire body and nervous system. So be it."

25. Roll to one side and gently stand up. Do not stretch for one hour.

26. Walk around the room feeling your feet on the floor and observing your balance in your body.

27. Either go to bed now, take a soak, or sit or lie down quietly for about fifteen minutes. Do not read, watch television, or do anything that involves focused use of your eyes for at least an hour, or longer if possible. Leave off your contacts and glasses for at least one hour, or longer if possible.

Other Dolphin Moves are available on tape, as explained at the end of the book, or they may be done in person with a Pleiadian Lightwork practitioner. The above exercises are the only Dolphin Moves appropriate to include in written text. The others are more complex and require your full attention on the movements. Although Dolphin Brain Repatterning work varies in some ways from Feldenkrais work, you may wish to read *Awareness Through*

Movement by Moshe Feldenkrais and continue movement work. The Dolphin Moves you have just completed may be repeated at a future time if you wish, but it is not necessary to do so. Once the information has been received by the motor cortex of your brain, it is permanently learned. Dolphin Moves are not like yoga or eye-strengthening exercises. However, after a few weeks or more, you may choose to repeat them in order to take your learning to a deeper level.

Etheric Hands-On Dolphin Brain Repatterning

In this case, the "hands" to which I refer are the etheric hands of the Pleiadian psychic surgeons. As I mentioned before, the Pleiadians have done extensive healing on me over the years with both Dolphin Brain Repatterning and Ka work. I have personally found that the Dolphin Brain Repatterning etheric hands-on work has corrected and alleviated skeletal and muscular pain with varying degrees of effectiveness. At times, pain relief and skeletal correction were immediate and complete. At other times, I needed the further assistance from a Dolphin Brain Repatterning practitioner or of movement work that I channeled for myself.

I make no promises or claims about how this work will affect you. Try it and see what happens. It cannot harm you. If it seems ineffective, wait until a time when you have an immediate need for healing and try it again. If you still notice nothing tangible, then use whatever methods you would normally choose for coping with skeletal and muscular pain or dislocation.

All you need to do is set aside an hour and fifteen minutes for the session, and another hour of quiet time afterward. Wear only loose, stretchy clothing with no bra, belt, jock strap, glasses, contacts, or jewelry. The Dolphin Brain Repatterning etheric hands-on work is ideal to do at bedtime since, after the invocation, you can just go to sleep. When you wake up, the session will be complete and you will have already integrated it into your nervous system and body.

Following is the procedure for setting up your Pleiadian etheric hands-on Dolphin Brain Repatterning sessions:

1. Lie down with a pillow under your knees. Place your feet

shoulder-width apart and your head flat on the bed, healing table, or floor, without a pillow.

2. Simply call on the Pleiadian Emissaries of Light and ask them to give you an etheric hands-on Dolphin Brain Repatterning session. If you have particular areas of pain, dislocation, or stiffness, tell them.

3. Silently affirm: "I now establish reciprocal balance between my pineal gland and the pineal gland of my enlightened future self relative to overall body, mind, spirit, and emotional balance and makeup."

4. Then relax or doze off. Allow your mind to be as still and empty as possible. This is not a time for meditation or processing; it is just a time be receptive and to relax or sleep.

5. When an hour and fifteen minutes is over, or when you awaken the next morning, silently say: "I affirm that my body, emotions, mind, and spirit will integrate this Dolphin Brain Repatterning lesson easily and graciously without replay of any healing trauma. I welcome the Dolphin Wave Effect throughout my entire body and nervous system. So be it."

6. Get up slowly without stretching. Walk around the room two or three times slowly, feeling your feet on the floor and noticing your balance.

7. Unless you did the session at bedtime and fell asleep, soak in a tub, or sit, or lie quietly for another fifteen minutes. Do not read, watch television, stretch, or use your glasses or contacts for at least an hour.

Feel free to request that Dolphin Brain Repatterning etheric hands-on sessions or Dolphin Moves be given to you during your sleep as often as you like. The Pleiadians will simply not come to work with you if it is inappropriate for any reason. There are also movement and healing groups that meet with the Pleiadians on a regular basis on the higher astral planes during sleep time. If you wish to be a part of them, just silently affirm your intention before going to sleep. Ask to remember your dreams if doing so is appropriate. You may remember or you may not. Either way, you will receive much benefit from the experience.

Always be sure to be very specific when you ask for work during your sleep. Ask that only beings who serve the Divine Plan of Light interact with your physical and astral bodies while you sleep. Also, ask for the Pleiadian Emissaries of Light by their full name when you set up sleep work or any other work with them. If you experience particular areas of pain or structural problems, always let the Pleiadians know at the beginning of each session.

Chapter 9

CHAMBERS OF LIGHT

O ne of the easiest and most exciting aspects of Pleiadian Lightwork is the use of healing chambers. These chambers etherically surround your entire body and aura with varying colors, frequencies, and light, each chamber with its own flow pattern and purpose in your ongoing quest for healing and spiritual mastery. In ancient Atlantis and Egypt, certain healing temples and pyramids contained small chamberlike rooms in which individuals, and sometimes couples, could receive energy balancing, spiritual alignment, and healing, or integration sessions following initiatic experiences. Occasionally these chambers were even used for the purpose of initiation. Each individual chamber room had its own unique energy grid and specific purpose, just like the Chamber-of-Light sessions you will experience in this chapter. Several of the types of chamber sessions to be revealed in the coming text had their own special chamber rooms in Atlantis and Egypt. All an individual had to do to receive a chamber session was enter the room, lie down on the table provided, and relax.

Today, setting up chamber sessions is as simple as saying an invocation and lying down for a few minutes to an hour. It is recommended that you follow the guidelines for each chamber with respect to time allowance, regularity of use, and establishing a clear intent. The Pleiadians have assured me, however, that they simply will not bring in a chamber if it is inappropriate at the requested time. So if nothing happens for you at times, tune in and see if you really need a chamber session or not. Perhaps you need a different chamber from the one you have asked for.

The following text contains descriptions and examples of some of my own and clients' experiences while doing chamber sessions. This information is intended to enhance your understanding of the purposes and possibilities of the individual types of chamber sessions rather than to imply what you should expect in your sessions. The form each Chamber of Light takes is uniquely determined by your need at the time you invoke it. Do not expect to duplicate the examples under each section or you may greatly limit your own experience. Follow the set-up steps, relax, and be receptive and open to new and wondrous healing adventures.

The opening of every Chamber-of-Light session is the same. Before beginning each individual session described in this chapter, follow the simple guidelines listed below:

1. Relax in a reclining position with your knees supported comfortably from below. (When your legs are perfectly straight, your knees tend to lock and inhibit full energy flow.)

2. When positioned, slowly take a few deep breaths while gently focusing on bringing your consciousness more fully present in your body.

3. Ground yourself.

4. Pull in your aura to two to three feet from your body in every direction. Make any needed changes in your aura boundary colors or roses.

5. Next, call in the Pleiadian Emissaries of Light and Ascended Master Jesus Christ to implement and oversee the healing session.

6. Ask them to bring above you the Interdimensional Cone of Light for divine alignment and clearing.

7. If there are other guides, angelic beings, or Ascended Masters you wish to have at the session, call them in now, always specifying that only beings of Divine Light may be present.

8. As in every healing situation, ask your Higher Self to be with you.

9. Now you are ready to invoke the particular Chamber-of-Light

session you wish to do. Instructions are in the individual sections on the chambers that follow.

PEMS Synchronization Chamber

PEMS is the abbreviation for "physical, emotional, mental, and spiritual." Your human self is made up of these four energy bodies. They are meant to work in balance and harmony with one another, even though each energy body has its own complete and individual function. If, for example, your work demands that you be extremely mental or physical, you may need to round out your life with more emotional and spiritual activities and focus when you are not working. Many indigenous tribes around the world, including Native American, Australian Aboriginal, and Celtic tribes, have used ceremonial circles and crosses with particular attention on the "four directions" to bring about this balance. In these circles and cross formations, the East is commonly used to symbolize the element of fire, which corresponds to your spiritual self. The South holds the energy of earth, which gives home to your physical body. West is the watery element and supports your emotional life. North is the home of air, your mental aspect.

Since before recorded time, rituals and healings have taken place inside these circles and crosses because conscious people have always recognized the importance of balance. "To everything there is a season. And a time for every purpose under heaven." Perhaps it is even more vital today to know how to bring about this balance again when you have lost it. Our life styles have become so polluted on every level that they are no longer conducive to natural balance and harmony. As well as the obvious environmental sources of this problem, there is contamination by radar, nuclear testing, chemical dumps and spills, televisions, microwaves, computers, and electrical light frequencies (ELFs). Subliminal programming via radio and television has intensified greed, fear, distrust, addiction, and shame in our culture in proportions beyond anything known on Earth since the last fall of Atlantis. Chemical ingredients in our foods, clothing, shampoos, soaps, cleansers, detergents, perfumes, and hair sprays have all but destroyed our nervous systems and mutated our brain functions due to the neurotoxins they contain. The list could go on and on. The point is: What the average person today might call balance and harmony is actually dysfunction and neurosis. The scary thing is, most people do not even know this and consider their dysfunctions normal.

The PEMS Synchronization Chamber opens up the communication between your energy bodies and redistributes the energy, leaving you feeling more balanced, present, and in harmony with yourself and others. What I have seen clairvoyantly, when using this chamber myself, are waves of energy coming down through my aura and body from above. These wavy lines appear to break up condensed energy spots and move the energy elsewhere in my body or aura where it is needed. Portions of the broken-up energy may be released all together. Sometimes I am temporarily drowsy as this is happening, or feel a need to stretch and yawn, or breathe deeply. I always feel the same sense of sacredness after this type of chamber session that I feel when I go out in nature for a long time or do a four-directions type of ceremony or prayer.

This process is not intended to take the place of circles, ceremonies, or nature time. It is simply a gift to assist you in busy times when you cannot create the space for a ceremony or a more time-consuming balancing process. Sometimes I use this chamber session prior to doing a ceremony or before teaching. When I do, I get even more from the experience because I start from a clearer place.

To experience a PEMS Synchronization Chamber of Light session, first follow the steps at the beginning of this chapter for opening a chamber session. Then simply invoke the PEMS Synchronization Chamber of Light to be brought around your body and entire auric field. Relax and enjoy. The healing takes ten to forty-five minutes. With this chamber, you can request a ten-minute session if you have time constraints. Otherwise, allow the maximum time in case it is needed.

When the chamber is pulled away and the session is over, you may experience a shift in or stabilization of your consciousness and body energy. Or, if you are clairaudient, you may hear a message telling you that you are complete. When either of these occurs, or you just know that it is complete, slowly get up, feel your balance on your feet before walking, and go on with your day. [⊙▭⊙]

Interdimensional Chamber of Light

This chamber could also be called the Soul Infusion Chamber, although the Pleiadians call it the Interdimensional Chamber of Light. Its function is to enhance and strengthen your feeling and awareness of your own soul essence throughout your body.

Approximately two to two-and-a-half inches inside your heart chakra in the center of your chest is the area called your "soul matrix." This matrix consists of two prismatic, diamondlike anchor points and the "sun of the soul," as I call it. This "sun of the soul" actually looks like a sun or star, glowing in beautiful starlight blue or sunlight gold. Since the Sun is a star, there is no contradiction in terms. This soul light is meant to shine brightly as you feel and know your worth and the value of your essential nature. The more you see the essential beauty in yourself and love yourself, God/Goddess/All That Is, other people, nature, and Creation in general, the brighter this light shines. And the brighter it shines, the more it helps you experience that inner beauty, worth, and love.

Any amount of self-doubt, self-judgment, lack of deservingness, or blame, judgment, or unlovingness toward others can dim the light of your soul. In other words, the more you value the sacredness of yourself, others, and existence, the more you likewise experience and express who you really are. Other things that can block or dim your soul's light are: dishonesty of any kind; sex without love; physical or emotional abuse; emotional repression; righteous justification for hate, anger, and blame; being ungrounded (your spirit not present in your body); and possession by entities. The list goes on and on.

The basic cure for any and all of these is love, acting from a place of integrity and goodwill, complete emotional honesty with yourself and loved ones, and taking responsibility for being an active creator of all aspects of your life. When you live this way, you begin to heal the past wounds inflicted by yourself and others, and your true essence can shine in your heart and body again.

To assist you as you heal and grow, the Pleiadians and the Christ have made available the Interdimensional Chamber of Light. When I use this chamber, I am aware of fine filaments of light shining like little lasers into my soul matrix and illuminating it from the inside out. The light coming in is somewhat akin to sunlight that shines inward instead of outward, with all its light aimed at a central core, as opposed to the usual sunlight that shines from the core of the Sun outward. This sunlight is so concentrated at the core of your soul that it accentuates the natural tendency of your soul to shine outward. As a result, it accelerates the gentle burning away of blocked energies inhibiting your soul from shining and allows you to feel like your true self. Whether these energy blocks are from self-hatred, judgment, abuse damage, or any other source, this Chamber of Light strengthens and enables your own soul light to burn through them.

At times when using this chamber, I feel this clearing in my body as a gentle pressure or low-grade pain. When I concentrate my breath on the affected area while consciously bringing my soul's radiance into it, at some point it releases and opens. This is generally accompanied by the feeling of energy waves rippling out from my soul through my body like ripples in water when a stone is tossed into it.

Some of my clients and friends have had out-of-body experiences while inside this chamber. This is usually caused by one of three things. First, there may be deep damage to a person's soul matrix that the Pleiadians are healing while the person is out of body. The person may need to leave his or her body simply to get out of the way so the healing can take place. A second reason a person may need to be out of body is to go into other dimensions for the purpose of soul retrieval. The third reason is the need for the person to receive either healing of, or a spiritual reference point in, his or her soul's origin and connection with God/Goddess/All That Is. When people leave their bodies for this third reason, they report feelings of not wanting to come back because where they were taken was so beautiful and peaceful.

Regardless of whether you stay in your body or are taken out for a time, you can expect to feel more peaceful and loving after these healings, as has consistently been the case with both myself and others. Your eyes will probably feel more relaxed and softer. Mine always do. Your eyes, as the windows of your soul, are cleared and opened and serve that function more fully after experiencing this chamber session.

At times, after doing an Interdimensional Chamber of Light session, I have experienced a delayed reaction in the form of a release of old emotions. For instance, after one such session I felt wonderful for about an hour and then went through a couple of hours of feeling lonely and depressed. Since I recognized these emotions as side effects of the clearing from the session, I affirmed to myself that these were old feelings leaving my body to make way for more love and soul union in my life. I made sure I kept my breathing open, was extra compassionate with myself rather than self-pitying, and allowed the feelings to pass gently and naturally.

It is important not to identify with emotions that surface after any type of chamber session but to see them for what they are: frozen emotions that have been freed so they can extinguish themselves through the transformational process that occurs as they move through your chakras. You can learn a lot about yourself in these sessions, both from the deeper experience of your own essence and from the nature of the emotions and thoughts you release during or afterward. Discovery of your own soul's myth is a vital part of your healing and reawakening.

If you have had a lot of heart or soul damage, you may not want to do an Interdimensional Chamber of Light session more than once every two weeks in the beginning. You can base your frequency of usage on the amount of clearing that occurs afterward. At times, however, even when numerous old blocks burn away, you may feel soft, open, and loving throughout the entire day with no adverse side effects at all. Your soul must be healed gently in order to create no more trauma through the healing process. Therefore, always allow for an integration period.

These Interdimensional Chamber of Light sessions are generally twenty minutes to an hour long. It would be best to allow for the maximum time, though they will seldom last that long. On one rare occasion, I was in this chamber for over two hours. During a large portion of that time, I constantly heard a distressed inner voice verbalizing limited beliefs I was holding about separation from men and God the Father. So I repeatedly used the technique for clearing beliefs described in chapter 6 until the voice quieted and the ripples of my soul light and love could flow throughout my body, bringing me peace once more.

Begin the session with the steps for opening chamber sessions at the beginning of this chapter. At the appropriate time, ask for the Interdimensional Chamber of Light to be placed around your entire auric field. Then affirm your desire to awaken your soul and allow its light to shine through every cell of your body. 🖭

Quantum Transfiguration Chamber

The primary purpose of the Quantum Transfiguration Chamber of Light is to break up cellular and emotional/mental patterning. Self-defeating behaviors, deep emotional traumas, ego- or fear-based resistance, erroneous self-protection holding patterns, implosion, pain, and even chemically caused damage can all cause cellular damage and erratic cellular movement and contraction. In a state of health and balance, your cells gently spin in a clockwise direction. While spinning, they constantly pull in light from your pineal gland, chakras, and bloodstream. This light is swirled around inside the cells as the cells continue their natural spinning motion, and then released, taking anything that needs to be sloughed off with it. As the light and life force continually fill up and spill over, they keep your cells energetically clear and free of disease.

When your breathing is shallow, whether from lack of exercise or from contraction created by emotional repression, the flow of oxygen, light, and life force slows down, and becomes sluggish. Then contraction or implosion occurs in your cells, and your physical, emotional, and mental bodies become rigid. This can result in tight muscles, body pain, lack of vitality, emotional and mental imbalance, or any of the many illnesses that plague the human species. Spiritually, such rigidity is a great contributor to feeling *stuck*.

The Quantum Transfiguration Chamber addresses these problems, whether they are manifesting in subtle and undefined ways or are blatantly causing blockages, degeneration, and pain. In this chamber, an etheric infusion of billions of microscopic lasers of colored light from several directions enters the cells. In a sense, this confuses the cells, causing them to release whatever is out of affinity and then resume a clockwise rotation. Other people's energy or programming, your own beliefs, stuck memories, emotions from the past, pain, or anything else that does not belong in your cells or energy bodies can be released.

The process used for accomplishing this laser light show in your cells requires your involvement in a more active way than did the previous chambers. Since this process tends to seem a little complicated when you first try it, it helps if you first go through the steps mentally and visually in increments. Therefore, practice the following steps prior to actually lying down and doing the chamber session:

1. Imagine a cube-shaped container made of clear glass floating in front of you.

2. Now imagine placing your hands above and below the cube and sending billions of tiny lasers of light through the cube from both hands at the same time.

3. Next, move your hands to the right and left sides of the cube and fill it full of lasers from those directions.

4. After that, place your hands behind and in front of the cube and once again infuse it with lasers.

5. Now that you have experienced the component parts of the light matrix generated in the chamber, visualize sending lasers from all three directions at the same time. In other words, imagine having three sets of hands, with one hand on each of the six sides of the cube. Then imagine sending billions of lasers through the cube from all six directions at the same time. (See illustration 9 on page 188.) You will see that the intersecting laser lines create many minuscule, linked cubes of light inside the original, larger cube, like a three-dimensional tapestry of finely woven threads of light.

6. Now, work with the same interlacing of laser lights but this time visualize them around your aura and body. Begin by imagining billions of lasers of light running from the left and right sides of your aura toward, and then through, your body. These lasers are small enough to go through every cell.

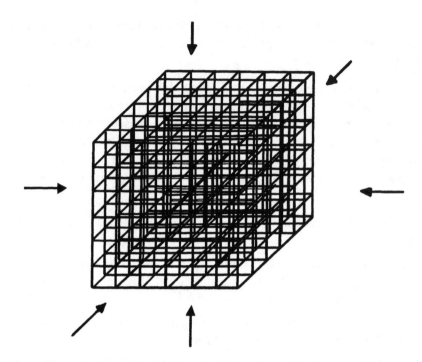

9. The grid structure used in the Quantum Transfiguration Chamber of Light with laser lights running from top to bottom, side to side, and front to back

7. Then, imagine lasers moving through your aura and body from above and below you.

8. Next, visualize lasers streaming from the front and back of your aura through your body.

9. Lastly, put all the lasers together. Visualize and/or intend the lasers moving through your aura and body from all six directions at once: above, below, right, left, front, and back.

If these steps feel confusing to you, especially from step 5 on, practice until the process feels more comfortable and natural. Then you will be ready to actually do the chamber session.

When invoking the Quantum Transfiguration Chamber of Light, it is necessary for you to hold the intention and vision of this interlaced grid of laser lights throughout your entire aura and physical body in order to help the Pleiadians anchor the frequencies and light patterns. Usually, you need to do this for the first two minutes of the chamber session before the Pleiadians are able to hold the light configuration in place. After that you can just relax until the session is complete.

The lasers can be any color or combination of colors you need at a given time. If you feel unsure of what color of light to visualize, simply imagine sunlight gold. The Pleiadians will bring in whatever energy and color are appropriate; they only require you to help establish the grid pattern. Once this grid is in place, they may change the colors from time to time, or they may keep them consistent, depending on your current need.

In the following chapters of this workbook section, you will be given other applications and uses for the grid patterning used in this chamber. For now, however, focus on using the light grid for your full body and aura to undo less-than-ideal cellular, emotional, and mental patterning. The repatterning that occurs as a result brings about healthier conditions that are more commensurate with who you are now and who you are becoming.

, After you complete the steps for opening a chamber session at the beginning of this chapter, invoke the Quantum Transfiguration Chamber of Light. Then visualize or imagine seeing the intersecting lasers of light shining from above your head and below your feet, from the right and left sides of your body, and from your front and back, all at the same time. (See illustration 10 on page 190.)

Remember, the lines all begin at the outer edge of your aura, which should be two to three feet from your body in every direction. If this image is still difficult or confusing for you, simply intend that the lasers all run simultaneously and visualize them one at a time, in sequence, repeatedly.

When the grid is fully anchored and made functional by the Pleiadians, I feel a shift in the energy, as if something clicks into place. When you feel this shift, or after two minutes, whichever comes first, simply relax, breathe deeply, and be receptive.

The chamber session lasts between ten minutes and an hour. I recommend doing the Quantum Transfiguration Chamber at a time when you can take a hot bath and relax afterward. Doing it a couple of hours before bedtime is ideal, since your body will do a lot of

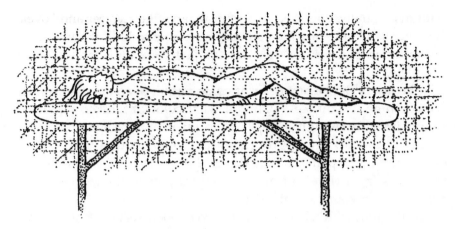

10. Person shown inside a Quantum Transfiguration Chamber of Light

releasing and reorienting after the chamber is complete. Hot water aids in the cellular and emotional release, especially if you have access to mineral water or use Epsom salts or bentonite clay in the bath. A hot shower is okay if a bath is not available, though it is not quite as effective. 🔲

Integration Acceleration Chamber

In these vastly accelerated times, you may find yourself feeling overwhelmed or "on overload" occasionally, or even frequently. The spiritual, mental, emotional, and even physical demands on you to change the basic structure of who you are, or think you are, are occurring so rapidly that becoming a "peaceful eye within the storm" is more and more a necessity. You may sometimes feel as though there is nothing tangible to hold onto; as if life is a roller coaster ride, an ongoing paradigm shift, a continual refinement process. You may find yourself experiencing the healing of several lifetimes in a single day, resulting in you becoming a different you over and over again. As Earth and this solar system move deeper into the Photon Band, this acceleration becomes more intense for all of us.

Sometimes the spiritual and etheric changes occur so rapidly that your body, mind, and emotions cannot keep up. At other times, the changes are so fundamental to your self identity that you may feel a sense of disorientation and general fuzziness. You may experience tiredness and weariness, or you may feel extremely hyper and "over-amped." You may feel like running away with nowhere to run to, or you may collapse and not be able to move. Overload can lead to undisciplined addictive behaviors unless you are aware of what is going on and can find other coping mechanisms. Using chocolate, sugar, or caffeine to mask emotional pressure or watching television to block the mental vomiting are examples of addictive coping devices. They are addictive because of their obsessiveness and urgency, and because you are using one thing to substitute for another that you are afraid of, resistant to, or in avoidance of.

Perhaps the experience you avoid at all costs is feeling loneliness, anger, or fear. Or perhaps overload occurs when you clear a lot of beliefs or past lives in a short amount of time. Maybe you hit overwhelm when you are repeatedly faced with your control and revenge issues. Or perhaps you experience overload when you go to a healer and do energy clearing just after you have read a book with a great deal of new spiritual information in it. The two together may use up your capacity for change, input, and newness. If you have ever done intensive spiritual or therapeutic trainings, you may be familiar with this syndrome. Regardless of the source of overload, it brings integration and learning from life experience to a halt and prevents further growth without damaging you.

This is where the Integration Acceleration Chamber comes in. Its sole purpose is to reduce overload on all levels and help you integrate healing, change, learning, and growth into your life and way of being. I was first introduced to this chamber in 1987 while doing the month-long intensive training during which I met the Pleiadians on a conscious level. You may find it easy to understand why I needed it at that time since I was being worked on and with twenty-four hours a day by the Pleiadians, waking and sleeping, while participating in an ongoing daily training program. The mental and emotional demands from the dual reality were wonderful, but taxing, to say the least. The chamber accelerated my own integration, which enabled me to continually keep learning and healing myself; this gift was greatly appreciated and used frequently. Therefore, I highly recommend this chamber if you are going through intensive trainings or workshops; it will help keep you present and available in as clear a way as possible. I wish I had known about it when I was studying for college semester exams years ago!

This chamber does not take the place of rest and relaxation, or exercise. You must still take responsibility for caring for your own needs in demanding or stressful times. It is no substitute for a day or a week off when you need it, and it is not intended to replace self-discipline and self-care. However, those times when you really need it, it is a godsend.

The chamber itself is perhaps the simplest one of all. It is a gentle field of silvery aquamarine light that permeates your aura and body. The Pleiadians tell me that it is one of several new colors that human beings will be able to see with their eyes in the fourth dimension; some people are beginning to see these colors clairvoyantly now. The closest you can come to it here and now is to imagine mixing equal parts soft metallic silver glow and pale aquamarine- or blue-topaz-colored light. This new color radiates a light, joyful, and relaxing frequency that helps cool and slow down the spiritual burning process that takes place in times of transformation. In addition, it helps bring about a more natural and peaceful body/soul balance and communication. It also tends to shut off your overworked mind and help you just *be* for awhile.

Even if you are not feeling overloaded, it is okay to experience the chamber now in order to establish a reference point and familiarity for when you truly need it. Besides that, it feels good.

Follow the steps at the beginning of this chapter for opening all chamber sessions, then simply invoke the Integration Acceleration Chamber of Light. If you visualize the silvery-aquamarine color at the beginning of the session and imagine it permeating your aura and cells, you may find that it enhances your experience. Then just relax and "let go." This type of chamber session takes only two to ten minutes and may be done as often as you feel a need for it. 🔲

Ascension Chamber

Using the Ascension Chamber of Light is a wonderful experience in Oneness. The rarefied points of light filling the chamber are of such a pure, peaceful, and high-frequency nature that they gently lighten your sense of body awareness. An actual experience of full-body ascension requires that your Ka Channels be open and that every cell in your body be karmically clear and able to hold a high-vibrational light frequency. This enables your Christed Self to make a full descension into matter. A state of ecstasy and enlightenment ensues, at which point your being has a choice to remain in your physical body in order to give and serve, or to ascend, in which case your body becomes lighter and vibrates at such a high frequency that it moves into the higher dimensions and is no longer visible to those on Earth.

My own past-life experience of ascension was initially a sense of weightlessness and buoyance. As the actual ascension occurred, the light frequencies in my cells were elevated, and my physical cells spun faster and faster. I felt joyful and light and had a deep sense of letting go. This continued until my body was made of pure light and levitated upward, disappearing from the physical world and arriving in the higher planes at its appointed destination. The most over-whelming feelings for me when I reexperienced this were ecstatic freedom, detachment from my individuality, and Oneness with the Light that exists in God/Goddess/All That Is.

The Ascension Chamber creates a bridge between where you are now and your own enlightenment and ascension. Allowing you the spiritual experience of Oneness with the omnipresent Light, which has also been called the Infinite Sun, is the main purpose of the Ascension Chamber. Even so, my own experiences in this chamber have been diverse. Usually I drift into a deep well of divine peace, sometimes accompanied by joy and pervasive love, while at other times it is devoid of any other feeling or thought.

Sometimes I experience a release in the first part of my session that clears out any obstacles to Oneness and peace. This release may come in the form of emotions being set free, negative thoughts or beliefs being cleared, or spontaneously making sounds to release ten-sion, just to name a few possibilities. Afterward, there seems to be a change in the frequencies that brings about the gradual lightening sensation and experience of divine peace. This latter change is how the chamber experience begins when there is no clearing to be done. From that point on, I most often sink into such a deep place of sur-render that my entire body feels like it is made only of bright points of light like a sun or a star. Then I feel myself joining with other bright, sunny, multiple points of light as if the bed or floor, the air, the building, and even the whole Earth are all made of the same light as I am—and this same light is endless, like the Infinite Sun.

At that point I sometimes experience myself freely moving around inside the Infinite Sun. Beautiful loving beings are often there with me. Sometimes they communicate with me, and sometimes I experience a silent communion with them. At other times I find myself with my Council of Elders. This Council of Elders is a group of four elder Light Beings who advise and guide me from lifetime to lifetime. Every human has his or her own Council of Elders; they know exactly what each person needs at all times and may make recommendations. However, people are totally free to choose what they do, and the Council of Elders always honors free will. Sometimes when I am with them I ask them questions, but they decide whether or not it is appropriate to answer.

Most often the experiences in the Ascension Chamber are more oriented toward states of *being* rather than *doing*. They offer opportunities to access deeper spiritual knowing, surrender, peace, and the elevation of light frequencies in your body. Once, while in this chamber, I was taken up a long flight of crystalline steps to a beautiful open temple called the Temple of the Sun, or the Temple of God the Father. There was a golden throne with a glowing being sitting on it. His radiance was so bright that his features were nondistinguishable. My feelings of being loved and valued, and of belonging, were overwhelming. I was taken inside the temple and blended with his energy field until we became a single golden sun, which then permeated all of existence. After that chamber session, I could not stop smiling for hours.

Your experience in the Ascension Chamber will be unique to your own next step toward enlightenment and ascension, and will tend to be oriented toward giving you a "spiritual reference point" in a higher state of beingness. So let go of expectations and allow the experience to be the most it can be for you right now.

After preparing yourself in a comfortable place and opening the chamber session as usual, simply invoke the Ascension Chamber of Light to be brought around your body and aura, and then relax.

Allow anywhere from twenty minutes to one and a half hours for this chamber experience, as it can go quite deep. When you feel or sense the chamber is complete, reground yourself before standing, as you may feel very expanded and spacey afterward. 🔲

Sleep Chamber

The Sleep Chamber of Light is to be used at bedtime or nap time when you are going to sleep and not just resting. When you are in the Sleep Chamber, the Pleiadians, the Christ, and any of your personal guides who wish to work with you can isolate aspects of your subconscious or higher consciousness that need education, healing, or illumination. The other function of this chamber is to assist you in creating your future. These functions can occur at any time when you are asleep, with the help of your guides. However, when you are in the Sleep Chamber, your physical and astral bodies are synchronized in such a way as to help you more efficiently and completely reap the benefits of your dream experiences.

During your sleep time, your physical body is held inside the chamber until you awaken the next morning or after your nap. This creates a very safe psychic environment for you to do deeper processing and healing in your dreams as well as to receive spiritual help. Any healing needed by your physical body and aura to enable you to integrate the dream experiences into your life is done by the Pleiadian healing team, while the Pleiadian Archangels work with your astral body in the higher realms. When I do Sleep Chamber sessions, I always sleep more deeply and experience my dreams as more lucid, easier to remember, and more profoundly symbolic and meaningful. Students have reported similar experiences and results as well. I generally ask for whatever is in my highest good at the time to take place in my dreams. You may choose to make this request also.

You may prefer to ask for dreams about specific issues you are working on in your life. For instance, if you are feeling a lack of self-confidence and are having a hard time asserting yourself as a result, ask the Pleiadians and the Christ to give you dreams that reveal the source of the problem and help you heal it. If you awaken remembering that in your dream you kept running into doors and walls, and that people around you laughed or jeered, work with that information when you wake up. After grounding yourself and pulling your aura in, run energy while replaying the dream in your mind and blowing roses. If certain images are especially strong, put the actual scene in a big rose and blow it up a few times. Then replay the movie the way you would like it to be: this is called "reframing." Reframing dreams is a powerful way to re-create your own reality and clear subconscious blocks.

You may also ask for instruction and teachings to be given to you during your sleep. If you do, be specific about what you want, unless you ask for whatever is in your highest good at this time. If, for example, you wish to learn about your higher purpose, or how to have more faith, simply specify your request after bringing the chamber around you. Then, first thing the next morning, either write down your dreams or go immediately into meditation to decipher and integrate the information.

These chamber sessions vary greatly every time you do them because your sleep and dream needs change very rapidly. It is difficult to adequately describe the details about the Sleep Chamber for this reason. When you are ready to experience the session, go to bed. Complete the usual steps for opening a chamber session listed at the beginning of this chapter. Then ask that the Sleep Chamber of Light be brought around your entire aura and body and kept there until the next morning or until your nap is over. Ask for assistance in being lucid during the dreams you need to remember, and in remembering them when you awaken. If you wish to focus on a specific issue or teaching, specify what it is now, and then relax and go to sleep. Otherwise, just ask for whatever is in your highest good at this time. Then, "to sleep, perchance to dream."

If you discover that being in the Sleep Chamber makes you more restless during the night, or if you find yourself overly involved in the processes taking place and wake up feeling tired, then ask the Pleiadians to make it a Deep Sleep Chamber next time. A few of my students, as well as myself, have found this necessary. [cassette icon]

Stress Reduction Chamber

The Stress Reduction Chamber of Light states its purpose obviously in its name. Due to these times of *faster, more,* and *better,* as well as to influences like electricity, radar, and microwave energies constantly playing havoc with our nervous systems, stress reduction has become a commonly used term. Even those of us in alternative professions do not escape the pressures that are building planetwide and locally every day.

At those times when all of this stress "gets to you," this chamber can be a godsend. Whether the stress originates from overwork, relationship conflict, overprocessing, emotional overload, worry, or having too much on your mind to sleep, the Stress Reduction Chamber can help tremendously. Of course, it cannot, nor is it intended to, take the place of a healthy, balanced lifestyle, and yet it can assist you when pressures build up and your nervous system and mind are overtaxed by pressure and stress.

When I use this chamber, I generally experience slow, gradual relaxation settling in. Often, gentle rippling waves of energy move through my body from left to right, creating a release of strain and tension. After a few sweeps of these wavy energy patterns, various things might occur. At times I feel as if the Pleiadians are holding my head in their hands, sending gentle relaxation and soothing light throughout my brain and nervous system. At other times I feel a soft, falling sensation that helps me let go and settle down in my body more. Sometimes I simply fall asleep and have no idea when I awaken what happened except that it obviously worked. When experiencing insomnia, I often use this chamber for assistance in relaxing enough to fall asleep.

After completing the start-up steps for a chamber session, simply invoke the Stress Reduction Chamber of Light, relax, and enjoy it for the next twenty minutes to an hour. Always allow for the full hour even though it may not be required. 📼

Dolphin Star-Link Chamber

Formerly called the Electrical Light Body Chamber, the Dolphin Star-Link Chamber is used both as an activation chamber and a healing chamber. Your electrical light body is actually the interfacing network in your body between your Ka Channels and your neurological and electrical systems. You might think of it as a network of channels with thousands of tiny secondary channels, or minuscule electrical circuits. Your Ka Channels feed this system with high-frequency, etheric, electrical light that activates your light body and keeps it vibrant and healthy. This vast electrical network has many juncture points that connect the circuits in an interlacing manner. When your Ka body is open and linked with your electrical system, the combination is literally a microcosm of the star systems in this galaxy. It is this merger of Ka and electrical energies that enables dolphins to be in harmony and synchronization with the planetary and galactic orbits and to receive communications and light from the star systems. Your electrical/Ka connection and interface are intended to eventually open you in the same way the dolphins are already open.

Some of your secondary channels, or smaller electrical circuits, may be damaged, broken, or jammed with foreign energy, your own energy blocks, or pain. When they are, the parts of your body affected by the problem cease to be fed electrically and begin to lose vitality, life force, resilience, and cosmic connectedness. Eventually disease and pain result if the problem is not corrected.

During Dolphin Star-Link Chamber sessions, the Pleiadians bring in the blueprint for your electrical light body and activate its circuits. When your healthy circuits are fully electrified, which you experience as warmth and relaxation, the circuits that are not fully functional are left darker by contrast and easy to see. It is like looking at a night sky that is brightly illuminated and noticing that the Big Dipper and the North Star are missing. The Pleiadians then work on your shut-down or damaged circuits, doing any repairs, unclogging them, and activating them if needed. Sometimes your circuits require psychic surgery, replacement, or pain removal, and these are things the Pleiadians cannot do unless they have human hands through which to work. However, there is much they can and will do to assist in your ongoing light-body healing and activation.

This chamber session takes between thirty minutes and an hour, and full time must be allowed. It is okay to do it as you go to bed and fall asleep. After completing the chamber set-up steps at the beginning of the chapter, ask that the Dolphin Star-Link Chamber of Light be brought around your aura and body. Then just relax, or fall asleep if you like.

Divine Axis Realignment Chamber

The Divine Axis Realignment Chamber of Light serves the function of clearing lower-frequency energies and preparing you to anchor your Higher Self more deeply in your body, which is described later on in this book. As explained in chapter 7, there is a tubular opening called the "tube of light" or "divine axis" that is like an extension of your own spine. It extends beneath your feet to the base of your aura, and above your head beyond the topmost point of your aura into the higher-dimensional realms of your own hologram. (See illustration 11 on page 200.) When you are in this "vertical alignment," you are in the best position to access higher truth and divine qualities, in general.

This chamber's function is to expand that of the Interdimensional Cone of Light, which also assists in bringing you into vertical alignment. The Divine Axis Realignment Chamber sessions allow the Pleiadians to actively work with your energy field to clear blockages and low frequencies, whereas the Cone of Light holds the environment for axis alignment in a more passive way. You may experience a pulling sensation as "horizontal" energies are freed from your body and aura. At times, you may feel a pulling sensation from your feet up, as though your spine is being stretched. At other times, you may feel energies pulling outward from your body into your aura, in your front or back, or anywhere in your body. I have also experienced energy waves moving from left to right. Basically, you receive whatever is needed at any given time to assist you in your next steps toward divine axis alignment. As always, the Pleiadians never do anything for you that you need to do for yourself in order to learn and grow.

After following the steps for opening chamber sessions at the beginning of this chapter, simply ask to be placed inside the Divine Axis Realignment Chamber of Light. Be aware of any thoughts, beliefs, or judgments that come to mind that you want to clear while in the chamber session. If you feel a strong localized pull on any part of your body for more than about two minutes, check for cords that need to be removed. The Pleiadians will clear extraneous cords, but not ones you need to be aware of for any reason. This chamber ses-

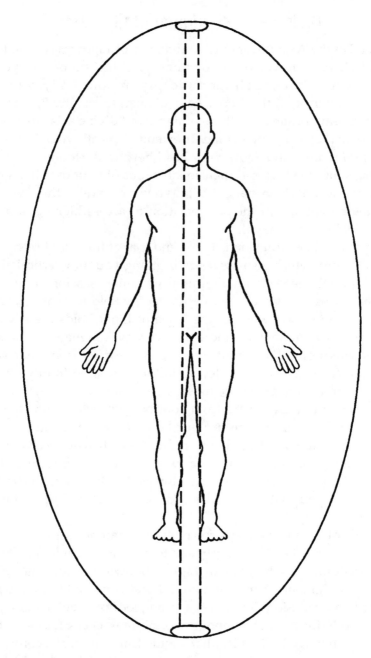

11. *The Tube of Light is shown running from the top apex of the aura through the body, around the spine, and to the bottom apex of the aura.*

sion lasts ten to forty minutes, and you should always allow for the maximum time in case it is needed. It is recommended that you repeat the Divine Axis Realignment Chamber session two or three times before you do chapter 13, "Higher Self Connection." [tape icon]

No Time and Space Chamber

The No Time and Space Chamber of Light has three different uses. They vary only slightly, based on circumstances. With all three uses, you are enabled to step outside of the impact of third-dimensional reality and be inside an environment that is not limited in the usual ways.

The first situation in which you may desire the use of this chamber is environmental. The best way I can explain it is to tell you the story of how I first discovered the No Time and Space Chamber. A friend and I were on vacation and had to pass through Salt Lake City. When we were about fifteen miles north of the city on the freeway, we entered heavy smog accompanied by equally heavy, thick psychic energy. The combination of pollution smells and etheric density was extremely oppressive, as if we had entered an area of condensed negative thoughtforms. I immediately went into a meditative state to clear the car and find out what could be done.

Pa-La, my Pleiadian guide, came right away and instructed me, "Command that the car and five feet in every direction around it be made into a No Time and Space Chamber in which the air and etheric-energy field are cleared of all physical and psychic pollutants. Also specify that until you rescind the command, the car and both of you be free of all influences outside the chamber. Hold an image of the chamber as a clear air space around and through the car until you feel it anchor into place on its own."

It took about two minutes for the chamber to feel solid. At that point, my friend, who was driving, turned toward me suddenly with surprise in his voice and said, "What did you just do to the car?" I asked him what he meant and he replied, "I was just about ready to ask you to drive because the energy was making it almost impossible for me to keep my focus. It was so thick and oppressive. Then all of a sudden the energy was clear, like being by the ocean."

About ten minutes later we both experienced the clarity and

purity fading; gradually the thick energy and smells seeped in again. I closed my eyes and reestablished the chamber, strengthening the commands even more than before. This time the chamber lasted until we arrived at our evening destination. I set up a No Time and Space Chamber in our motel room that night as well. We stayed on the southwest side of Salt Lake away from the city, and the energy in the motel, though not as dense as that on the eastside freeway, was still quite uncomfortable for us. The motel was also very noisy due to the presence of a class reunion at which heavy drinking was going on. When the chamber was in place, we noticed an immediate drop in the noise level, a reduction of smells, and an etheric quality of clarity and freshness.

Usually I can effectively use the techniques for clearing the home (given in chapter 5) for clearing motels, cars, or other spaces. However, under extreme environmental circumstances when those techniques are not enough, the No Time and Space Chamber works. Because you live in a world of time and space, it is not advisable to use this chamber all the time for clearing purposes.

The second use of this chamber is for multidimensional communications. For those of you who feel you are ready to tune into guidance and interaction with Light Beings of a higher-dimensional nature, especially your own Higher Self, this chamber can assist you by pulling your consciousness out of third-dimensional reality and opening your mind to normally inaccessible frequencies. If you have not been meditating for very long, or if you have a particularly overactive mind, the chamber may not bring immediate results. It will, however, bring a refreshing sense of calm, clarity, and focus.

When you use this chamber, it is important that you relax and let go of effort and thoughts as much as possible. The nature of the chamber itself greatly augments this process. At the beginning of the chamber session, ask for any guidance that is in your highest good to be given at this time. Since you will already have stipulated that only beings of Divine Light may be present, you will be in a safe space for opening up. At times, the guidance may come as sudden thoughts in the midst of a state of "no-mind." If you are naturally more clairaudient and telepathic, you will clearly hear spoken messages when appropriate.

There are other times, however, when guidance is not what you really need. Then the chamber operates in its third capacity, which is to bring about effects as if you had spent an afternoon on the beach, or in a flotation tank session. You can also specify that this is what you want instead of guidance. When you use the chamber in this way, you find yourself feeling expanded, freer from the pull of gravity, and lighter. Every time I experience the No Time and Space Chamber in any of the three ways, I feel relaxed and recharged, as if I am breathing negative-ion–filled air, as is prevalent near the ocean. The same freshness and openness seem to actually permeate the air in the chamber. The No Time and Space Chamber experience can also help you access the alpha state in meditation, which is healing and rejuvenating for your nervous system; it fills you with a deep sense of calm and well-being.

It is not recommended that you use this chamber consistently for meditation. Rather, use it specifically when you need a break from third-dimensional reality. Meditation with a focus on pulling your spirit more into your body and feeling divine energies is very important in the goal of mastery and ascension. Overuse of the No Time and Space Chamber might interfere with this goal. Frequency of use varies from person to person, and it will fluctuate for you with changes in your life circumstances. In general, the second and third uses of the No Time and Space Chamber are recommended about once a week if you are so inclined, and more frequently only if you feel personally guided to do so.

For your first experience with this chamber, set up the space as outlined in the beginning of the chapter, then ask for the No Time and Space Chamber of Light to surround your body and aura. Request that it bring you deep rejuvenation and opening to divine guidance as appropriate. Then simply relax, let go of all agendas, and enjoy. When you request guidance in this chamber, it is best to wait and listen passively instead of actively focusing on waiting and listening. You need forty minutes to an hour and a half for the session and may stipulate the time frame yourself if it is more advantageous than leaving it open-ended.

Emotional Healing Chamber

The Emotional Healing Chamber is a blessing during those emotionally raw times when grieving or emotional release leave you feeling wiped out. It can also be used when emotional demands in your life are overwhelming or draining. When you are emotionally drained or in overwhelm, you tend to have an aura that is either sulphur-yellowish-green or orange and pulsating. When you are in this condition, you need soothing, relaxing healing and not more emotional release and issue processing.

This chamber can affect you like a soak in hot mineral water and a gentle massage. It soothes, eases, smoothes out the rough edges, and helps you relax and let go of problems for awhile. It is wonderful to do at bedtime when you can just drift into sleep, but it also works well any time you need it.

If you have a history of emotional trauma from physical, mental, or emotional abuse, deep grief from losses, or unresolved past-life emotional karma, you can benefit from experiencing this type of chamber session. Whether you have an ongoing source of emotional pain, or damage and buildup from the past, emotional-body healing takes place. The emotional buildup may involve fear, paranoia, anger, rage, self-pity, shame, depression, sadness, hurt, or grief; the chamber addresses the problem by lifting, lightening, and soothing the excess emotions, and repairing any emotional-body damage. As with other areas of Pleiadian Lightwork, the Pleiadians cannot do psychic surgery and certain other specific types of deep healing, but they can do a lot.

This chamber cannot to be used as a substitute for emotional expression; the Pleiadians simply do not work in that way. However, when you are taking responsibility for expressing and clearing emotions in present-time situations and for learning from past experiences, they gladly assist you when healing is needed.

Whether or not you have an immediate emotional problem, you can still experience the chamber and receive any needed emotional-body healing. The Emotional Healing Chamber sessions vary in length from fifteen minutes to forty minutes, and you always need to allow for the maximum time in case it is needed. After doing the steps for opening a chamber session, ask for the Emotional Healing Chamber of Light to surround you. Then just relax and be receptive.

[cassette icon]

Multidimensional Healing and Integration Chamber

If you have incurred damage between your third-dimensional and higher-dimensional aspects, you can use the Multidimensional Chamber of Light to assist in healing it. Perhaps this damage occurred due to past- or present-lifetime abuse; drug, sex, or alcohol addiction; rape; or extreme emotional or physical damage accompanied by shock. Such experiences can sever your connection to the higher-dimensional planes altogether. If you grew up with alcoholic or violent parents, you probably lived in a psychic environment filled with lower astral energies and disincarnate entities, parasites, and negative thoughtforms. Access to etheric light sources beyond your body was most likely cut off, and you would have lived in an atmosphere of fear and illusion.

Your personal hologram extends deep within and far above your aura. When it becomes a lower astral field instead of a light field, you feel separate, negative, and even hopeless at times. Connection with your Higher Self and with the spiritual realms is then possible only via out-of-body experience. Rips occur in the etheric structures of your geometric configuration. Open channels and spaces become filled with foreign and dense energies. Meditation, positive thinking, emotional and past-life healing, and spiritual awareness, in general, help you clear these blocks and begin the journey home to your true self.

The Multidimensional Healing and Integration Chamber of Light can greatly augment and accelerate this recovery and healing process. The Pleiadians assist by bringing in higher-frequency energies that "burn off" and transmute lower-frequency, denser energies. They can also assist in repairing and reconnecting you to as much of your own divinity as you are ready for at any given time.

This chamber may also be used when you have had an extremely expanded spiritual experience beyond your body and you need assistance integrating it into your human energy field and life. Often these out-of-body experiences cannot filter into your time-and-space reality, and leave you feeling letdown and with a sense of futility in terms of the experience making a real difference in your life. This can be especially true if you tend to always go out-of-body to meditate or are generally ungrounded. The ability to down-step higher frequencies and experiences and allow them to make a real difference in your life and who you are is critical to your spiritual evolution.

If you use, or have used, drugs to access higher realms, you create the same dilemma for yourself as you do by always meditating out-of-body. Your body frequency actually gets lower by virtue of drug use or ongoing absence of your spirit in your body. You become more and more dependent on going out of your body to have spiritual highs, whether through drug use or meditation, and become incapable of integrating the experiences into your in-body conscious daily living. This same problem is created by being ungrounded and out of your body all the time in order to avoid feeling emotions or taking responsibility.

The Multidimensional Healing and Integration Chamber facilitates in-body spiritual experiences by repairing holographic damage and opening the pathways to more fulfilling and tangible multidimensional connectedness and communications, especially with your own Higher Self, though it is not limited to that. It assists you in bridging the gap between your spirit and body and the higher dimensions in a way that changes your life by accelerating your Higher Self's descension into your body, or "human space suit" as José Argüelles calls it.

Another use for this chamber is the integration of initiatic experiences. Whether the initiation is a new one that has just taken place or a past-life initiation you are reliving in order to bring it into your present-time reality, the Multidimensional Healing and Integration Chamber of Light can assist greatly. Initiatic experiences are always multidimensional and can leave you feeling quite altered and disoriented. This is especially true when you reexperience a past-life initiation since you are bridging the normal gap in the time-space continuum as well as interfacing with other-dimensional realities. In this case the Pleiadians and the Christ work with your body, consciousness, aura, and hologram to help you align and integrate the experience in such a way that it can make a difference in your current life instead of just being a "far out" experience.

During a recent Pleiadian Lightwork Intensive that I taught, two students who were paired for a Ka Channel opening both experienced very profound past-life initiations. Initial clearing was followed by deep altered states and a sense of expansion beyond their bodies into other dimensions and time realities. Afterward, both felt somewhat dazed, disoriented, and in need of stillness and quiet time. After doing the Multidimensional Healing and Integration Chamber of Light, they began to adjust to being different from before and were not so disoriented by the change. Harvey, one of the two reinitiates, forgot to ask for the chamber before going to bed but remembered it around 4 A.M. At 8:50 A.M. his wife, Pat, who was visiting, informed me that Harvey had invoked the chamber a few hours ago and still could not move. Class was scheduled to start in ten minutes, and he was in bed in the classroom. When I went down to check on him, all he could move was his eyes. He had not only invoked the chamber but had told the Pleiadians to do anything else he needed. I was able to speak with the Pleiadians and find a way to accelerate his completion of the session; about two minutes later, he was on his feet again. The joke in class that day was that you need to be careful what you ask for and to specify that it is complete at least an hour before class time. Harvey was not paralyzed in a dangerous sense—he was only so deeply into the energy state of the work with the Pleiadians that he was temporarily nonfunctional.

This example demonstrates that there are those rare occasions when the transition you are going through is so extensive that the Pleiadian Lightwork chambers and healing sessions can take a long time. If you know you have had an unusually life-changing spiritual experience or healing and you want to do this chamber to assist in the integration process, it is recommended that you do so at bedtime or on a day off when you have nothing scheduled. It may take only the normally allotted time—but who knows?

When you are ready to experience this chamber, always allow for the maximum time. Sessions range from twenty minutes to an hour and a half. After following the steps for opening chamber sessions, ask that the Multidimensional Healing and Integration Chamber of

Light be brought around your body and aura. Remain receptive and relaxed. You may occasionally find negative thoughts and judgments arising for clearing while in this chamber. Allow them to come into your awareness naturally, if they do at all, without trying to seek them out. Then simply use the techniques for clearing judgments, pictures, and beliefs given in chapter 6. ▱

Chapter 10

LOVE CONFIGURATION CHAMBERS OF LIGHT

T he Love Configuration Chambers focus on bringing divine love to your physical body cellularly as well as to your emotional, mental, and spiritual bodies. Because of their multiple uses and unique content, an entire chapter is devoted to these chambers. Perhaps the only source of healing is love; at the very least, healing must be done with loving intent to really make a difference. Clinical healing without love and caring may sometimes alleviate symptoms, but I do not believe it can truly effect deep and lasting change with respect to the source of problems.

How many people experience the purity and sweetness of unselfish love with any consistency in their lives? Certainly there are those who do, and yet it appears at this time on Earth that divine love is still the exception rather than the rule. This statement is not intended to point a finger at anyone, just to point out an area in which we as a species need to evolve. Divine love might be defined as: (1) pure love given without expectations, ulterior motives, guilt, manipulation, or "dumping on" others; (2) love given as a natural outpouring of the essential nature of the self who cares about others without the need for a reason; (3) the natural response to witnessing the essence of another person, animal, plant, or anything else in creation; (4) God/Goddess essence flowing through all that exists.

Today's society teaches that love is defined by feelings such as: worrying about people; being afraid of losing them; requiring others around in order to feel good or safe; something you feel toward others when they meet your needs, validate you, or give you what you want; telling people you cannot bear to live without them; pitying others and sympathizing with them. This last description is what most people call love, or the symptoms of love.

Recently, a client was staying at my home for a three-day private healing intensive. He was having an emotionally tough time coping with what was coming up in the work and was stuck in "poor me." I was required to step into the "tough love" role in order to keep the work moving. After a session, I smiled and looked directly into his big sad eyes and said, "I love you." He replied, "It's been pretty hard to tell sometimes." I said, "That's because I love you. I do *not* feel sorry for you." He got my meaning at once and said, "I don't think I've ever known the difference. I've always gone for pity." This was a deep realization for him.

Society teaches you to constantly vie for love by playing "poor me," "misery loves company," and "ain't it awful" games, which are all closely related. Can you remember a time when you were accused, or when you accused someone else, of being unloving and insensitive because of not feeling sorry for another person and giving the "you poor thing" response? Pitying people actually disempowers them. It validates their powerlessness and inability to help themselves. This does not mean you have to be cold and distant. It just means: keep loving people, be compassionate, but do not negate their ability to learn, grow, and change their lives by feeling sorry for them.

There is quite a difference between the definitions of divine love and the definitions society gives to "love." You probably learned early in childhood that if you wanted to be loved you had to do what your parents wanted and expected of you. You either adapted to that behavior or rebelled and refused love altogether. Either way your ability to receive divine love was greatly reduced or blocked completely by the game of vying for energy and attention from others.

As an adult, this misunderstanding about the nature of love translates into unrealistic expectations of mates and friends. If people do not call when you think they should, you assume they are being unloving. If your best friend makes a new friend, you feel unloved and jealous because she was supposed to be giving you all her attention. "He" does not hold your hand or kiss you when you want him to, so you accuse him of being unloving because he didn't anticipate your wants and needs.

The majority of people today have forgotten that humans are intended to choose mates and closest friends with whom they are compatible, ones toward whom they naturally feel loving and caring, and who naturally return those feelings. Instead, many people constantly create sexually bonded relationships or friendships with people before they get to know them, before they share with each other their wants and needs, before a basis for compatibility is determined. Then they get hurt when other people's way of loving does not meet their expectations, and instead of seeing it simply as other people's way of loving, they blame and accuse others of being unloving. Maybe some of these people are unloving and maybe not. If these agendas and attitudes are familiar to you, it is important that you realize that you are responsible for using discernment and making more conscious choices in the first place.

A very loving man once told me, "I don't want to involve myself in relationships of any kind in which anyone is depreciated. We are meant only to appreciate one another, and if we can't do that with people, we should not be involved with them." You probably have not escaped such lessons somewhere along the way.

Because of such dilemmas about loving, as well as many others, you may have shut down your ability to receive divine love, as well as the other things that have been called love. You may even be afraid to let in the joy of true love because you so closely associate it with giving up control to another, being hurt and disappointed, or becoming dependent. Love in its pure form never involves fear, resistance, contraction, loss, control, hurt, or dependency.

When what you call love does bring about these types of pain, you must take responsibility for examining your discernment, or what you are holding within yourself vibrationally that magnetized the situation or person to you. What unfair or unrealistic expectations are you holding? Did you get to know the person enough to find out if he or she was caring and giving before you got involved?

Do you believe you deserve to be loved and to have your love received? Are you able to let the person be who he or she really is, or do you think you have a right to change people to suit your needs? Do you even like the person when he or she is simply being genuine and doing what he or she naturally does? If you feel a need to work on these issues and understand them better, I recommend a little book by Erich Fromm called *The Art of Loving*.

The Love Configuration Chambers help you open to and receive divine love, let it heal you and soften your resistance, and become more discerning about whom and what you let into your life in the future. They also tend to bring you to a state of feeling more loving as well as feeling more loved. They may make you an even better person just by virtue of the experience if you are willing to let it do so. During the chamber sessions, you are surrounded by and filled with Divine Love from various Light Beings and Father God and Mother Goddess. You may experience their love touching your heart and penetrating your body. Though each type of Love Configuration Chamber has a slightly different focus and intent, each one brings in Divine Love.

Love Configuration Chamber sessions begin with the same eight steps given in chapter 9 for opening all chamber sessions. Once you complete these steps, invoke the chamber around you. Then you will need to stipulate which of the types of Love Configuration Chambers you want to do: (1) Unification, (2) Angelic and Archangelic, (3) Divine Feminine, (4) Divine Masculine, or (5) Yin/Yang The following sections explain the unique functions of each type of chamber and guide you into each of the individual chamber sessions.

It is recommended that you wait a minimum of eight hours between these individual chamber sessions in order to fully experience the contrasts among them. All Love Configuration Chamber sessions last thirty minutes to an hour. You may stipulate the amount of time if you wish; however, when it is practical to do so, allow for the maximum time.

Unification

The Unification Love Configuration Chamber is the most general and broad-based of the five types of Love Configuration Chambers.

Its purpose is to align you with universal divine love from a variety of sources and bring you a feeling of unity and oneness through love with All That Is. It requires your conscious participation at several stages of its setup. Review these as listed below before you actually experience the chamber session.

At the beginning of the Unification Love Configuration Chamber session, you will do the preliminary steps, as always, and then invoke the chamber itself. Then you will ask to receive the love from God the Father through the Sun. You will envision, even though you are most likely indoors, that the light of the Sun is shining above you, filling the air above and through your body with the tiniest, finest rays of light that you can imagine. These multiple tiny light rays carry the energy of God's love, so that as they touch and penetrate your body from above, you are filled with love-light. As you continue to envision this love-light streaming through every cell of your body, you will see it entering your front, penetrating your entire body, and pouring out your back and into the Earth. This process may take a few minutes. The love-light will flow through you in a continuum until the session is over, and you stipulate that fact before proceeding.

Earth is used as the vessel of Mother Goddess love. You will ask her to fill you with streams of light and love just as the Sun is doing. Using your breath and visualization, bring the Goddess love from Earth into and through the cells of your body from behind you. (Actually, beneath you, since you will be lying down.) You will continue holding this vision until the Earth's Goddess love fills your body and overflows out your front. Again, you will ask that the love-light continue flowing through you until the chamber session is completed.

At this point, divine love will be flowing through your body from front to back and from back to front. Next, ask the Pleiadians and the Christ to fill you with their love. Then call on any guides, Ascended Masters, angels, archangels, and Light Beings from whom you want to receive love. You may wish to invoke devas and overlighting devas, Buddha, Quan-Yin, Mother Mary, Saint Francis, or any other Light Beings with whom you feel a connection or would like to feel a connection. You may also opt to make a general appeal to "all beings of Light and Divine Love who wish to participate at this time."

Then just relax until the session is over. Allow yourself to feel the love coming to and through you. Let it make a difference. If tears or other emotions arise, feel and express them in whatever way is most natural to you. Soon you will return to a state of peace and feeling only the love you are being given. If negative thoughts, beliefs, or judgments come to mind, clear them using techniques you learned earlier in this book.

I always end a Love Configuration Chamber session with a "Namaste" (see Glossary) and an expression of gratitude to those who have been present and giving to me.

The following is the complete procedure for using the Unification Love Configuration Chamber:

1-8. Do the steps for opening a chamber session as described in chapter 9, page 180.

9. Ask that the Unification Love Configuration Chamber of Light be brought around your aura and body.

10. Envision the Sun shining into the room and on the front of your body (above you, since you are lying down).

11. Ask that the Sun be used as a source of God the Father's love to be given to you.

12. See the fine rays of love-light entering your aura and the front of your body from your head to your toes. Breathe it into the front of you until it streams out the back of your body and into Earth.

13. Ask that love-light from Father God continue to flow through you until the session is over.

14. Next, call on Mother Earth to be a vehicle for Mother Goddess, or Holy Mother, love.

15. Envision fine streams of love-light flowing from Earth toward the back of your body (beneath you, since you are lying down) and breathe them in. Continue this process until you feel love-light overflowing out the front of your body and filling your aura.

16. Ask that this love-light continue to flow through every cell of your body until the session is complete.

17. Ask the Pleiadian Emissaries of Light and Ascended Master Jesus Christ to fill you with their love.

18. Call on any guides, Ascended Masters, angels, archangels, or any other Light Beings you want to have join the Love Configuration Chamber circle around you.

19. If you wish, say this invocation: "I welcome any and all beings of Divine Love and Light who wish to participate in this Love Configuration Chamber session to come forth now. I am ready to receive your love completely and fully."

20. Be as open and receptive as you are able to be at this time. Allow the love to flow through every cell in your body from every direction at once. If you need extra help to open up and let go, repeat the following affirmation until you feel relaxed and more open: "I deserve divine love, and I am willing to receive divine love now."

21. When you sense that the session is coming to an end and the Light Beings are pulling away, close with them in any way that feels genuine to you. For example: say, "Namaste," or express your gratitude.

22. Open your eyes and come back to the room slowly, bringing the feeling quality of the chamber session back to your day with you. Reground yourself if necessary.

Angelic and Archangelic

In this chamber session, the basic format is the same as for the Unification Chamber session. The major difference in the process takes place after you bring in the solar and Earth love energies from Father God and Mother Goddess. At that point, you will call on *only* angels and archangels to form a circle around you and fill you with their love. The reason for this is that angelic love is a unique and wonderful love frequency with its own type of purity, joy, peace, and innocence. Angels, in general, strongly carry the energy of devotion, adoration, and service to God/Goddess and the divine in all things and people. After you experience this chamber, you will understand the uniqueness of this energy more fully.

When calling on angels and archangels, you may be specific or general. You may choose to invoke all angels and archangels of divine love, asking them to create a circle of love-light around and through you. Or you may choose to invoke specific angels and archangels with whom you want to connect. There are many types of angels from which to choose: healing angels; angels of love, mercy, peace, innocence, faith, or any other divine quality you can think of; protective angels; messenger of God angels; angels of guidance; angels who watch over children; angels who watch over sexual relationships; music angels; death transition angels; angels of birth and rebirth; angels of divine female healing; angels of divine male healing; and many more.

The archangels are as many and varied as the angels. You can call on them according to the quality they emit or the role they play. Each of the following major archangels is in charge of a host or league of angels and archangels who serve him/her. Though the male names have become more widely known, the archangels are male and female divine counterparts. Archangel Michael and his divine counterpart, Michaella, or Faith, as some call her, are keepers and protectors of divine truth, and the Legions of Light. Archangels Gabriel/Gabriella are messengers of God and guards of free will. Archangels Uriel/Uriella watch over the peacekeepers on Earth and in the heavens. Archangels Raphael/Raphaella are the protectors of, and hold the quality of, divine love. Archangels Chamuel/Chamuella hold dominion in the areas of divine harmony and music. Archangels Zadkiel/Zadkiella are the keepers and protectors of divine mind and spiritual commitment. Archangels Jophiel/Jophiella hold the quality of divine wisdom and the ability to gain wisdom from all life experience, including suffering. Jophiel/Jophiella also lead the angels who work with death transition.

When experiencing the Angelic and Archangelic Love Configuration Chamber, you may ask for individual angels or for a host of angels to serve a specific function. For example, if you wish to call on Archangel Zadkiel/Zadkiella to bring in divine mind and spiritual-commitment frequencies, you may request that the host of angels in service to Zadkiel/Zadkiella join the chamber session as well. Or if you wish to call on the healing angels, you may call on them individually or as a group.

You may also want to include the cherubim and seraphim kingdoms. The cherubim are like the little cupids depicted on Valentine's Day cards. They are childlike and carry the vibration of sweet youthful love and innocence. The cherubim can bring wonderful healing and soothing to your emotional body and inner child. The seraphim are also childlike angels who protect the purity and innocence of the minds of children and help restore those qualities in adults.

Following are the steps for using the Angelic and Archangelic Love Configuration Chamber:

1-8. Do the steps to open a chamber session at the beginning of chapter 9.

9. Bring Father God's love-light through your body from front to back, using the Sun as the vehicle of that love.

10. Invoke and envision Mother Goddess's love-light streaming through your body from back to front as you receive it from Earth.

11. Call on any specific angels or archangels you wish to have present; or state: "I call on all angels and archangels of divine love, including the cherubim and seraphim, who wish to be present for this Love Configuration Chamber session and ask that they come forth now, surrounding and filling me with their love-light."

12. Relax, remain open and receptive, and enjoy.

13. When the session is complete, close with the angels as you wish.

14. Come back to waking consciousness slowly, and open your eyes. Reground yourself if necessary.

Divine Feminine

Whether you are male or female, heterosexual or homosexual, you need to receive divine feminine love, as well as experience your own inner female loving nature. It is fairly commonly understood nowadays that all people have an inner male or animus, and inner female or anima, regardless of physical gender. These parts of yourself must be in some semblance of health and balance in order to create health, balance, and creativity in your life.

Opening to divine feminine love requires you to use the receptive quality of your feminine nature in order to let love, or anything else, come to you. The feeling quality and vibrational nature of each gender are unique and wonderful. The purpose of this chamber is to open you to the specific energy and feeling of feminine love in its highest form.

If you have had a painful relationship with your mother, women friends, or female lovers or mates, this chamber can facilitate deep healing internally, as well as in those relationships. If you have had positive and satisfying relationships with women, this chamber session can bring you another step closer to ending any remaining sense of separation you may have from Mother Goddess and assist you in opening to more oneness, nurturing, and female love.

Before beginning the session, I would like to suggest a few female Light Beings on whom you may wish to call. Quan Yin (whose name is also spelled Kwan Yin, Kuan Yin, and Kanseon) lived on Earth and was enlightened long before the time of Gautama the Buddha. She is worshiped in most Buddhist practices as the keeper of Divine Compassion and Mother of the World. Her extreme gentleness and nurturing nature bring peace; she is often depicted with tigers or dragons whom her sweetness and compassion have tamed.

Mother Mary was an enlightened priestess and the mother of Jesus Christ. She and a large group of other females who were enlightened prior to or as a result of meeting Christ, form a group called the Sisterhood of the Ray of the Ascended Christ. Mary Magdalene, Martha, Saint Anne—who was Mother Mary's mother—Ruth, Rachel, Elizabeth, Sarah, Judith, and many more work together as a collective of feminine enlightenment and Christ consciousness. They also maintain one-on-one roles as guides and Ascended Masters for individual humans. I always call on this group when I do female healing of any kind.

Others you may want to call on are: Isis; Shakti, whose divine counterpart is Lord Shiva; Radha, whose divine counterpart is

Krishna; Kali, the destroyer of ego and all that is false, a "tough love" goddess; White Buffalo Calf Woman; Tara; Deodata, whose divine counterpart is Gautama the Buddha; any of the female archangels; Saint Catherine; Saint Bernadette; Saint Joan of Arc; or any other female saints or deities with whom you feel a particular kinship or with whom you wish to establish one.

When you are ready to begin the session, follow the same steps given for the Angelic and Archangelic Love Configuration Chamber. However, substitute the following for the earlier step 11:

11. Call forth any female guides, Ascended Masters, and Light Beings you wish to have present. If you do not desire to call on specific beings, then simply use the following invocation: "I call forth the Sisterhood of the Ray of the Ascended Christ, and all female angels, archangels, masters, and guides who are of Divine Light and love. Surround and fill me now with your divine feminine love that I may be reunited completely with the Holy Mother Goddess." If you need healing in specific female relationships, ask for that now as well.

Divine Masculine

Once again, your gender and sexual preference have no bearing on this type of chamber session whatsoever. Western culture has tended to make heterosexual men very homophobic, and as a result, they often shut down to masculine love, even on the level of divine love from Father God. Most American and European families, in particular, create very little space and time for fathers to nurture and actively show love to their children. Western society, therefore, needs a major renaissance in the area of male lovingness and ability to receive love.

Regardless of your history with males, this chamber helps you open to healthier and more fulfilling, loving relationships with men and with Father God, if you are ready and willing. If you have a painful history with males, you stand to benefit even more deeply and profoundly than if you have been fortunate enough to experience the unique and wonderful quality of masculine love. If your experiences with males have been damaging, you may first release old hurt and painful emotions prior to feeling the nurturing and love during the chamber session.

As with the divine feminine Love Configuration Chamber, there are male Light Beings you may call on if you choose to do so. Ascended Master Jesus Christ is in charge of a group of men who have become enlightened through connection with him or the Christ realm. They are called the Brotherhood of the Ray of the Ascended Christ. This Brotherhood includes males who have attained to Christ consciousness such as: all twelve known disciples, including Judas; Father Joseph; all the saints, including Saint Francis, Saint Christopher, Saint Barnabas, and Saint Germain; Father Abraham; and King David.

The Order of Melchizedek of Divine Light is also a male group. Melchizedek is named in the Bible as a teacher of Jesus Christ. However, this group predates Christ's time by many thousands of years. They were first anchored on Earth as a human initiatic group of priests during the first era of Atlantis. When the third and most recent Atlantean period ended, their teachings and practices were taken to Egypt and established in the temples there. That was where Christ connected with the order. Unfortunately, since the order became divided between allegiance to the light and to the dark during the second Atlantean era, it is especially important that you always use the words "of Divine Light" when you call on the Order of Melchizedek.

You may also wish to invoke: the male archangels; Gautama the Buddha; Lord Maitreya, the upcoming Buddha; Chenreysi, Lord of Compassionate Wisdom; Shiva; Krishna; Osiris; Quetzalcoatl; Manjushri, Buddhist Lord of Wisdom and Truth; Hiawatha; and any other male Light Beings with whom you wish to connect.

Again, the format is identical to that of the Angelic and Archangelic Love Configuration Chamber. However, substitute the following for step 11:

11. Invoke any male guides and deities you wish to have present. Then state the following invocation: "I call forth the Brotherhood of the Ray of the Ascended Christ, and all other male beings of Divine Light and love who wish to join me at this time. Surround and fill me

with your love-light that I may open to divine masculine love and the love of the Holy Father God." If you need healing in specific male relationships, you may specify that at this time. 🔲

Yin/Yang

The Yin/Yang Love Configuration Chamber is specifically for healing and balancing your inner and outer male/female relationships. This chamber can be done both by individuals and by couples who wish to heal or deepen their relationship with one another and with God/Goddess/All That Is.

If you are doing the chamber individually, it is a wonderful opportunity to ask for a healing of your relationship to your Earth parents. If you have had a particularly traumatic relationship with your parents, it is recommended that you specify this at the appropriate time as you do your first Yin/Yang Love Configuration Chamber. If your relationship to your Earth parents has not been a problem, then you may wish to focus on healing your sexual relationships, or on the *sacred marriage* between your own inner male and female, body and spirit.

Whatever you choose to focus on, your relationships to Father God and Mother Goddess will both be affected, which will in turn affect all your other relationships. In aligning yourself to receive balanced divine feminine and divine masculine love simultaneously, you can embrace and experience a wonderful wholeness.

If you are a couple doing this chamber session, it is best if you both do the Divine Feminine, Divine Masculine, and Yin/Yang Love Configuration Chambers individually prior to doing the Yin/Yang Love Configuration Chamber together. That way you will each go into the couples chamber with more of a sense of your own uniqueness and wholeness, and you will be less likely to project onto your mate that he or she is the *only* source of love. I think it is also a good idea to know your individual relationship to God/Goddess/All That Is as the source of divine love prior to sharing the experience. There is a wonderful line in one of Ferron's songs that says, "It's a woman's dream, this autonomy, where the lines connect but the points stay free." The Runes say, "Let the winds of heaven blow between you." This in no way negates surrender to divine love through relationship;

it just adds the elements of appropriate individual wholeness, relationship to Divinity, and autonomy.

Begin the session by doing the standard first eight steps. Then you will envision Yin/Yang symbols ☯ floating above your head, beneath your feet, in front of you, and behind you. You will command that the symbols remain throughout the chamber session. After you bring through the God and Goddess love from the Sun and Earth, you will bring in the Sisterhood of the Ray of the Ascended Christ and the Brotherhood of the Ray of the Ascended Christ. Then you will ask that the male and female archangels be present.

The last invocation will be to the Divine Couples of the Seven Rays as follows: (1) Violet Ray: Quan Yin and Lord Maitreya; (2) Blue Ray: Jesus Christ and Mother Mary; (3) Green Ray: Chenreysi and Tara; (4) Golden Yellow Ray: Buddha and Deodata; (5) Orange Ray: Krishna and Radha; (6) Red Ray: Hiawatha and White Buffalo Calf Woman, or Shiva and Shakti; (7) White Ray: Osiris and Isis.

The format for the Yin/Yang Love Configuration Chamber is the same for couples and individuals, except that in the case of a couple, you may each want to do the invocations out loud. The steps for doing this chamber session are as follows:

1–8. Do the steps to open a chamber session at the beginning of chapter 9.

9. Ask that the Yin/Yang Love Configuration Chamber of Light be brought around your body and aura.

10. Envision Yin/Yang symbols above your head, below your feet, in front of you, and behind you. Command that they remain there throughout the chamber session.

11. Envision and invoke the Sun as a vessel emanating the love of the Holy Father God; its rays penetrate your aura and body from your front through your back.

12. Envision and invoke Earth as a vessel emanating the love of the Holy Mother Goddess; this love flows from behind you, through your body, and out your front.

13. Ask that the Sisterhood of the Ray of the Ascended Christ and

the Brotherhood of the Ray of the Ascended Christ form a circle around you and fill you with their divine love.

14. Invoke the male and female archangels of light to surround you and fill you with their love.

15. Call forth the Divine Couples of the Seven Rays to surround you and fill you with love and balance.

16. Relax, be open and receptive, and enjoy the session.

17. When the chamber session is complete, do a closing with the Light Beings who are present in whatever way you wish.

18. Open your eyes and slowly return to waking consciousness. Reground yourself if necessary. 🖭

Feel free to repeat any of the Love Configuration Chambers as often as you would like. Eventually, you can evolve to a state in which you receive and give divine love through and from every cell of your body all the time.

I often do a meditation in which I call on and envision God's divine love and the Goddess's divine love flowing through me as described previously. I use this flow of love as the entire focus of the meditation and come out feeling peaceful, joyful, and very much in love with everything and everyone in the divine sense. At the end of the meditation, as my body fills and overflows, I see the love continuing out into the plants and trees, animals and people, and the planet and its atmosphere.

As the love is pouring out, I silently speak as follows: "I send this love to all the trees on this Earth so that you know there is a human who loves you and sees your sacredness. I send this love to all the animals on this Earth so that you know there is a human who loves you and sees your sacredness." I continue with the air, water sources, humans, Earth, all plants, and then out to the stars and Light Beings. You may wish to do your own version of this meditation. It could only help.

Chapter 11
SUBPERSONALITIES

A subpersonality is any aspect of yourself that has a specific function, attitude, or identity that operates in an individual and rec-
ognizable manner. For instance, you have an Inner Child who
feels and responds to life emotionally and from a place of needing to
feel cared for and safe. This part of you exists whether you are newborn, 100 years old, or any age in between. Many books and healing
modalities focus exclusively or largely on assisting you in becoming
familiar with and creating healthy subpersonalities. Psychosynthesis,
Alchemical Hypnotherapy, Regression Facilitation (a modality I originated and teach), Voice Dialogue, and Inner Child work are some of
the more contemporary examples of such modalities.

Since early times, communication with and balancing of subpersonalities have held vital roles in various cultures. Long before Jung
or Freud "originated" subpersonality work, certain Native American
tribes, African tribes, Druids, Goddess-based spiritual traditions, and
other cultures recognized the need to honor the existence of diversity
within the individual. This has been done through ceremonial rituals, personal inner-focus time, healing sessions, and medicine
wheels. A medicine wheel is a circular area outdoors either outlined
in small rocks to create a container for the circle, or marked with larger rocks in four or more directions. Ceremonies, gatherings, and personal spiritual activities are all held inside the medicine wheel from
time to time. Throughout the ages, humans have also designed and
worn masks, created costumes, painted their faces, mimicked other
beings, and performed rites of passage to facilitate the incorporation
and health of different aspects of themselves.

There are two categories of subpersonalities. The first category
consists of aspects of yourself that develop relative to your individual personality needs or expression. For example, if you have a lot of

sexual denial, you may have an Inner Prude and an Inner Whore. They have developed due to neglect and judgment of parts of yourself that are whole and natural but that have been denied their freedom of expression. Another example is the subpersonality that might be called the Inner Critic. This aspect may have grown in you if you were invalidated and scolded excessively as a child. Some part of your personality adopted the behavior of your parents and teachers and took over where they left off. These types of dysfunctional subpersonalities need to be healed, educated, and reintegrated into your wholeness and self-esteem.

The second category is made up of aspects of yourself that will always be a part of you. This is the category on which this chapter focuses. The four subpersonalities of this category are: the Inner Nurturer, the Inner Child, the Inner Warrior/Warrioress, and the Inner Spirit. Their states of health are reflections of both your inner and outer lives. Your freedom to be emotionally spontaneous and honest, your ability to carry through on commitments and accept responsibility, and your spiritual connection are among the many things that create health or imbalance in these aspects of yourself.

Whole books have been written about subpersonality work, so this workbook does not cover the subject in its totality by any means. It is a vast subject that you could explore in much more depth. However, it is important that you understand the basic format of subpersonality work, since the Ka work, Chamber of Light sessions, and even basic psychic self-care processes can and do bring issues to the surface that are most easily resolved through communication with and healing of your subpersonalities.

Integrating and Healing Your Subpersonalities

The subpersonality process used in this book has its origins in a specific Native American tradition that I am told dates back at least 25,000 years. I am using "artistic license" in this presentation and in some of the material, but the fundamentals are directly from the tradition I was taught. The process is based on teachings about the medicine wheel and four directions that, regardless of the individual ceremony or personal focus, are always aimed at balancing and harmonizing. Honoring and balancing the four directions are parts of most medicine wheels. If you know the traditional symbolism of each direction, this will assist in further understanding how they apply to the four main subpersonalities. Though there are variables in traditional symbolism and interpretation among the different tribes, the symbolism used in my work is as follows: (1) South represents planet Earth, the earth element, and the physical body. The Inner Nurturer is associated with this direction. (2) West represents the water element and the emotional body. The Inner Child is located here. (3) North is the direction of the air element and the mental body. The Inner Warrior/Warrioress is associated with the North. (4) East represents the fire element, light, and the spirit body. It is the direction of the Inner Spirit. If you already have four-directional interpretations that you use for spiritual purposes, simply interchange the placements of the elements and subpersonalities as appropriate. For instance, if you traditionally call South the direction of water, then read the section on the Inner Child for your interpretation of South, as the Inner Child is associated with the water element. The Inner Nurturer would then be located in the West instead of the South.

When working with the four subpersonalities, or places on your "personal shield," as the whole subpersonality system is called in some Native American teachings, it is important to know that each subpersonality has a positive and important function in your life regardless of any imbalances or dysfunction being expressed. Each subpersonality should be treated like a sacred being. The purpose of meeting your subpersonalities of your personal shield is to balance them through awareness, understanding, communication, and action.

Awareness comes first from meeting your subpersonalities and finding out how they are doing and what their needs and wants are. Upon initially meeting these aspects of your personal shield, you will ask the subpersonalities what their names are. You will see an image for each subpersonality with your inner eyes and talk to it as if you were addressing a physical person. Then you will listen. In order to understand how that part of you thinks and feels and what its needs are, you will ask questions. These questions are listed in the individual sections in the guided process for meeting your subpersonalities. The subpersonality may tell you ways in which it feels unfulfilled and stifled, or joyful and fulfilled. Your job is to listen with caring and understanding as that part of you shares its feelings, its hopes and dreams, and its little wishes. When you have heard the answers to all your questions, you will be complete with the initial meeting. You will say your goodbye for the time being and agree to connect at a later time.

The decision on how often to meet with your subpersonalities, or "balance your personal shield," is up to you. The particular Native American people from whom I learned this practice recommend balancing your personal shield daily. I have find that I tend to do so about once a week unless I feel a specific immediate need. My other spiritual practices are time consuming and take precedence in my daily practice. However, this may be different for you. The process may be so profound and vital that it becomes your most important daily focus. There was a time when it was a vital daily practice for me. When I leave the medicine wheel after each session of balancing my personal shield, I tell the aspects in the four directions approximately when I will see them again. This communication is important for making the process real and meaningful for yourself and your inner parts.

The next step is action. If your Inner Nurturer tells you that you are watching too much television and that you need to spend more time being in nature or taking long baths, you need to listen and follow through on these suggestions to the best of your ability. If you cannot comply for some reason, be honest with your Inner Nurturer and tell it why you cannot heed the advice given. What your subpersonalities ask for is genuinely intended to bring you back into balance with yourself and your life. It is important that you intend to take action, however possible, based on the feedback; without this intention not only is the process useless, but your self-trust will deteriorate as well. Instructions for what to do when you go back into the medicine wheel after the initial meeting are given in the last section of this chapter.

In the particular Native American tradition that I learned, you meet each part of your personal shield in a vision quest. You find a spot in nature to which you are drawn, and you make an offering of tobacco, smudge, corn, or some other gift. This spot is ideally one in which you feel a particularly strong connection with the element that direction represents: South representing earth element, for example. Next, you sit on the earth and sing sacred songs or go into a silent meditation, asking the aspect with whom you desire contact to come forth. Then you wait for this aspect to present itself. You may hear a voice speak to you or see an image of what your subpersonality looks like. You will need to establish both the image and the communication before you are through. Then the dialogue takes place. After the communication is complete, you may take an item from the quest location back to your altar or outdoor medicine wheel as a physical symbol of the relationship. This can be a rock, a leaf, a piece of tree bark, or anything else that feels right. You will choose a separate quest location for each of the four parts of your personal shield.

If you do not wish to do this process by going into the outdoors, you may also do it through meditation. After entering into a relaxed state, you will offer prayers to the Great Spirit, God/Goddess/All That Is, or whatever you call the Divine Oneness. Give thanks and ask for clarity and assistance as you meditatively quest to meet your four subpersonalities. Directions for meeting your four subpersonalities are given in the following sections.

Subpersonality Harmonization Chamber of Light

This chamber session is ideal to do after meeting each individual aspect of your personal shield for the first time, and subsequently after balancing your shield. The focus of the Subpersonality Harmonization Chamber is to redistribute energies, open and soften inner communications, and bring you back into balance with yourself. I always find that I feel more in self-affinity, or more like myself, after experiencing one of these chamber sessions.

This chamber is also ideal to use after any kind of subpersonality work such as hypnosis, Psychosynthesis, Voice Dialogue, or shadow work. You may also work with your own inner voices and subpersonalities and do the Subpersonality Harmonization Chamber session afterward.

The first time you do this chamber session, do it after meeting one of your four subpersonalities. You will use the same opening steps as you use for all chamber sessions; these steps are given at the beginning of chapter 9. At the appropriate time, simply ask that the Subpersonality Harmonization Chamber of Light be brought around your entire body and aura. Then relax and be open and receptive for the next twenty minutes to an hour. When you are experiencing a time shortage, you may specifically ask that the session be only twenty minutes long. Otherwise, allow for the full time and enjoy the session however long it lasts.

Meeting Your Inner Nurturer

The first direction to work with is the South, which in this practice represents the earth element. Earth is the source point of your physical birth, your connection with your physical mother and the Goddess, your physical body, grounding, security, and nurturing. From the South you receive food, shelter, clothing, and all things physical. In this medicine wheel teaching, you honor and thank the South, or the earth, for all of these gifts of sustenance, including your body, which sustain your spirit here on planet Earth.

The subpersonality that lives in the South part of your medicine wheel is your Inner Nurturer. Your Inner Nurturer is the part of you that knows about and takes care of your needs, as well as keeps other parts of your personality in balance. If you are out of touch with your Inner Nurturer, you tend to be out of balance in life. You may experience symptoms such as feeling overly needy of attention and nurturing from others because you are not giving these things to yourself. Maybe your whole life focuses on work and you never take time to play or spend intimate time with yourself or your loved ones.

When you are out of balance, and you get in touch with your Inner Nurturer, he or she knows what is needed to bring you back into balance again. Even if your needs are emotional or spiritual, your Inner Nurturer keeps track of your overall balance and well-being. If your needs are specific to self-nurturing, you may need to get more massages, or take quiet, unscheduled time alone. Perhaps your diet is not truly nourishing your body and giving you what you need. Maybe you need to take long baths, or do yoga, or sing and play music more. Whatever you need, your Inner Nurturer knows. If this subpersonality has become extremely dysfunctional and damaged, communications can be confusing at first. He or she may be hurt and frustrated and not want to talk to you. This is a symbolic reflection of the fact that you are feeling betrayed and angry with yourself for not paying attention to your own needs. If you can take responsibility, without guilt, for creating the dilemma, the subpersonality will usually come around and tell you what is needed and why he or she feels so out of balance. Remember, your job is to listen with sincere understanding and nonjudgment and then to plan with the subpersonality how you will correct the problems through action in your life.

Whether you are meditating indoors or doing a vision quest outdoors to meet your Inner Nurturer, and your other subpersonalities, write down your questions on a piece of paper. Leave space between the questions to record the answers you are given so you will have them to refer back to.

Following are the steps for meeting your Inner Nurturer:

1. After you have found a spot in nature where you feel connected to the earth element, or are comfortably seated indoors for your quest, center yourself and go into a meditative state.

2. Send your prayers of gratitude to planet Earth, the earth element, and the direction of South in your own way. You may also say any other prayers and invocations at this time.

3. Ask your Inner Nurturer to come forth so that you may see, and communicate with, him or her.

4. When an image and voice come into focus, refer to your paper and ask the following questions, writing down the answers you receive.

    a. What is your name?

    b. How are you?

    c. What do you need?

    d. What do you want?

    e. Is there anything else you would like to share with me at this time?

5. Close the quest in whatever way feels appropriate to you. Tell your Inner Nurturer when you plan to return.

6. *Optional*: You may choose to invoke the Pleiadian Emissaries of Light, your Higher Self, and Ascended Master Jesus Christ at this time and ask them to place you inside the Subpersonality Harmonization Chamber of Light.

Meeting Your Inner Child

The Inner Child lives in the West of your medicine wheel. The West, in my teachings, is the home of water and your emotions. Dreams, feelings, the shadow side of your personality, your subconscious, and inner journeying are all functions of the West.

In your personal shield, your Inner Child holds the qualities of emotional spontaneity and honesty, curiosity, and freedom to be playful and joyful. He or she approaches the world and other people with awe and wonder. Your Inner Child never takes anyone or anything for granted and finds exploring and learning about life and other people to be most fun when they are done experientially. He or she loves to examine the details of the tiniest wildflower, or gaze at the monumental stature of trees, in awe of the complexity and perfection of nature. Watching a bumble bee or an ant colony and being delighted can take up a whole afternoon. Your Inner Child is fully absorbed in whatever he or she is doing unless feeling stifled and bored by lack of freedom. This subpersonality shows enthusiasm and expresses pleasure easily, and cherishes his or her dreams and fantasies.

When your Inner Child is out of balance, you may feel restless, agitated, frustrated, bored, or apathetic. All of these are signs that your Inner Child needs more freedom of expression. Have you become too sophisticated to share your dreams, or to feel awe and wonder in the presence of a busy squirrel or a brightly colored insect? Do you hide your true feelings because you think it would be uncouth or immature to express them? Do you look at your mate and close friends with the inquisitiveness and excitement of wanting to know more about the vastly conscious beings before you? Are your relationships alive, loving, and ever changing, or boring and predictable? Do you let yourself cry and laugh out loud at special moments in your life or at good movies? Or do you drink, smoke, eat sweets, watch movies, or overindulge in any way when you feel uncomfortable emotions coming to the surface? Most addictions are due to a repressed and controlled Inner Child.

When you go into your vision quest to meet your Inner Child, it is important that you be available for full emotional and verbal expression. If your Inner Child is lifeless and sad, or distrusting and sulky, it may take a little time to win his or her trust. Be very honest with this part of yourself, because even the slightest deception will be seen as a reason for distrust and feelings of hurt and betrayal. Your Inner Child needs you to support its freedom, joy, and a vast array of feeling states. The rewards for giving yourself this needed support are a happier, more balanced life, and more self-respect and self-love.

Follow the instructions in the section on your Inner Nurturer for setting up your vision quest to meet and communicate with your Inner Child.

Meeting Your Inner Warrior/Warrioress

The North is the direction in which your Inner Warrior/ Warrioress lives. In this practice, the North is the direction of air and the mind, or mental body. It is the home of learning, teaching, clarity, responsibility, organizational ability, purpose in the world, and linear accomplishment.

Your Inner Warrior/Warrioress is responsible for taking care of the practical and linear aspects of your life. This subpersonality pays your bills, keeps your house clean, cooks food, shops, balances your checkbook, goes to school, has a profession, and in general functions in all of the areas of labor and your mind. He or she also serves as your protector and guardian. Your Inner Warrior/Warrioress stands up for you when needed, deals with confrontations with others, and keeps your Inner Child feeling safe and secure.

When your Inner Warrior/Warrioress is out of balance, you are either a workaholic, overbearing and domineering, or confused, ineffectual, wimpy, and lazy, or prone to procrastination. Maybe you spend so much time being responsible for work and physical survival that you neglect your spiritual life or emotional needs. You may be so worried about not having the energy to get everything done that you spin your wheels and actually accomplish very little. Your mind may be in such a state of confusion that you need more meditation, or a vacation to help you focus on one thing at a time. Problems such as an overdrawn bank account, a dirty messy home, or lethargy due to emotional imbalances that are affecting your mental balance may plague your life. You may control everyone around you and your environment in overprotection of your vulnerable Inner Child, who needs healing. Whatever is going on, your Inner Warrior/Warrioress can help you understand it when you establish contact and communication.

The process for contacting your Inner Warrior/Warrioress is identical to the one given in the section above on contacting your Inner Nurturer (see pages 230–232). Use the same steps to set up your quest in the North of your personal shield.

Meeting Your Inner Spirit

The East, which is the home of your Inner Spirit, is also the direction representing fire and light. In the East, the direction of the sunrise, lie hope, aspirations, inspiration, creativity, spiritual beliefs and practices, your spirit itself, enlightenment, ascension, and connection with Great Spirit, God/Goddess/All That Is, or the Divine Oneness.

The functions of your Inner Spirit include obvious things such as meditation, prayer, and your spiritual life. Whether your spiritual activities consist of quiet meditation, reading spiritual books, connecting with a spiritual teacher or Ascended Master, praying, spending time in nature, or going to rituals and ceremonies, your Inner Spirit is the one who does these things. This subpersonality's less obvious areas of focus are sexuality, creativity, magic, dance, music, and connection with yourself, others, and Divinity.

When your Inner Spirit is out of balance, you are probably giving too much attention to other aspects of life and too little to spirit, or vice versa. Regardless, the imbalance will show up in the East of your personal shield. You may experience it as feelings of hopelessness, defeatism, and futility. Lack of spiritual faith and connection leave you feeling uninspired, only taking care of what you have to in life but not experiencing the magic. Or you may meditate all the time and never get in touch with your emotions or sexual nature. Being a spiritual hermit may be an excuse for feeling inadequate or awkward socially. Are you too stoic to dance, appreciate or create art or music, or make love under the full moon? When was the last time you experienced being in nature and feeling connected to God/Goddess, or Oneness in all things? Do you practice what you preach and live in integrity and truth in your life? Do you celebrate the accomplishments of others, or feel envious and threatened by them? When you make love, is it just for the local release and lusty sensations, or do you really care about the other person and give to him or her as well as receive? Do you move sexual energy through your chakras and use sex as a way of opening more deeply and vulnerably to yourself, your partner, and God/Goddess/All That Is? Do you allow true intimacy in your life? Are you excited and inspired by life's lessons and opportunities for growth, or do you try to maintain the status quo, or believe you are so evolved that you have nothing left to learn? All of these are questions for your Inner Spirit, and the answers imply his or her health and balance, or dysfunction.

With these issues and any of your own that come to mind, prepare for the meeting with your Inner Spirit. Be open and receptive and carry as few preconceived ideas and ideals as possible. When you are ready, do the quest for your Inner Spirit using the same guidelines as those given for the quest to meet your Inner Nurturer.

Balancing Your Personal Shield

Now that you have met each of your subpersonalities, you are ready to balance your personal shield. To do so, go into a meditative state, imagine yourself entering a medicine-wheel circle made of stones in which your four subpersonalities live, and move around the circle, meeting and communicating with each one. Ask the following questions of each of your four subpersonalities in the four directions: (1) How are you? (2) How are the changes I've made, since our last meeting, working for you? (3) What do you need? (4) What do you want?

In the tradition I learned, you enter in the East, and immediately walk in a clockwise, or sunwise, direction, first to the South. After connecting with your Inner Nurturer in the South, move on in a clockwise direction to the West, where you have a dialogue with your Inner Child. From there, continue to move clockwise to the North, where your Inner Warrior/Warrioress awaits. Lastly, you move clockwise to the East and finish by meeting with your Inner Spirit. When you are done, imagine walking out of the circle. Now you have balanced your personal shield.

If you wish, you may follow this process with the Subpersonality Harmonization Chamber of Light. It can smooth out the rough edges and add a finishing touch when needed. Most of the time when I come out of the circle, I already feel very balanced, at peace, and warm inside, just from communicating and being with the four sacred parts of myself. If you feel this way, you do not need to do the chamber session.

Chapter 12

ADDITIONAL PLEIADIAN LIGHTWORK HEALING SESSIONS

T his chapter contains additional healing processes available through the Pleiadians and the Christ that they deem important at this time. As with all of the other healing methods in this workbook, the purpose of these techniques is to bring you more into your divine alignment, not only etherically and spiritually, but behaviorally and attitudinally in your day-to-day life. When you are willing to embrace divine truth at all times and in all places, enlightenment and ascension are made possible.

Cocoon Healing

"Cocoons" are protective enclosures used for the transport of damaged souls and spirits for healing and preparation for reincarnation. When major planetary changes such as catastrophic quakes or explosions occur, many beings can get stuck on the lower astral planes or suffer extreme soul fragmentation and damage. These beings need a spiritual life-support system and slow regeneration through loving, nurturing, and light, such as the dolphins and whales on Earth can provide.

I have vivid soul memories of being blown apart when the planet Maldek exploded, flying through space out of control and fragmented, and unable to move my consciousness at will. Beautiful angelic Light Beings called the Pleiadian Angels of Mercy "caught" me, entwined me in a lustrous light cocoon and took me to a Pleiadian lightship for transport to Earth. (See illustration 12 on page 239.)

The dolphins came to me at the bottom of the fourth-dimensional sea and gently rotated the cocoon with their snouts while sending joyful loving energy to me inside the cocoon. They swam around the cocoon in pods, singing to me with their magical sonar, and slowly strengthening and preparing me for my next step.

This original type of cocoon is like the womb of the cosmic Holy Mother; it is surrounded by many wonderful nursemaids who attend to a soul's needs until it is time for the soul to be born. It is required as a safe container for a soul recovering from extreme trauma. The cocoons described in this chapter are simpler, yet more versatile versions of the original. These simpler cocoons are easy to work with at any time by yourself, with the assistance of the Pleiadians and a being called the Overlighting Deva of Healing. The circumstances under which you might call for cocoons are variable, as are the types of cocoon available to meet your needs. Cocoons may sound much like Chambers of Light, but their function is actually quite different. When you are inside a Chamber of Light, you must set aside time for the ongoing healing or energy work to take place. This occurs in stages until the desired result is achieved. A cocoon holds a consistent quality of energy and serves both as a protective container for your body and aura and as a generator of a specific energy. Once the cocoon is brought around you, there is no actual session time required. You just go on with whatever you are doing while the cocoon remains around your aura, serving whatever function you have requested.

One type of cocoon helps you embrace divine qualities. Divine qualities are spiritually aligned states of being in which your attitudes, emotions, and identity are attuned with your Higher Self, as opposed to your ego-based personality. Examples of divine qualities are: faith, hope, charity, compassion, understanding, forgiveness, love, tenderness, caring, lightness, humility, peace, harmlessness, inspiration, clarity, courage, strength, humor, sincerity, patience, generosity, honesty, acceptance (nonjudgmentalness), beauty (as an essential attribute, not necessarily physical beauty), harmony, balance, devotion, prayerfulness, playfulness, joy, presence, willingness,

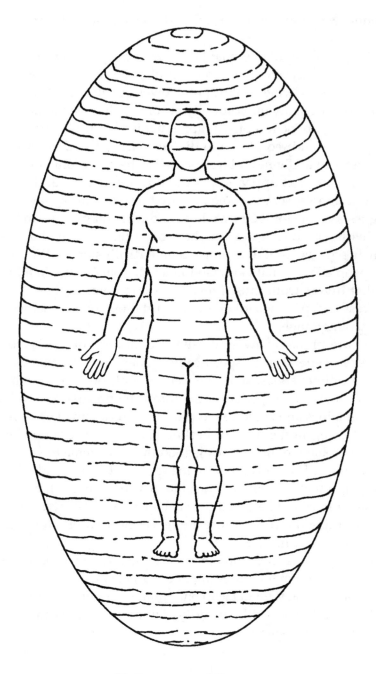

12. Cocoon around the aura

confidence, surrender, receptivity, discernment, detachment, and bliss.

Many of these divine qualities have corresponding lower qualities. For example, receptivity to harmful or destructive people or situations is not a divine quality, but a lower quality. People experiencing the lower quality of receptivity at some point need to evolve into experiencing divine receptivity, accompanied by discernment, implying openness and receptivity to divine or truth-based energies only. This reference to divine and truth-based as being synonymous means that anything that appears less than divine is illusion-based. As another example, some people practice blind faith as a way of never being responsible for their own lives and what they create. In turning their lives over to God in faith, they forget that they are intended to do their part as well, and they become disillusioned. With divine faith, people know that God/Goddess/All That Is lives in all things and that divine truth must prevail at some point in time. They do their best and put their divine faith in the outcome, whether short range or long range.

You are probably aware of divine qualities you need more of, whether in general or in specifically challenging situations. Maybe you misapply energies, as in the examples of lower receptivity and faith given above; or perhaps you are in the process of developing certain qualities and could use assistance. You can invoke the desired states of being in the form of healing cocoons. For example, if you have the problem of not allowing good things to come to you, working with the healing cocoon of divine receptivity may gradually help you open to that attribute in your life. If you have much experience with being hurt and betrayed in this lifetime or past lives, you may wish to utilize the cocoon to experience more divine forgiveness, courage, or strength.

You may also ask for combinations of qualities in a cocoon. Some of the more common mixtures might be: divine love with acceptance; divine compassion with detachment; divine receptivity with discernment; divine humor with sincerity; divine honesty with courage; divine faith with inspiration.

Follow the steps below to experience a healing cocoon:

1. Choose a divine quality or combination of qualities you would like to have more of in your life and your being.

2. Invoke the Pleiadian Emissaries of Light.

3. Invoke the presence of Ascended Master Jesus Christ and other Ascended Masters.

4. Invoke the presence of the Overlighting Deva of Healing.

5. Invoke the presence of your own Higher Self.

6. Ask these beloved ones to cocoon your entire aura in the divine quality or qualities you have chosen.

7. Meditate on the feeling and awareness of the quality. Relax and make this your focus. Do this meditation at least five to ten minutes, or longer if you wish. However, you can go on with your day as soon as the cocoon is around you if you need to; this will simply limit your conscious awareness of the energy state.

8. When your meditation is complete, you may ask that the cocoon be left around you, or that it be removed. If you leave it in place, it will naturally dissipate after awhile.

Another type of cocoon can help you when you are experiencing emotional rawness or vulnerability. Perhaps you are coming from a particularly intense session of emotional release with a healer or therapist. Or you are having an emotionally traumatic experience in your life, such as a relationship ending, or a loved one dying. You may feel shaken and insecure from your own processing and release of past lives, or from reliving early traumatic experiences. You may temporarily feel very vulnerable and be in need of more security, protection, and clearer boundaries.

At these vulnerable times, you can use the same process given above for invoking a divine quality cocoon, with some minor changes, as indicated below:

1. Invoke the Pleiadian Emissaries of Light.

2. Invoke Ascended Master Jesus Christ and other Ascended Masters.

3. Invoke the Overlighting Deva of Healing.

4. Invoke your own Higher Self.

5. Now state: "Please place me inside a protective and healing cocoon for the next twenty-four hours while I am integrating and strengthening from this emotional (or spiritual) experience."

6. Sit or lie down with your eyes closed as long as it takes for you to feel the energy shift that occurs when the cocoon is brought around you. Then proceed as you like with your day.

When the twenty-four-hour period is up, you may reestablish the cocoon if you still need it. [cassette icon]

If you are a healer or therapist, you can invoke a cocoon for a client who has just experienced a deeply unnerving or emotionally painful release. Envision the cocoon being wrapped around the outside of the client's aura, and assist in the creation of it by seeing gold strands of light encircling the outside of the client's aura like the wrapping around a mummy. Then ask that the cocoon be kept in place for twenty-four hours while the person integrates the healing experience.

Clearing Erroneous Neural Pathways

Neural pathways are minuscule electrical circuits in the brain through which sensory input from life is received, interpreted, and acted on. These pathways are divided into three main sections. (See illustration 13 on page 243.) The information on neural pathways in this chapter was taught to me exclusively by the Pleiadians and in no way implies any medical or scientific sources. So, when I speak of neural pathways, I speak in terms of etheric images and energy functions as they correspond to behaviors and attitudes.

The three sections of a neural pathway, as shown in the illustration, are:

(1) the upper brain receiving segment; (2) the middle brain segment, which has an interpretive function and determines the

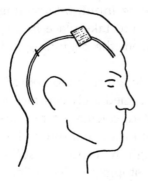

13. *An erroneous neural pathway with a neural plate between the first and second sections. Beginning at the forehead, the first section is for neurological input; the second section is for interpretation and decision-making relative to action; and the third stimulates the body-mind to act.*

response to input received from the first section; and (3) the lower brain segment, which stimulates the body, voice, or other aspect of the self to take action. In order for your spirit to live in your body fully, your neural pathways must be clear, open, and available for spontaneity based on truth. In other words, when you do not respond in your most natural and honest way to any given situation, your spirit experiences this as a slowdown and contraction of energy; this creates a lower-vibrational frequency in which your spirit cannot live.

Think of the implications of this. If you honestly and sincerely are dedicated to living spiritually and are a seeker of divine truth, you can never be even subtly dishonest and expect your spirit to remain embodied. Here is an example: Your boss comes up to you and asks you what you think of his new proposal. You dislike the proposal and think it is doomed to fail, but, out of fear or subservience, you contract and reply, "It's fine, Herb." What takes place neurologically is this: The boss's question is the input into the first segment of your neural pathway. If you were to respond without calculating, hiding, or deception, you would spontaneously say, "Quite frankly, Herb, I don't think it will work. Something similar was tried by the Ajax Company two years ago and it was a disaster." The entire process of receiving input, interpreting, determining what to do, and acting on it would take place in a split second, or roughly at the speed of light, from the beginning to the end of your neural pathway.

When instead you do not respond honestly, what happens is this: You receive the input, immediately contract before the second part of the loop can be activated, calculate a response you think your boss will like, then send that message through the rest of the loop for it to be acted on. Even though the process is still fairly quick from beginning to end, there is a stopgap called a "neural plate" between the first and second segments. (See illustration 13 on page 243.) This neural plate is where the calculated, deceptive response is "encoded." When the electrical stimulus moves through the first segment of your neural pathway and hits the neural plate, the electrical current stops and scans the neural plate from top to bottom, "reading the instructions" on the neural plate before it can access the rest of the pathway. The neural plate reads something like this: "Never disagree with your parents, teachers, or employers or you may be punished." When the electrical impulse reads this message on the plate, it creates a fear warning in your body, causing contraction, even if very subtle, and you tell a lie.

Of course, you may justify your response because everyone says the same thing, or because your boss is a moody man who does not accept constructive criticism well. But, essentially, as far as your spirit is concerned, you are lying and kicking your spontaneous, free, honest, impeccable spirit out of your body and giving way to ego identity. When your neural pathway is blocked by a neural plate, it is called an "erroneous neural pathway" because it no longer has the ability to function in a natural and spontaneous way. The more of these erroneous neural pathways you have, the less your spirit is able to fully embody.

The spiritual teaching of these neural pathways is that all humans are responsible for completely impeccable, spontaneous honesty at all times in order to truly progress spiritually to the point of enlightenment and ascension. Luckily, contrary to most psychological dictates, erroneous neural pathways can be cleared, neural plates can be removed, and open pathways for spontaneous right action can be re-created.

In order to identify your erroneous neural pathways and neural plates that need to be cleared, you need to use clairvoyance, intuition, clairaudience, or creative visualization. Creative visualization, in the guided process that follows, consists of going into a deep meditative state, then imagining a movie screen at the outside edge of your aura. On the screen you project an image of your own head. Then you ask to see or feel places in your brain where you have created neural plates that usurp your spontaneity and honest responsiveness. It would not be uncommon for you to have one to four erroneous neural pathways with neural plates all pertaining to a single issue. You may have numerous sets of erroneous pathways covering a wide array of personal issues. It is recommended that you work on only one set of these pathways with a common theme at a given time. Once you are shown where these pathways are, and how many there are to be cleared at any given time, you can use the step-by-step clearing process given later in this section.

Basically, the process is to first identify the functions of the erroneous neural pathways. You may touch the screen with your hands in order to feel the energy, or ask for messages, or ask for a movie to demonstrate the erroneous behavior. After you have identified the behavioral pattern, which is crucial if you hope to be conscious enough to change it, you will utilize the grid pattern of the Quantum Transfiguration Chamber of Light. (See illustration 9 on page 188.) Visualize a cube image crisscrossed with lasers of ultraviolet light going horizontally, vertically, and from front to back. Ultraviolet is a slightly reddish-purple color like the ultraviolet rays from the Sun. This color is the only one I know of that is capable of dissolving neural plates. You will then imagine placing your hands around a neural plate and bombarding it with thousands of microscopic lasers. You may do this on the screen or by imagining projecting your hands etherically into your own head in the location of the neural plate. Then hold your hands around the neural plate, keeping the visualization or intention until the plate is completely dissolved. You will ask the Pleiadians to assist you with this process, yet it is essential that you participate in order for it to work.

When the neural plate has been dissolved, you will place your physical hands on the screen, one at your forehead and one at the base of your occipital ridge at the back of your head. Visualize sending a tiny electrical current, like a small lightning bolt, from each hand through the neural pathway. When the lightning bolts from both hands meet each other, the pathway should be clear. Then you will bring the tips of both of your index fingers together at the point where the neural plate was removed. There will be a break in the neural pathway at this point, and the neural pathway must be woven back together. Ask the Pleiadians to help you while you envision fine strands of golden white light sewing the broken ends of the neural pathway back together again. This is like a small network of fiber optics being fused together after being broken. When you think your work is complete, you will test it by running golden sunlight from the front of the neural pathway all the way through to the back. If the light runs through the pathway smoothly and without leaks at the rewoven spot, the circuit is complete. If not, resume the reweaving process until the golden light flows through the neural pathway without leaking.

If you find this process really impossible to do for yourself, find a friend (who is also reading this book) with whom to exchange the clearing. In this case, each of you in turn will work exclusively with a reading screen outside your aura. Make sure you are grounded and that your aura is pulled in to within two feet of your body and has violet light on the outside of it before working on each other. If necessary, give yourself new roses outside your aura before and after the healing. When each healing is complete, create a large rose with your friend's face on it and place it in front of your aura with the intention that it will pick up any of his or her energy you might have taken on. When the rose has absorbed all it can, blow it up outside both your auras. Then create a rose with your own image inside it and place it outside your friend's aura with the intention that it will retrieve any of your energy that you might have left in your friend's energy field. Again, when the rose is full, blow it up outside both of your auras and your energy will be returned to you. If this process still does not work for you, contact a Pleiadian Lightwork practitioner for assistance.

Following is an example of an actual experience of clearing neural pathways. The first time I was taught about erroneous neural pathways, I was doing a clairvoyant reading and healing session for a client I will call Alice. This woman was in an open relationship and had been living with her lover, whom I will call Lover A, for over four years. They were both free to see other people and had no need to lie to one another about other lovers at all. When the woman came to me, she was very upset because she had taken a new lover, whom I will call Lover B, about six months before, and the new lover had just moved into Alice's home with Alice and Lover A. Alice had not told Lover A about Lover B; she was deliberately concealing the nature of the new relationship and was in fear that Lover A would find out and leave. As a spiritual advisor, I was, of course, responsible for recommending honesty, but also for helping this woman get to the bottom of why she was needlessly lying and creating the dilemma in the first place.

In the clairvoyant session, I saw pictures and pain energy caused by Alice's childhood beatings from her father, to whom she had chronically lied in order to avoid more abuse. Unless she had told him what he wanted to hear, violence had almost always ensued. As a young child, Alice had chosen to create erroneous neural pathways in order to survive.

There were three pathways with neural plates in Alice's brain that established the criteria for her safety. The message on the first one was basically, "Figure out what other people want to hear and always tell them or you might get killed or badly harmed." The message on the second neural plate was, "Hide your true feelings and act unaffected by other people's emotions and words." The third pathway was programmed with, "If you are not sure what to say, plead ignorance. Act like you don't know what the person is talking about."

The fear and pain in Alice's heart chakra were very intense, and had been triggered by Lover B coming into her life. Although her fear was completely irrational, it was preventing her from telling Lover A the truth. Alice was creating lie after lie to cover herself. Needless to say, she was extremely relieved to finally understand why she was doing this, and was able to be compassionate and forgive herself. She took the tape from the session home and had both lovers listen to it in the hopes that they would also be able to understand and forgive her when she revealed the truth. Fortunately for her, both lovers were very understanding and forgiving, which gave her a powerful new reference point for safety in truth. Alice also understood that because the pattern was so longstanding, it was also an unconscious habit that would require conscious pattern breaking in order to prevent it from re-creating erroneous neural pathways.

At that time, the Pleiadians also showed me one other side effect of erroneous neural pathways. Whenever you tell a lie, whether overtly or by simply not being spontaneously truthful, a small, web-like, dark energy begins to form around the soul area of your heart chakra. The more you hide, calculate, withhold, or lie, the more webs you create. The Pleiadians, when pointing this out, very compassionately said, " 'Oh what a tangled web we weave, when first we practice to deceive.' This saying, like so many others that have become well known, points to a literal truth." Over time, the dark, sticky webs around your soul cut you off partially or completely from your ability to feel and express your own soul essence. These webs can be transmuted and dissolved with violet flame. Saint Germain will assist in this process since he is the keeper of the violet flame for alchemical transmutation. This process can also be done on a movie screen if that technique is easier for you.

Before you begin the clearing process, make sure you have at least an hour of free time, just in case it takes that long. Following are the steps for clearing erroneous neural pathways and webbing around your soul:

1. Ground yourself.

2. Pull in your aura to within two feet of your body in all directions.

3. Check your aura boundary colors and roses and adjust them if necessary.

4. Place a movie screen just outside your aura with a grounding cord going just beneath the Earth's surface.

5. Invoke the Pleiadian Emissaries of Light.

6. Ask Ascended Masters Jesus Christ and Saint Germain to be present and assist in the healing.

7. Invoke your own Higher Self.

8. Tell the Pleiadians, Ascended Masters, and your Higher Self that your purpose for calling on them is to ask their guidance and assistance in clearing any erroneous neural pathways in your brain that are appropriate to clear at this time.

9. Project the image of your chest onto the screen, imagining that you can see the inside of your chest as if you are using an etheric X-ray. Ask to be shown your soul matrix area, which is approximately one-and-a-half inches inside your heart chakra; notice the amount of webbing around it.

10. Lift your physical hands to the screen and feel the energy of your soul projected there. Ask Saint Germain to bring in the violet flame and help you transmute any webbing around your soul matrix. Visualize violet flame coming from your hands, which are cupped around your soul matrix on the screen. Continue until the webbing feels or looks completely clear, or until you receive a message that you are complete.

11. Clear the screen by placing the image of your chest in a rose and blowing up the rose.

12. Project the front view of your head onto the screen.

13. Ask to see, feel, intuit, or hear how many erroneous neural pathways you have that are ready to be cleared at this time and where they are located.

14. When you have located the pathways, identify the purpose they are serving by feeling their energy, receiving a message, using your intuition, or asking for a movie that shows the behavioral pattern. This information is on the neural plates between the first and second segments of the erroneous neural pathways.

15. Once you have identified the behavioral pattern, follow the remaining steps for each individual pathway involved in that pattern. Place your hands around the neural plate to be cleared. Visualize many tiny ultraviolet lasers, in the Quantum Transfiguration Chamber

grid pattern, being projected at and through the neural plate. Ask the Pleiadians to assist you in holding the laser grid around the neural plate to dissolve it.

16. When the neural plate is completely gone, move your hands to your forehead and the occipital ridge area of your head on the screen. Visualize or intend to send tiny lightning bolts of electrical energy through the neural pathway until the two bolts meet one another in the middle.

17. Bring both index fingertips together at the point where the neural plate was removed and the ends of the channel are broken. Visualize or postulate many tiny threads of golden white light weaving the neural pathway back together, while asking the Pleiadians and guides to help you. Hold the vision or intention until you sense the work is done.

18. Test the neural pathway to make sure it is not leaking by running golden sunlight from the front of the pathway all the way through to the back of it. If the golden light runs smoothly with no leaks, the healing of the pathway is finished. If the pathway does leak, continue step 17 until the leak is gone.

19. Repeat steps 15 through 18 for each remaining erroneous neural pathway to be cleared and healed.

20. Take a few minutes to contemplate the behavioral pattern you need to change in order to keep your neural pathways clear. Imagine yourself in some actual life situations in which the pathways were still operating erroneously. Observe yourself to see and feel what was happening in those situations. Notice where and when your body contracted. Observe the reactions of other people to you. Notice how you were breathing and whether or not you were able to look at the people you were with. How did you feel emotionally?

21. Now imagine those identical situations again, only this time with your neural pathways clear so that you behave in a spontaneously truthful manner. What are the differences? Notice the new freedom from contraction in your body. Observe how the other people involved respond to you differently. How do you respond? Is

your breathing freer? Are you able to look at the people? How do you feel emotionally?

If the new, more truthful, pattern is still effortful or difficult, exaggerate the feelings you are having in order to clear them. Running energy and blowing roses may help. If negative thoughts, beliefs, or judgments arise, take time to clear them. Practice your new behavior until it is light, natural, and spontaneously flowing.

22. When you are complete, place the screen in a rose and blow it up outside your aura.

23. It is recommended that you do a Dolphin Brain Repatterning session with the Pleiadians as soon as it is convenient. Ask them to clear any holding patterns in your body that correspond to the erroneous neural pathways that were cleared. Instructions for these sessions are in chapter 8.

You can also use this clearing technique on another person. Simply substitute images of his or her brain, chest, soul matrix, and so on. When the clearing is complete, advise the person to do a Dolphin Brain Repatterning session as suggested in step 23. Then make psychic separations by visualizing a rose with the person's face in it outside your aura. When the rose has collected any of his or her energy you may have taken on during the session, blow it up outside your aura.

Then visualize a rose with your own face inside it. Place the rose outside the other person's aura with the intention that the rose will collect any of your energy you may have left in his or her space during the session. When the rose no longer collects energy, blow it up outside both of your auras. Your energy, if any, will return to you.

Self-Healing with the Quantum Transfiguration Grid

The grid from the Quantum Transfiguration Chamber, which you used on a small scale to clear neural plates, can be used for other applications as well. The grid structure is such that it has a unique capacity to clear energies that are normally time-consuming and difficult to clear through other methods.

First are examples of other specific uses for the ultraviolet Quantum Transfiguration grid. Frequently, my clients report having seen spiders, bats, or snakes moving around in their auras or chakras, especially accompanying the release of dark pain energy or old repressed emotions. These spiders, bats, and snakes have no apparent relationship to physical creatures but are parasitic entities living on a lower astral level. They feed on repressed emotions, dead energy such as pain, and lower-frequency energies, in general, such as you find around people who drink or do drugs, indulge in negative thinking, or who have experienced much trauma in their lives. The more you meditate, become positive and loving, bring light into your body, eat healthily, and clear all repressed energies, the less "feeding ground" these parasites have within you.

If you do see or sense spiders, bats, or snakes in your energy field or that of a client or friend, you can test to find out if they are astral parasites by envisioning ultraviolet light and throwing it at them. If the ultraviolet freezes them so they can no longer move, they are astral parasites, because these entities cannot tolerate this frequency of light. Once they are frozen, place them inside an ultraviolet Quantum Transfiguration grid just big enough to fit completely around them, and keep the grid in place until the parasites are completely dissolved. You can ask the Pleiadians for help with this. There is no reason to be afraid. If these parasites were already there and you had not noticed them, you are simply better off knowing about them so you can eliminate them now.

Another use for ultraviolet light in general or in a Quantum Transfiguration grid is helping people with chemical poisoning, radiation toxicity, and/or allergies. Although ultraviolet light cannot usually eliminate these problems altogether or immediately, it can work on them gradually, and faster than anything else I have found. The purification properties of ultraviolet light from the Sun constantly do so much more for people than most realize, yet many people hardly spend any time in the Sun at all, especially with the holes in the ozone layer intensifying the Sun's radiation. However, I believe that people need some direct sunlight frequently to be healthy and to feel more alive. Even if you can only be in the Sun for two minutes per day, it can help tremendously, especially if you spend that time using your intent and breath consciously to absorb the sunlight into your body.

Ultraviolet rays have the capacity over time to break down chemical and toxic-radiation poisoning on the Earth and in the human body. If you have a known problem of this type, using the ultraviolet light Quantum Transfiguration grid can help you. Isolate the part of your body from which you want to clear toxins, such as your liver, brain, or colon, and concentrate the grid of ultraviolet light on that area. If the toxins are throughout your bloodstream, you may want to do a full-body and aura chamber session of ultraviolet light, using the instructions in the section of chapter 9 entitled "Quantum Transfiguration Chamber."

Begin by using the grid for only about ten minutes at a time, until you find out how much physical detoxing the ultraviolet grid brings about. If you discover that ten minutes is too long because too much detoxification occurs, then use the grid for an even shorter period of time when you repeat the treatment. You will need to determine how often to do the grid by observing your own body and emotional responses to it. Remember, this type of clearing happens in stages, and it is better to go slowly than to tax your body.

You may also experience benefits from ultraviolet light if you have immune-system weakness or disorder. Place your thymus gland inside a Quantum Transfiguration grid of ultraviolet light to stimulate your etheric body to stimulate your physical body and to assist in the clearing of illness and infection-causing energy blocks. The ultraviolet grid may also be localized around areas of infection, wounds, abrasions, boils, blisters, and so on.

There are also uses for the Quantum Transfiguration grid other than those involving ultraviolet light. For example, if you have tight muscles, they may benefit from a localized grid of sparkling silver light. Any place in your body that tends to hold contraction and tension can usually be eased to some degree by silver light, whether it be in the Quantum Transfiguration grid or simply by visualizing radiant silver light in that area of your body. However, for more chronic holding and tension, the silver light grid can relax the areas, as well as begin to break up energy blocks. This technique works wonderfully for blocks in the colon area. The relaxing properties of the silver light help the colon relax, allowing it to empty more easily. This light grid could be helpful for hemorrhoids, as well.

With intense pain, such as that accompanying a sprain, dislocation, or broken bone, a Quantum Transfiguration grid of golden light may assist in speeding up the regeneration and bringing warmth and relief to the area. This golden light can also ease PMS and menstrual pain, hernias, ulcers, sore throats, heart pain, indigestion, earaches, and headaches, including migraines.

Golden light grids are also good for tight or blocked chakras. If a particular chakra area is obviously not very open, use the golden grid around the entire chakra for as long as you feel it brings results. It not only soothes and helps the chakra to open, it can bring etheric healing to a damaged chakra, clear foreign energy, and assist in the regenerative process. At times, you may feel a need to use another color or combination of colors of light for a particular chakra area; trust your intuition and guidance. Gold is the most universal healing color, but it is by no means the only one for chakras.

If you have arthritis, rheumatism, or problems with calcium deposits, you may benefit from localized grids or full-body Quantum Transfiguration Chambers. For these problems, use a sequential series of three different colors of light during the chamber session. The first color of light to use is rose-gold, which breaks up calcification and holding. Rose-gold light is the color of the pink-gold metal in Black Hills tri-tone gold jewelry. You can also imagine it as an equal blend of copper and metallic gold that creates a new color and not just a fusion. The second color of light to use is silver, which relaxes the area and flushes the broken-up energies away, helping them release. Golden sunlight is the third color to use. Gold regenerates, strengthens, and stimulates self-healing and self-affinity.

When you do a Quantum Transfiguration Chamber or localized grid for arthritis, rheumatism, or calcium deposits, allow thirty minutes. Run each of the three colors in the session for ten minutes. You may find that this chamber brings anger to the surface because arthritis is a result of implosion of your own and/or other people's anger that settles in your bones. As the energy pattern breaks up, leaving your body free to heal itself, the anger needs to be felt and released in order to prevent it from settling in your body again. If you need to work with a primal therapist or bioenergetics practition-er, or simply work with the anger on your own, it is highly recom-mended that you do so in order to affect a cure and not just give yourself temporary relief. Lazarus audio tapes on releasing anger can help greatly as well.

These chamber or grid sessions can be repeated as often as you feel a need or desire for them and your body and emotions can keep up with the releases stimulated by the sessions. It is probably best to do no more than two sessions per week for most people. But as always, trust your own intuition and guidance as to your timing.

The specific steps for using the Quantum Transfiguration Chamber of Light or localized grid for working with arthritis, rheumatism, or calcium deposits are as follows:

1–8. Perform the steps at the beginning of chapter 9 for opening a chamber session.

9. Invoke the Quantum Transfiguration Chamber of Light or localized grid for your specific physical need.

10. Visualize the three-dimensional grid structure, as shown in illustration 9 on page 188, using rose-gold light around and through your entire aura and body, or around the localized area. After you feel that the chamber or grid is secured around you, just relax. Continue to gently hold the intent of rose-gold light in the specific grid for ten minutes while the Pleiadians and the Christ work with it as well.

11. Now focus on visualizing sparkling silver light in the grid pattern until it feels anchored. Then relax and lightly hold the gener-al intent while being receptive for ten minutes.

12. Switch the color to golden sunlight, once again holding your focus until it feels stable on its own. Then relax and hold the intent for ten more minutes.

13. When the chamber session or localized grid clearing is com-plete, it is advisable to soak in a hot bath as long as you would like, but no less than ten minutes. Use peppermint oil or eucalyptus oil in the bath water to assist in the continued release, soothing, and stabi-lization.

[Author Note: This process is not included on my tape for this book since it is for specific circumstances only. If you need a tape for it, you could make one yourself, leaving ten minutes of silence between each of the three stages of healing, or order the tape entitled "Quantum Transfiguration Grid for Arthritis Sufferers" at the address in the back of the book.]

Beyond what is included in this chapter, be creative using the Quantum Transfiguration grids for specific energy blocks or physical problems. When you use a localized grid for cellular or very concentrated clearing of organs or glands, arthritis, or areas of the body with particularly chronic ailments, you can expect the healing to be about forty to sixty percent as effective as physical hands-on healing. You are encouraged to pair up with a friend to do hands-on sessions, or to work with a Pleiadian Lightwork practitioner if the results of the above processes are not extensive enough.

When experimenting with this form of energy work for physical illness and pain, do not expect instant cures. Try the work, moderately at first, until you determine its impact on physical and emotional releases, and then pace yourself accordingly. I would love to hear from you about your results and creative uses for the localized grids and full-body Quantum Transfiguration Chamber.

Cellular Reorientation and Repatterning

Cellular Reorientation and Repatterning sessions are unique in that they are never the same twice, they are personally tailored to your individual needs, and they are a blend of many forms of Pleiadian Lightwork. These sessions are called for when you have been working on many issues centered around a core issue and have reached a standstill. Perhaps you are at a loss for what to do next, or you simply feel stuck; or perhaps you have done all you can to process the issue and just need help "mopping up" and taking care of the loose ends.

If you have been working on your own healing and spiritual growth for a long time, you probably know there are times when you meditate, pray, clear emotions, work with light for healing, get bodywork, clear beliefs and judgments, and forgive. At these points, you may feel "washed out," or, at the very least, like things are not totally clear, yet there is nothing left for you to do. You can continue meditating, working with violet flame, and doing your best to keep the vibrations as high as possible, but it would be wonderful to have some way of magically smoothing out all those loose ends so that you could just get on with whatever is next. This is one example of a time when a Cellular Reorientation and Repatterning session could greatly help.

Another example is when you are really stuck: your feelings are still strong, you have done everything you know to get through them, and you know there is something else very important to understand or clear, but you just cannot seem to find it. You even find yourself in the middle of saying or doing something that you truly intend not to say or do, but you seem incapable of changing. Your self-esteem and self-respect are suffering, as well as your ability to focus and be totally present and available for life.

These times are examples of when Cellular Reorientation and Repatterning can help the most. Turning-point times can be very frustrating. You feel yourself almost at a new doorway to the future, but something vague or not quite tangible is blocking the way. Unresolution and stuckness have many possible origins, and often a combination of origins. Some examples of these origins are: cellular patterns; stuck energies; neuro-muscular-cortical holding patterns that keep re-creating problems you have worked on spiritually or emotionally; densely concentrated energy blocks and residues left in organs, glands, and other parts of the body; foreign energy; stuck pictures you cannot find; shame and hurt that you need help to completely release; and sluggishness in chakras that have been cleared but still need "a tune up" or deeper healing.

To receive a Cellular Reorientation and Repatterning session, you must have already learned the lesson you need to learn, and have transcended its accompanying behavioral patterns. These are prerequisites for experiencing this session in which the remaining unresolved or stuck energy is cleared. If you have learned the lesson and transcended it behaviorally, then you are ready for grace to do the rest; and that is exactly the purpose of this process.

If you are newer to self-healing and spiritual growth work, this process can still be helpful for clearing outmoded patterns and energies that are no longer commensurate with who you are and who you are becoming. You can receive healing, clearing, and balancing work that will assist in bringing all of your energy bodies to a more compatible place with each other so that they are ready for whatever is next.

As mentioned previously, you have four main energy bodies: your mental, emotional, spiritual, and physical bodies. When you clear all of the beliefs in your mental body relative to a specific issue, your emotional body must be cleansed of the accompanying emotions. Your spiritual body must reclaim the cleared part of you with new, higher truths and feelings of forgiveness, love, and anticipation of new and better ways of being. Your physical body must release holding patterns that were keeping the beliefs and emotions intact. When you are growing and changing, it is not always easy to know if you are taking care of all these areas, but if you are learning the lessons, you can use a Cellular Reorientation and Repatterning session for troubleshooting and refining; in the session the Pleiadians, the Christ, and your Higher Self do the troubleshooting and cleanup healing for you. They will use a combination of any or all of the following during the session: Dolphin Brain Repatterning work, Ka work, divine axis alignment clearing, cellular flushing and regeneration, any type of chamber of light, a localized Quantum Transfiguration grid, chakra balancing and healing, nervous-system energy work and soothing, lifting of excess emotions outside your body for neutralization, messages of guidance, or Dolphin Star-Link work.

Whether or not you have a particular issue for which you consciously need this type of work, do the session and you will receive whatever you need at this time. The process for receiving a Cellular Reorientation and Repatterning session is as follows:

1. Lie down comfortably with a pillow under your knees, your feet shoulder-width apart, and your eyes closed.

2. Ground yourself.

3. Pull in your aura, or push it out, to two to three feet around your body in every direction. Check your aura boundary colors and roses if you wish.

4. Invoke the Pleiadian Emissaries of Light.

5. Invoke your own Higher Self to be present with you.

6. Ask Ascended Master Jesus Christ to come forth.

7. Invoke the presence of the Overlighting Deva of Healing.

8. Invite any other guides, angels, or Ascended Masters you wish to be a part of the session to join you now.

9. Silently say the following (or use your own words): "I call upon the Law of Divine Grace, asking that Ascended Master Jesus Christ, the Pleiadian Emissaries of Light, the Overlighting Deva of Healing, _____ (any other Light Beings you wish to call on), and my own Higher Self now lift and heal all painful emotions, physical holding patterns, thoughts or beliefs, spiritual karma, or energies belonging to myself or to other people that I do not need to process or know about in order to learn and grow. I ask that these energies be lifted from my body and aura, transmuted into pure, creative life force, and returned to me."

10. Breathe deeply but gently, imagining that each exhalation releases the old unneeded energies and that each inhalation brings in new creative life force to replace the energy that is leaving. When the release is complete, go to the next step.

11. Ask to receive a Cellular Reorientation and Repatterning session. Relax and be as open and receptive as possible. If you feel pressure or discomfort on any level, increase your breathing and assist in the release. You will need one to two hours for this session and should always allow for the maximum time. If you use this technique at bedtime, you may fall asleep at any time during the session.

12. If you are not doing the session at bedtime, when it is complete, take a few deep breaths before getting up. Sit up and reground yourself before going on with your day.

You may also do a brief session that stops at step 10. This can assist in the completion of an emotional release; you can use it to ask that shame, hurt, humiliation, grief, fear, blame, or rage be lifted after you have processed and moved all of the emotions you can on your own. 🔲

Restoring Life Force to Food

Because we live in a world in which foods are filled with chemical additives, sprayed with pesticides, color enhanced, bleached, destructured in microwaves, and in general *mutated*, it is difficult to eat all whole-grain, organic, unadulterated food. Even if you do manage to do so, the life force in the food is diminished greatly between the time it is harvested, delivered, and cooked. This might be less of a problem if you had grown up eating healthily from the time of birth, but you probably ingested a lot of mutated foods such as white sugar, white flour, white rice, meats, cooked oils, and nonorganic food early in life. What is the impact of this way of eating on your body and spirit? Humans and animals eating mutated foods manifest the same mutations in their own cellular structures and chromosomes as have been demonstrated in plants. Therefore, your body's health, as well as your spirit's ability to live in your body in a fully functional way, is dependent in part on the nature of what you eat.

The Pleiadians have expressed concern about this simple fact and have assisted me in devising a way to improve this situation. First of all, common sense would tell you to buy organic food whenever it is available. The Pleiadians have said that, after five generations of seed production from organically grown foods, any mutations will correct themselves if the plants from which the seeds are harvested are properly nourished during their growth.

Secondly, use whole grains and whole foods whenever possible. Plants were created to contain a complete energy pattern and all of the necessary enzymes needed for digestion. Plants have "geometric creation signatures" that match similar or identical ones in human bodies. They were designed this way by the Pleiadians and the Devic Kingdoms so that everything you need to be healthy and nourished, and to heal illness, exists on Earth in the natural world. If the bran and germ are removed from grains before they are eaten, or if cane and beets are stripped down to their simplest sugar forms, the signatures of the plants are altered and enter your body in incomplete and mutated ways. Your body then tries to complete the picture so that what is being ingested makes sense to it. Vitamins B and C are pulled from places where they have been temporarily stored in your body to create balance and health; they are used to help get these mutated grains and sugars through your system. Extra enzymes that would not be required if the foods were in their whole form are produced by your body to aid digestion. In the long run, the result is Vitamin B and C deficiency, premature exhaustion of your body's enzyme supply, immune system problems, propensity to allergies, and nervous system and brain damage. Your colon cannot eliminate properly due to the paste formed by the white grains and sticky sugars, and toxins are sent back into your body through the walls of your colon due to ongoing putrefaction there. Your chromosomes and cells become mutated, spin erratically, begin to create disease, and cannot create a home in which your spirit is capable of living.

Eating whole foods that are organically grown can eradicate this problem and even begin to heal and restore the natural balance within. Of course, if damage has already built up, you may need to fast and do enemas or colonics occasionally, or go on an enzyme therapy program for awhile. Supplements may be required until your body recovers from past mutations and functions normally again. You can learn about these protocols from books, or from a good nutritionist, herbologist, iridologist, homeopath, or naturopath.

You may find it necessary (or fun), no matter how careful you are at home, to eat in restaurants or at other people's homes occasionally. Grabbing food on the run is an American trademark as well. The process given below for "healing your food" and restoring the life force cannot completely rid foods of chemicals and mutations. However, it will help you recover from mutation to varying extents and make your body more available for your spirit to dwell within:

1. Envision an ultraviolet Quantum Transfiguration grid around the food you are about to eat. Hold your hands around the edges of the dish or the food itself to assist in localizing the grid. Hold the grid firmly in your awareness for about thirty seconds to one minute, or longer if it feels right.

2. While holding the grid in place, you may wish to express gratitude or blessings of any type that you normally do.

3. Envision an infinity symbol, which looks like a horizontal

number eight, made of golden light. This golden light flows through the symbol continually. Place one end of the infinity symbol near the food while you say the following invocation or one of your own: "I send gratitude to all of the sources of this food, including the plants, animals, sentient beings, humans, and Earth. I ask that all of the life force that has been lost since this food was harvested, shipped, and prepared be returned to the food through the infinity symbol now." Continue to hold the image of the golden light flowing through the infinity symbol until you sense that the life force has been restored as much as possible. This usually takes between thirty seconds and a minute.

4. Enjoy your meal.

After you "heal" and restore your food in this manner a few times, you will be able to hold the Quantum Transfiguration grid and the infinity symbol in your awareness simultaneously, which will reduce the time needed for the process.

Chapter 13

HIGHER SELF CONNECTION

Your Higher Self is the aspect of your individual conscious spirit that exists beyond your body from the fourth through the ninth dimensions. Beyond the ninth dimension, individuated consciousness is no longer discernible. (See Glossary listing for "dimension" for a broader description.) Your Higher Self has a different level of awareness, function, and form in each dimension. What you may refer to as your Higher Self is that part of you that lives in the fifth and sixth dimensions and still maintains a humanoid type of form even though it is no longer physical. Your Higher Self is always available for conscious connection with you whenever you want it and are ready, and yet it will not interfere with your free will in order to make itself known or influence your life. You must want to evolve spiritually, and know that you are a valuable soul and spirit beyond your body, in order to connect with your Higher Self directly. Otherwise your consciousness in your body identifies with your ego and personality self as your whole self.

If you are just awakening spiritually, you may or may not have realized that you have a divine counterpart, or you may believe that it is separate from you. Through meditation, instruction, dreams, or revelations, you may begin to realize that there is divinity within your body, as well. At that point, it becomes natural to ask for assistance from guides, Ascended Masters, angels, and your own Higher Self in unveiling the divine, or true, self within. With their help, karmic issues, beliefs, judgments, emotions, and anything else that is blocking the way to accessing this divinity within you, surface and you start the clearing and healing aspect of spiritual awakening.

When you realize that the only thing blocking access to God consciousness is what human ego/personality self has created, you are ready to take responsibility for creating your reality in a more conscious and harmonious way. Being connected with your Higher Self in your body is the most direct way I know of to create reference points in higher love, spiritual integrity, and connection with God/Goddess/All That Is, and to accelerate the release of limited and denser energies.

You may have experienced your Higher Self as a Light Being with whom you can only connect outside your body. This experience arises from a spirituality based on duality and the need to be nonphysical in order to experience higher states of consciousness and understanding. If you view your human self as being exclusively a "lower self," and therefore your physical life as a "less than" reality, this will greatly block your spiritual progress and joy. Your human self is only what you make it, or believe it is. If you are fortunate enough to have loving parents and peers who encourage you to think for yourself, and know that you are a divine part of God/Goddess/All That Is, and that you are a sacred spirit living in a body, then from the time of birth you need not consider your human self a limited "lower self." You become identified as your body consciousness only because you live in a society that does not yet encourage and acknowledge awareness of your divine self from birth throughout life. Thus your human self perceives itself to be physical, impure, spiritually at the mercy of an all-powerful God, and powerless to help itself. This "lower self" lives only to survive and avoid pain as much as possible, and it subconsciously feels deep shame for the fact that it is a human, and, therefore, a "lower" form of consciousness. Dogmatic religions have complicated matters even more by programming people to believe themselves sinful, lower creatures in need of salvation, yet incapable of helping themselves without the authority of the church. In many cases, these religious teachings join with societal standards to convince you that you are the body, and that is all.

"Shame of being" is a symptom of this planetwide, religious, and societal indoctrination. It includes shame about the need to eat in order to live, shame about body smells, shame about being undeserving, shame about self-loathing, and simply shame about being in physical form as mentioned above. Shame about the desire for sex and companionship is a symptom of the deeper "shame of being," and has to do with the shame and accompanying fear of feeling separate. I vividly remember when I was a child hearing my mother say many times, "She has no shame" or "Have you no shame?" as if shame was a virtuous quality and one that determined whether you were a "good person" or a "bad person." The person who was judged as having no shame was always a "bad person" and one to be shunned in my mother's eyes. I always found it sad that people viewed one another in such judgmental and separate ways, and sad that my mother clung so desperately to her own shame as a saving grace.

The two major missing links in modern culture that appear to cause this kind of judgment and separation by their absence are: (1) the knowing that, by birthright, as a child of God/Goddess, you deserve love, fulfillment, and joy without the need to earn it; and (2) the awareness that you are a spirit with a soul made of light and love who is here to evolve. When you know and feel these two spiritual understandings about your inherent worth and purpose deeply within yourself, great change and spiritual progress can happen quickly. Bringing your Higher Self's energy and consciousness into your body, instead of leaving your body to access this consciousness, is a great affirmation of the value and connectedness of your human self to divinity, and a big step in letting go of belief in separation.

If you feel "shame of being" and hold onto beliefs that tend to create this shame, it is suggested that you focus on tuning into and releasing those beliefs using the technique in chapter 6 for clearing beliefs and judgments. Examples of such beliefs are:

1. I have to be punished and serve penance for my "badness" before I can hope for redemption and mercy.

2. Something must be wrong with me because I just do not feel God's love.

3. The need for food and shelter is shameful because it takes from the planet, my parents, people in other countries, and so on.

4. My love is not good enough because it does not make others happy.

5. Wanting sex or having sexual feelings is not spiritual.

6. Because I am afraid to be alone, I am needy and unworthy.

7. Being born caused my mother pain and therefore was bad and shameful of me.

8. I must not deserve what I want or I would have it.

9. Having a body is proof that I am "less than" and a "fallen" being.

10. Because I am the gender I am, I am a disappointment to my parents, and I can never make up for that.

These are only a few examples, but they are hopefully enough to help you identify your own "shame of being" issues and clear them.

The next two sections of this chapter are dedicated to actual processes for consciously connecting with your Higher Self in your body. As you move closer to enlightenment and ascension, the initial aspects of your Higher Self with whom you connect will integrate into your body one by one, until they finally dwell there in a permanently blended state. At those stages, the form you see your Higher Self taking will change. This is due to the fact that you are connecting with the next higher aspect of your Higher Self beyond the one you have just integrated into your consciousness and body. Eventually, you will experience your Higher Self as a ball of light, a star, a spiral of light, or some other essential form that is no longer human in appearance. This is an indication that you are reaching higher-dimensional parts of yourself.

You are highly encouraged to incorporate the techniques that follow into your daily, or at least regular, spiritual practice in order to accelerate and stabilize your identity as one with your spiritual essence.

Meeting and Blending with Your Higher Self

As mentioned previously, your Higher Self is not ultimately in human form but does have aspects in the fifth and sixth dimensions that appear in humanlike light bodies. The part of your Higher Self that is vibrationally and dimensionally closest to you in your body is the one you will contact first.

In illustrations 14a and 14b on pages 268 and 269, you can see that your Higher Self first bonds with you by connecting its palms with the palms of your hands. Then, on a chakra level, the front of your Higher Self's body connects to the back of yours. In the first stage, while your hands are touching, there is an energy flow from your Higher Self into your body through the hands. As you are filled with the energy, you will be instructed to ask your Higher Self if it has a name you may use when calling on him or her. Your Higher Self may not choose to give you a name for some reason. This can happen if your Higher Self believes that a name would limit your perception of it in some way; therefore, if no name is given, it is okay. You may or may not receive one at another time.

In the second stage of the meditation, when you connect the back of your chakras with the front of your Higher Self's chakras, your Higher Self will drop the hand contact and stand behind you. This is because the subconscious parts of your chakras are located in the back of your body directly behind the conscious parts of your chakras, which are in front. For example, your heart chakra is located in the center of your chest in front, and between the shoulder blades in the area of your fourth to seventh thoracic vertebrae in back. Each subconscious chakra location is specified in the guided meditation that follows.

When your Higher Self connects with all seven chakras, you will feel a gentle surge of energy as your Higher Self's form comes in from behind you and blends fully with your physical body. Once this blending is completed, you exchange gifts with your Higher Self. You will be guided to give your Higher Self something for which it asks. If your Higher Self asks you for the pain in your heart, or the shame of feeling not good enough, or anything else that seems to you like a poor gift to give, realize that when you give up limitations, you and your Higher Self can experience more closeness and intimacy. So, giving the gift of something you might consider negative is a wonderful gift to your Higher Self, since what it wants most is to be deeply and lovingly connected with you. You may also be asked for

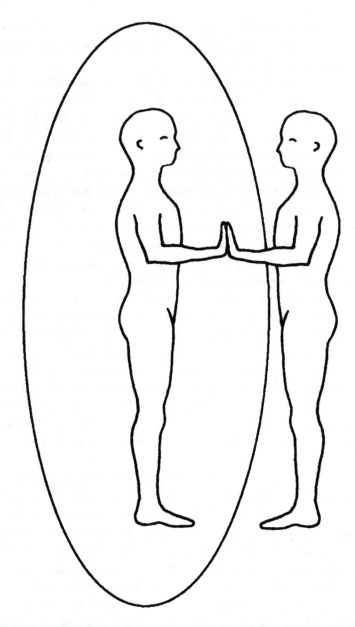

14a. The Higher Self and the human self making hand-to-hand contact for the purpose of exchanging energy

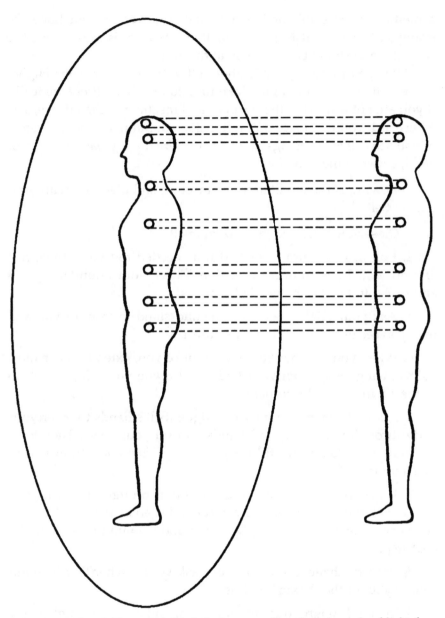

14b. The Higher Self stands behind the human self and sends cords of light from each of its chakras into the back of each chakra in the human body

something more symbolic like a crystal, a flower, or your hope, for example. Whatever it is, just know that it is what is most needed to strengthen the bond between you at this time.

After you present your Higher Self with your gift, your Higher Self will then give you a gift. Take time to feel this gift energetically. If you are not sure what the purpose and meaning of the gift are, ask. Afterward, you will place that gift inside your aura or body, wherever you sense that it belongs. It will always be there, creating a link, or bond, between the two of you.

Following is the meditation for meeting and blending with your Higher Self:

1. Close your eyes and ground yourself.

2. Pull in your aura or extend it as needed to two to three feet around your body in every direction. Check your boundary colors and roses, and make any needed changes.

3. Ask your Higher Self to come and stand in front of you and help you see or sense its humanlike form.

4. When your Higher Self is in front of you, extend your hands, palms facing away from your body, and invite your Higher Self to connect with you palm-to-palm.

5. Allow the energy from your Higher Self's hands to enter your body through your arms and hands and fill your heart. Then let it overflow your heart and fill up your body. This takes from two to five minutes.

6. When you sense the energy running through you, ask your Higher Self if it has a name you can call it. Listen in as relaxed a manner as possible. If no name is given after about a minute, go on to the next step.

7. Drop the hand connection and ask your Higher Self to stand behind you for the chakra bonding.

8. Inhale through your crown chakra, and ask your Higher Self for a cord of light from its crown to yours. When you feel the connection, move on.

9. Inhale through the center of the back of your head, and ask

your Higher Self to send a cord of light from its third eye, or sixth chakra, to the back of your third eye. When you feel the connection, continue with the next step.

10. Inhale through the back of your neck, and ask your Higher Self to send a cord of light from its throat chakra, or fifth chakra, into the back of your throat chakra. When you feel the connection, move on.

11. Inhale through the back of your heart chakra between your shoulder blades, and ask your Higher Self to send a cord of light from its heart chakra, or fourth chakra, to the back of your heart chakra. When you feel the connection, move on.

12. Inhale through the small of your back, directly opposite your solar plexus, and ask your Higher Self to send a cord of light from the front of its solar plexus, or third chakra, into the back of your solar plexus. When you sense the connection, move on.

13. Inhale through your sacrum, and ask your Higher Self to send a cord of light from its sacral chakra, or second chakra, to the back of your sacral chakra. When the connection is made, move on.

14. Inhale through your tailbone, and ask your Higher Self to send a cord of light from its root chakra, or first chakra, into your root chakra. At this point, feel the gentle surge or wave of energy move from behind you through your body to your front. This is your Higher Self fully blending with your body. You may feel more expansive, light, peaceful, joyful, filled with love, or just a general sense of well-being. Relax into that space for as long as you want before you move to the next step. If there is any part of your body in which the blending seems not to be occurring, breathe into that area and relax it until you feel the energy shift as your Higher Self is able to blend with you there.

15. Ask your Higher Self what gift it would like to receive from you. Then give it. If you want an explanation about the significance of this gift, ask now.

16. Now extend your hands in front of you and receive a gift from your Higher Self. Hold the gift, feeling its energy, and look at it. If you want to ask your Higher Self what the gift means, do so.

17. When you are ready, place the gift in your body or aura wherever you sense it belongs.

18. Ask your Higher Self if it has anything to communicate to you at this time. Remain relaxed and receptive, and feel the connection as you listen for a reply. You may or may not receive a message.

19. When you feel complete, tell your Higher Self that you want to become permanently bonded with it. Ask your Higher Self to help you with that goal in any way that is appropriate. Tell your Higher Self that you will connect again soon, and ask it to remain bonded with you to whatever extent possible at this time, even when you are not meditating.

20. Become aware of the air in the room flowing in and out of your nostrils. Then become aware of your physical environment, and open your eyes slowly and gradually. Before going on with your day, take a few moments to feel the energy connection with your Higher Self with your eyes open. Notice how you feel centered and calm. Remain present with whatever you do from one moment to the next to assist in maintaining the connection. ▭

Divine Axis Alignment with Your Higher Self

This meditation technique is the most important one in this book for assisting you in coming into Divine Axis Alignment and bringing your Higher Self energies into your body in an ongoing way. When you begin doing the meditation, it is recommended that you do it every day; it can take as little as five minutes or as long as you like.

In illustration 11 on page 200, there is a tubular area about two to two-and-a-half inches in diameter that extends from the topmost point of your aura, through your crown, down and around your spinal column, and between your legs to the bottom point of your aura.

This "tube of light" is the divine axis described previously. It also continues above your aura through the center of all the aspects of your Higher Self from the fifth through ninth dimensions. (See illustration 15 on page 273.) It is what links you and all of these aspects inside your own personal hologram. This link-up runs light from the higher dimensions down into the "tube of light" in your body and

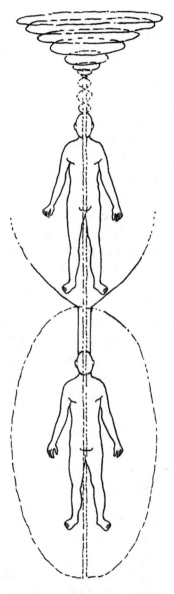

15. *Divine Axis alignment by way of the tube of light and silver cord from the Higher Self and higher dimensions into the human aura and body. The solid lines that cap the entire top of the human head represent the silver cord. The tube of light is represented by the narrower tube that extends from the aura below the body, through the body, out the top of the aura, through the Higher Self, and on into and through the upper dimensions.*

aura, and is the key to bringing your higher consciousness into your body permanently. When this Divine Axis Alignment is accompanied by the opening and awakening of your Divine Ka, and by your living in spiritual integrity, you are ready for the step-by-step descension of your Christed Self into your physical form—in readiness for ascension, when your time is right.

Bringing your Higher Self into your body through this tube of light is a very blissful and vitalizing experience for most people, though you may find it to be very subtle in the beginning. If you keep your intention and attention on the process while you are doing it, you will strengthen the effectiveness of the meditation technique. Once you have made the connection with your Higher Self and the energies are running the full length of the tube of light, you can relax and go into a more receptive and passive type of meditation.

Prior to opening the tube of light, it is important to connect with and activate the "silver cord" to your Higher Self, as shown in illustration 15. The silver cord is about six to eight inches in diameter and circles the top of your head roughly in the area of the hairline at the top of your forehead. When you anchor the silver cord there, the first step to Divine Axis Alignment is complete. This is accomplished by simply invoking your Higher Self, asking that the silver cord from your Higher Self be attached to the top of your head, and committing yourself to becoming one with your divinity, or I Am Presence, in your body. You will physically lift your arms above your head as far as they reach easily, and with your hands open, feel the silver cord being brought into your aura by your Higher Self. Then you will hold the silver cord between your hands and assist your Higher Self by slowly pulling it down around the top of your head, until you feel it solidly anchor and remain there when you take your hands away. After this is done, you will open the tube of light by asking your Higher Self to fill it with your own divine light and love. Breathe in through your crown and exhale down your spine and out between your legs to assist your Higher Self in clearing and filling the tube of light.

Following is the meditation for accomplishing Divine Axis Alignment:

1. Sit with your spine as straight as possible and your hands uncrossed, your body in a comfortable position. It is fine to sit cross-legged if you are comfortable that way. Otherwise, sit in a chair that supports your spine.

2. Ground yourself.

3. Pull in your aura, or push it out, to two to three feet around your body in every direction, including beneath your feet. Make any desired adjustments to your boundary colors and roses.

4. Call in the Pleiadian Emissaries of Light and the Ascended Master Jesus Christ.

5. Ask the Pleiadians and the Christ to bring in the Interdimensional Cone of Light around the top of your aura for divine alignment and clearing.

6. Tell the Pleiadians and the Christ that you are going to bring in the silver cord and activate the tube of light to your Higher Self. Ask for their assistance if it is needed to clear the way.

7. Lift your arms above your head and invoke your Higher Self by stating: "I ask my beloved Higher Self to bring the silver cord of light into my aura. I am ready to bring my own divinity fully into this body, to nurture the relationship between my body and spirit, and to become enlightened and prepare for ascension now. I intend to work with you, beloved Higher Self, to make this silver cord attachment to my body permanent." Of course, you can always use your own wording; use this prepared statement as a guideline or as an actual invocation, depending on your preference.

8. As you feel the energy of the silver cord touch your hands above your head, place your hands around the silver cord and slowly and gently pull it toward the top of your head. Hold it around the top of your head until you feel it anchor firmly and remain there even when you remove your hands. Breathe deeply to assist in the process.

9. After the silver cord is connected, ask your Higher Self to fill the tube of light with your own divine light and love all the way from the top of your aura through your body to the bottom of your aura. Inhale through your crown to pull in your Higher Self's light

and love through the tube. When you exhale, push your breath gently down your spine and out between your legs to the end of the tube of light. Continue with this breathing pattern, visualization, and intention until you feel, see, or sense that the tube of light is filled with light all the way to the bottom of your aura. This will most likely take a few minutes. Hold the tips of each thumb and middle finger together, with your palms up and hands resting in your lap, to help anchor the energies in your tube of light. This hand position is a *mudra*. (See Glossary.)

10. Tell your Higher Self to continue filling the tube of light and help you stay in divine axis alignment at all times, and especially to keep the energy flowing throughout the rest of the meditation.

11. Remain in meditation as long as you wish, but stay a minimum of ten minutes the first time you do this meditation.

12. Tell your Higher Self when you plan to do the meditation again, and ask your Higher Self to maintain as much connection with you as is possible until then.

13. Open your eyes slowly, maintaining the connection with your Higher Self as you come back to normal waking consciousness. 〔▭〕

After you practice Divine Axis Alignment a few times, you may wish to ask your Higher Self to run its energy and light out of the tube into any or all of your chakras. This is not a substitute for running cosmic gold energy through your body channels and chakras. That process does a more thorough healing and clearing job than the Higher Self meditation does. When your Higher Self energy runs through your body and chakras, it activates some clearing, but its main function is to bring your Higher Self into your body and gradually assist you in reaching a state of identification with your own divinity, instead of with your ego-based personality. Running your Higher Self energy into and through the chakras accelerates this process and brings your chakras into self-affinity and alignment with your higher purpose, as well as raising your vibrational frequency.

This meditation is also not intended to replace the first Higher Self meditation in which you and your Higher Self bond through your chakras and blend with one another. That first meditation brings about more intimacy and bonding with your Higher Self, while this second one specifically brings you into divine axis align-

ment within your hologram. It is up to you to determine which meditation you need at any given time, although, as mentioned before, it
is recommended that you do the Divine Axis Alignment daily, if possible. This accelerates your process of becoming vertically aligned on
your divine axis at all times. When the time comes that the silver
cord is already in place when you start the meditation, just move
straight to the part of the meditation involving the tube of light.
Eventually the silver cord and tube of light will be activated and
flowing in your aura and body continually.

Allow this meditation technique to be as personal and intimate
as you can. It is easy to slip into doing a meditation by rote and miss
the deeper qualities of spiritual connectedness it is intended to bring
about. The technique without the intimacy is like a relationship without love. You can nurture the relationship with your Higher Self just
as much as your Higher Self nurtures its relationship with you.
Eventually, the time will arrive when your consciousnesses meld into
one again.

Chapter 14
SUSTAINING THE KA WORK

By now, if you have been doing the exercises and healing sessions in this workbook, most or all of your Ka Channels have been worked on by the Pleiadians and you are running as much Ka energy as you are capable of at this time without receiving physical hands-on work. There will be an ongoing acceleration and expansion of your Ka flow from this point forth, leading to deeper clearing of energy blocks, more spiritual connection, and greater opening to the higher functions of the Ka that were previously discussed. In order to assure the maximum continuation of the work and to prevent your channels from shutting down and becoming blocked again, you need to participate in a maintenance program for awhile.

The keys to keeping the Ka energy flowing, maintaining the openness of your channels, and expanding the flow are: spontaneous emotional honesty and expressiveness, living in the integrity of spiritual morality, hiding nothing, committing to healing and releasing the past, connecting with your Higher Self through the tube of light regularly, and doing the maintenance exercises given in this chapter. The Pleiadians are fully committed to assisting you with your spiritual growth, evolution, enlightenment, and becoming your Christed Self as long as you are committed to doing your part. The Pleiadians will not do your spiritual work for you, but they are by your side when you are doing your best and need them to assist in some way. Any path or spiritual group that promises to do it for you is one you will most likely wish to turn and walk away from if you truly hope to embody the Christ Presence that you already are. Humans, in general, are not here to be rescued; humans are here to evolve, master third-dimensional reality, and then ascend.

Ka Maintenance Process

The Ka maintenance process is quite simple. It involves Higher Self connection, breath, and intention, and takes only about one to two minutes of your time per day once you are accustomed to doing it. Illustrations 16a, b, and c on page 281 show the three portals in your body through which the Ka energy enters from your higher-dimensional self. They are: (1) your crown chakra via the Ka Template, which channels the Ka flow into your pineal gland, as shown in illustration 16a; (2) the back of your heart chakra extending into your soul matrix in the central interior of your chest, as shown in illustration 16b; and (3) your perineum with a channel extending into your navel center, as shown in illustration 16c. The perineum is the puckered skin area located between the anus and vulva in women, and between the anus and scrotum in men. Approximately one-quarter to one-half inch inside the skin, there is an energy center that is key for bringing sexual energy up your spine as well as receiving and distributing Ka energy throughout your lower body. Stop reading for a moment, close your eyes, and breathe into your perineum in order to feel its location. You may need to touch it with your fingertip and then breathe into it if you find it difficult to isolate with your awareness.

When doing the Ka maintenance process, you will always begin with connection of the silver cord to your head and activation of the tube of light with your Higher Self's energy. Once this energy is flowing freely, you will breathe in through your Ka Template and crown, into and back out of your pineal gland, as per illustration 16a. Inhale by sucking in deeply, as if you are slurping the last of a drink through a straw, but without swallowing. Then exhale in a normal, relaxed fashion. After the crown-pineal connection is activated, you will repeat the deep sucking inhalation, this time with your concentration on bringing the Ka energy in through the back of your heart chakra, as per illustration 16b. Then you will repeat the deep sucking inhalation, pulling the Ka energy in through your perineum and up

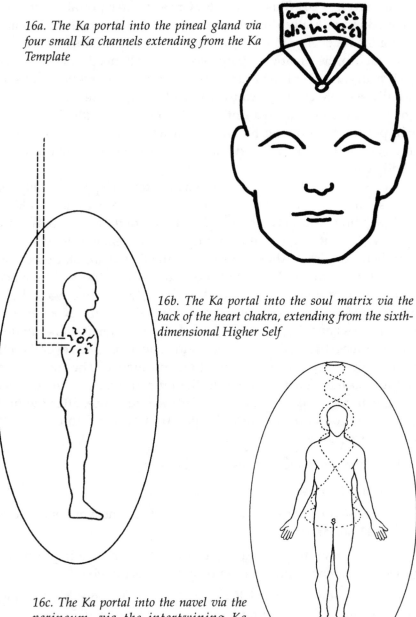

16a. The Ka portal into the pineal gland via four small Ka channels extending from the Ka Template

16b. The Ka portal into the soul matrix via the back of the heart chakra, extending from the sixth-dimensional Higher Self

16c. The Ka portal into the navel via the perineum, via the intertwining Ka Channels around the body from the top of the aura to your navel, as per illustration 16c. Once all three portals have been activated individually, do the same kind of breath while envisioning pulling the Ka energy in through all three portals at the same time.

If you do the breath properly, you will only need to take one or two breaths at each of the four stages. You will know when you successfully activate the Ka because you will feel or sense an increase of light and energy in the areas into which you have breathed. When all three portals are flowing together, you will probably feel or sense more energy flow in your body and a balancing effect on your overall body energy level.

It is recommended that you do the maintenance process daily for about six months. After that, you can do it twice per week to keep the flow going. You may, of course, continue to do the process daily if you wish, or if you are in doubt that the Ka remains activated on the in-between days. About a year after the Pleiadians started opening my Ka Channels, I reduced the frequency of the maintenance process to only when I am guided to do so, which averages about once per week. The exception seems to be when I am experiencing unusual stress and responsibility, or a lot of emotional vulnerability. At those times, I sometimes do the maintenance process several days in a row until my lifestyle or emotions normalize. The increase in need for Ka maintenance is due to the human tendency to contract during extreme situations. Follow your own guidance, after the first six months, to determine how frequently you need to do the Ka maintenance process.

The Ka maintenance process is as follows:

1. Ground yourself.

2. Pull in your aura to two to three feet around you, and check your aura boundaries.

3. Take a few deep breaths with the intention of bringing your conscious awareness into your body as much as possible.

4. Call in your Higher Self and ask it to assist you in activating the silver cord and connecting it to the top of your head.

5. When the silver cord is connected, ask your Higher Self to fill

the tube of light. Feel the energy travel from above your head, into your crown, around and through your entire spine, and down to the bottom apex of your aura beneath your feet. Assist in the filling of the tube by breathing in through your crown to welcome the energy, and by exhaling down your spine and out between your legs through your perineum.

6. When the tube of light is activated, call in the Pleiadian Emissaries of Light and Ascended Master Jesus Christ.

7. Ask that the Interdimensional Cone of Light be brought above you for clearing and divine alignment.

8. Ask the Pleiadians and the Christ to assist you and your Higher Self in fully activating your Divine Ka.

9. Inhale into your crown and pineal gland with a deep sucking breath, and exhale normally. Repeat this breath until you sense the activation of the Ka energy.

10. Inhale into the back of your heart chakra, pulling the Ka energy into the soul area inside your chest with a deep sucking breath, and exhale normally. Repeat this breath until you sense the activation and energy flow in this area.

11. Inhale through your perineum and up to your navel with a deep sucking breath; exhale normally. Repeat this breath until you sense an increase in energy flow between your perineum and navel.

12. Using the same deep sucking breath, visualize all three portal areas at once and breathe in through them together. Exhale normally. One or two complete breaths should be adequate.

13. Ask the Pleiadians, the Christ, and your Higher Self to assist you in keeping the Ka energy flowing and expanding.

14. Continue with your normal meditation, or open your eyes and go on with your day. [▣▭▭]

Ka Balancing Chamber of Light

The Ka Balancing Chamber session takes only about ten minutes to do, and is definitely one of my favorites energetically. The purpose of this chamber is to balance the flow of the Ka energy between the right and left sides of your body, between your upper and lower body, and between the front and back of your body. It also helps distribute the energy more evenly throughout your aura in all directions, including beneath your feet. Simultaneously, the flow of your cerebrospinal fluid is activated and balanced similarly to the Ka energy flow. This latter function is important because your cerebrospinal fluid is a conductor of electrical frequencies of the central nervous system and the interface between your Ka Channels and your physical body. If you have ever received cranial-sacral work, you will recognize similar sensations and effects. The difference is that you may feel as if you had received the work on your whole body and not just on your cranium and sacrum. When receiving a Ka balancing, whether in a chamber session or hands-on, I have experienced the same wavelike effect that I have experienced during cranial-sacral work or Dolphin Brain Repatterning sessions.

This chamber session can be done as often as you wish, but you may need it more frequently during the earlier stages of Ka activation. After the Ka Channels have been opened, maintained, and balanced for awhile, they tend to learn to maintain the balance more easily on their own. After experiencing a couple of Ka Balancing Chamber sessions, you will begin to recognize when you are out of balance and need a session. Always precede the chamber session by doing the Ka maintenance process to assure that the Ka energy is flowing at its current peak potential. It is fine to do this chamber session at night, and to fall asleep whenever you like.

After doing the maintenance process—since the Pleiadians, the Christ, and your Higher Self are already present with you—all you need to do is ask that the Ka Balancing Chamber of Light be brought around your entire body and aura. Lie on your back with pillows under your knees, your feet shoulder-width apart, and eyes closed for ten minutes while the balancing is done. [cassette icon]

Recommendations for Ongoing Pleiadian Lightwork

Now that you have experienced all of the techniques and healing sessions in this workbook, I would like to give a summary of my recommendations for continuing Pleiadian Lightwork on your own. If you choose to do a minimal amount of ongoing conscious focus on Pleiadian Lightwork, the Ka maintenance process in this chapter is the most important thing to do daily, if possible.

If you wish to maximize your healing connection with the Pleiadians, the following is a sample outline for daily, weekly, and monthly healings or energy sessions. Please remember that this is only intended as a sample outline. Your intuition about your own needs and spiritual activities is always the most important factor in determining your choices of ongoing energy sessions.

Daily Agenda: Mornings

1. Ground yourself.

2. Adjust your aura to within two to three feet of your body.

3. Check your aura boundary colors and the five roses outside your aura. Make any desired adjustments.

4. Run cosmic gold and Earth energies through your body channels for ten minutes or more. (See "Owning Your Spinal Pathway," chapter 5.)

5. While running these energies on Automatic, call in your Higher Self to activate your silver cord and fill your tube of light. (See "Divine Axis Alignment with Your Higher Self," chapter 13.)

6. Invoke the Pleiadian Emissaries of Light and Ascended Master Jesus Christ and ask them to assist while you do the Ka maintenance process. (See "Ka Maintenance Process," chapter 14.)

7. Meditate for as long as you want.

Daily Agenda: Bedtime

1. Ground yourself.

2. Pull in your aura to within two to three feet of your body, and surround it with violet flame.

3. Invoke your Higher Self, the Pleiadian Emissaries of Light, and the Ascended Master Jesus Christ, as well as any other Ascended Masters, guides, or guardian angels you wish to have with you.

4. Ask these beings to place you inside a Sleep Chamber of Light for protection and healing while you sleep. Tell them you are

available for any healing during your sleep that they deem to be in your highest good at this time. (See "Sleep Chamber," chapter 9.)

5. Tell your guides and helpers that you want your astral body to go only to the planes of divine light while you are sleeping.

6. If there are any specific chambers or types of healing you feel a need for, specify them at this time. (*Note:* The Sleep Chamber cannot be done simultaneously with other chamber sessions.)

7. Say the following invocation or one of your own: "In the name of the I Am Presence that I Am, I call forth the golden light from the City of Light where the Ascended Masters dwell to fill my aura, this room, this house (apartment), and the entire property, making them holy temples as in the City of Light, where only that which is of divine truth may enter. All that is less than the divine truth is illusion and must leave now. So be it."

8. *Optional:* Meditate as long as you desire at this time.

9. Sleep well.

Weekly Agenda

1. After doing the daily Ka maintenance process, do a Ka Balancing Chamber of Light session for ten minutes. You can do this session any time of day or night, as long as you lie down for it. (See "Ka Maintenance Process" and "Ka Balancing Chamber of Light," chapter 14.)

2. Violet flame your entire home and property. Then place a wide border of violet light or flame around your home and property. Ask Ascended Master St. Germain to help you with this if you wish. Afterward, say the City of Light invocation as listed above as step 7 in the daily agenda for bedtime. (See "Keeping Your Home Psychically Clear and Safe," chapter 5.)

3. During your morning meditation, visualize violet flame filling and cleansing your aura, and if you feel a need for it, run violet light through the front and back of your chakras. Then do the golden rain shower through your aura. (See "Healing Your Aura and Keeping It Clear," chapter 5.)

4. Run cosmic gold light out the front and back of each chakra,

one at a time. Between one and three minutes should be enough for each chakra. (See "Clearing Your Chakras," chapter 6.)

5. Do the meditation in which you bond each chakra and then blend with your Higher Self. (See "Meeting and Blending with Your Higher Self," chapter 13.)

6. Check yourself for cords and clear them as needed. (See "De-Cording," chapter 6.)

7. Check yourself on a screen or with a friend for erroneous neural pathways that are ready to be cleared. You may prefer to do this monthly. (See "Clearing Erroneous Neural Pathways," chapter 12.)

8. Bring yourself into present time. This may also be done more frequently if needed. (See "Being in Present Time," chapter 6.)

9. Connect with your four medicine-wheel subpersonalities and balance your personal shield. This may be done more often if desired. (See "Balancing Your Personal Shield," chapter 11.)

Monthly Agenda

1. Do a Quantum Transfiguration Chamber of Light to keep your cellular clearing going. (See chapter 9.)

2. Do a Love Configuration Chamber of Light of your choice to consciously receive divine love in a receptive way. This may be done as often as you would like, but once a month is a recommended minimum. (See any section in chapter 10.)

3. Do an Interdimensional Chamber of Light to continue your soul-level healing and your essence connection with yourself throughout your body. (See chapter 9.)

4. Do a Divine Axis Realignment Chamber of Light to continue clearing blocks to your Higher Self and holographic alignment. (See chapter 9.)

5. At bedtime, ask for a Dolphin Brain Repatterning session which will keep the neurological and skeletal clearing updated. Lie on your back with a pillow under your knees and no pillow under your head. This session may be done more often and at any time of day you prefer, especially if you are experiencing skeletal and mus-

cular stiffness or discomfort. (See "Etheric Hands-On Dolphin Brain Repatterning," chapter 8.)

For easy reference, the following is a list of chambers and healing sessions categorized according to their uses for various symptoms and needs. This may give you ideas about what types of Pleiadian Lightwork are ideal for common situations. Use your discernment to determine which session is appropriate at any given time.

Feeling Scattered, Ungrounded, or Overwhelmed

1. PEMS Synchronization Chamber of Light (as listed in chapter 9)

2. Integration Acceleration Chamber of Light (as listed in chapter 9)

3. Stress Reduction Chamber of Light (as listed in chapter 9)

4. Emotional Healing Chamber of Light (as listed in chapter 9)

5. Cocoon of divine peace, balance, acceptance, forgiveness, or any other divine quality you feel is absent in your life. (See "Cocoon Healing," chapter 12.)

Need or Desire for Spiritual Expansion and Connection

1. Blend with your Higher Self (as listed in chapter 13).

2. Divine Axis Alignment with your Higher Self (as listed in chapter 13)

3. Ascension Chamber of Light (as listed in chapter 9)

4. Dolphin Star-Link Chamber of Light (as listed in chapter 9)

5. Multidimensional Healing and Integration Chamber of Light (as listed in chapter 9)

6. Love Configuration Chamber of Light (any section in chapter 10)

Body Pain or Physical Energy Imbalance

1. For skeletal, muscular, or neurological pain or imbalance: Dolphin Brain Repatterning (as listed in chapter 8)

2. For blocked energy flows or numbness: Dolphin Star-Link Chamber of Light (as listed in chapter 9)

3. Cellular Reorientation and Repatterning session (as listed in chapter 12)

4. PEMS Synchronization Chamber of Light (as listed in chapter 9)

5. Quantum Transfiguration grid healing on localized areas. (See "Self-Healing with the Quantum Transfiguration Grid," chapter 12.)

6. Run gold energy through the troubled area while blowing roses. (See "Clearing with Roses," chapter 6.)

Emotional or Psychic Vulnerability

1. Emotional Healing Chamber of Light (as listed in chapter 9)

2. No Time and Space Chamber of Light (as listed in chapter 9)

3. Healing and psychic protection cocoon. (See "Cocoon Healing," chapter 12.)

4. Violet flame throughout your aura, and place violet flame around your aura (See "Healing Your Aura and Keeping It Clear," chapter 5.)

5. Angelic and Archangelic Love Configuration Chamber of Light (as listed in chapter 10)

6. Subpersonality Harmonization Chamber of Light (as listed in chapter 11)

7. Chakra bonding and blending with your Higher Self. (See "Meeting and Blending with Your Higher Self," chapter 13.)

8. Run energy and blow roses with a symbol for the problem, such as panic, fear, deep hurt, or betrayal. (See "Clearing with Roses," chapter 6.)

9. Ask to have the excess emotions lifted and healed. (See "Cellular Reorientation and Repatterning," step 9 of the guided process, chapter 12.)

Need to Integrate a Deep Healing Experience

1. Integration Acceleration Chamber of Light (as listed in chapter 9)

2. Cellular Reorientation and Repatterning session (as listed in chapter 12)

3. Ground and bring yourself into present time. (See "Grounding," chapter 5, and "Present-Time Consciousness," chapter 6.)

4. Healing and psychic protection cocoon. (See "Cocoon Healing," chapter 12.)

5. Emotional Healing Chamber of Light (as listed in chapter 9)

6. PEMS Synchronization Chamber of Light (as listed in chapter 9)

7. Subpersonality Harmonization Chamber of Light (as listed in chapter 11)

8. Multidimensional Healing and Integration Chamber of Light (as listed in chapter 9)

9. Ask to have excess emotions and pain lifted and healed. (See "Cellular Reorientation and Repatterning," step 9 of the guided process, chapter 12.)

Feeling Stuck

1. Balance your personal shield, and do the Subpersonality Harmonization Chamber of Light afterward (both as listed in chapter 11).

2. Cellular Reorientation and Repatterning (as listed in chapter 12)

3. Dolphin Star-Link Chamber of Light (as listed in chapter 9)

4. Run energy through the individual chakras and use roses to clear the energy blocks. (See "Clearing Your Chakras," chapter 12.)

5. De-cord yourself (as listed in chapter 6).

6. Clear beliefs, judgments, perfect pictures, and/or contracts (as listed in chapter 6).

7. Bring yourself into present time (as listed in chapter 6).

8. Cocoon of divine clarity, willingness, acceptance, peace, or any other divine quality or combination of qualities. (See "Cocoon Healing," chapter 12.)

9. Divine Axis Alignment with your Higher Self (chapter 13, second section)

10. Do the Sleep Chamber of Light at bedtime and ask for dreams that will show you what is causing the stuckness (as listed in chapter 9).

11. Check for and clear erroneous neural pathways (as listed in chapter 12).

These are only some of the most common challenges for which you may wish to use Pleiadian Lightwork. Beyond the recommendations given here, find your own creative ways of applying what you have learned and experienced in this workbook. When you are in doubt about what to do, quiet yourself, slowly go over the options, and check to see which technique *feels right* when you say it aloud or think about it. Trust your own guidance and intuition. If you know how to use a pendulum or do muscle-testing—a form of kinesiology—you may use these methods to determine what you need to do. If you still cannot decide, call in the Pleiadians, the Christ, and your Higher Self, and tell them your circumstance. Ask them to do whatever is in your highest good at this time to assist your healing and clearing process. When you set up a connection with your healing team in this way, it is best to allow up to one-and-a-half hours for the session in case it is needed.

I wholeheartedly welcome your comments and discoveries. I would love to know how Pleiadian Lightwork is contributing to your life and what new ways of using it you discover as a result of doing the processes given in this book. My address is listed in the Postlogue.

We—the Pleiadians and I—hope you have enjoyed and benefited from this book which is, as all that the Pleiadian Emissaries of Light offer, given in love, faith in the Divine Plan, and gratitude and respect for your willingness to receive and utilize it on your path to mastery.

Namaste . . .

Postlogue

ADVANCED PLEIADIAN LIGHTWORK

If you feel pulled to pursue more direct experience with the Pleiadian Emissaries of Light and the Pleiadian Lightwork, the following is an outline of the work available at this time either through me or through certified Pleiadian Lightwork practitioners who have completed the trainings I offer and are prepared to teach it and do private work with individuals.

Individual work sessions available through graduate students and rarely by myself include:

1. clairvoyant readings and spiritual healing sessions by phone or in person, depending on where you live

2. hands-on Pleiadian Lightwork, including Dolphin Brain Repatterning, Ka activation sessions, Dolphin Star-Linking, cellular and soul clearing and healing; and phone sessions or sessions done in person for clearing neural pathways, clearing blocks to Higher Self connection, and kundalini clearing

3. Pleiadian Lightwork private intensives if you do not live near a practitioner; you stay in the area where the practitioner lives for about one to two weeks while having your Ka Channels opened with hands-on work, being guided through Dolphin Moves, and given other Pleiadian Lightwork sessions as needed

4. one-to-three-day private intensives designed to fit your personal and spiritual needs that include any or all of the following: clairvoyant reading/healing sessions; hands-on healing; regression facilitation; Dolphin Brain Repatterning; Dolphin Star-Linking; crystal and gemstone layouts and energy balancing; individual ceremonies; communication with your Higher Self, Ascended Master

teachers, and guides; emotional release work; spiritual instruction; bodywork; soul retrieval; and depossession

Training Programs available from students and myself are:

1. Pleiadian Lightwork Intensive I: a training program for becoming a Pleiadian Lightwork practitioner over a period of twenty-eight consecutive days, with every fourth day off. You may take the training just to receive the hands-on work in the group setting, even if you do not intend to become a practitioner. This is an accelerated and spiritually intense way to receive healing and awakening.

2. Pleiadian Lightwork Intensives II and III: the second and third levels of the program. You may take these if you wish to become a Pleiadian Lightwork practitioner or if you prefer group intensives to private work. Each intensive is eleven consecutive days, with every fourth day off. Processes included are: cellular clearing and healing; paradigm clearing in the original eight cells; soul clearing, healing, and depossession; anchoring the Pillar of Light, or *Laoesh Shekinah*; conscious accessing of multidimensional realities; Dolphin Tantra; advanced Dolphin Brain Repatterning hands-on; Dolphin Star-Linking; Dolphin Moves; Assemblage Point shifting; using the Ka energy for localized healing in the body; Ka linking to other meridian systems; merkabah clearing and activation; and accessing original soul memory and purpose.

3. Clairvoyant and Full Sensory Perception Training Program: twenty-four separate day-long classes taught in varying formats, depending upon their location. The program includes all of the basic information for becoming a clairvoyant reader and spiritual healer, and for deepening your own healing process, full-sensory abilities, and spiritual growth.

Weekend Workshops are available, once you have completed this book, as follow:

1. Kundalini Healing, Clearing, and Opening: Beginner Level

2. Advanced Kundalini (once you complete the beginner-level workshop)

3. Becoming Who You Really Are: spiritual teachings on impecca-

bility, clearing processes, multidimensional meditation techniques and activations, and soul healing

4. Solar and Galactic Initiations: teachings, ceremonies, activation and initiation experiences, soul healing, and activating your soul's blueprint

5. Others are offered from time to time.

Sacred Sites Ceremonial Trips may be arranged with myself, or with myself and other teachers and speakers.

Tapes and tape sets are available as follows:

#1. The Pleiadian Workbook tapes: set of four 90-minute and two 60-minute tapes covering all of the processes in this workbook ($53.50)

#2. Dolphin Moves tapes (numerous guided floor movement sessions may be purchased individually): one 90-minute tape including both Dolphin Moves in chapter 8 ($12.20)

#3. Quantum Transfiguration Grid for Arthritis Sufferers ($12.20)

#4. Higher Self Meditation tape: includes both meditations in chapter 13 ($12.20)

Others tapes are also offered from time to time; please inquire below.

Brochures with more details and schedules are available upon request. You may also get on the Pleiadian Lightwork mailing list or set up workshops by contacting:

Pleiadian Lightwork Associates/Dolphin Star Temple
P. O. Box 1581/310 E. Ivy Street
Mt. Shasta, CA 96067
Phone: 530-926-1122   Fax: 530-926-1112
email: pleiades@jps.net
Web: www.jps.net/aquanyin

BIBLIOGRAPHY

Argüelles, José, *Dreamspell*. Makawao, Maui, HI: Chelsea Pacific, 1990.

Bryner, Michael and Ariel Spilsbury, *The Mayan Oracle: Return Path to the Stars*. Santa Fe, NM: Bear & Company, 1992.

Burmester, Helen S., *The Seven Rays Made Visual*. Marina del Rey, CA: DeVorss & Co., 1986.

Carey, Ken, *Return of the Bird Tribes*. Kansas City, MO: UniSun, 1988.

Clow, Barbara Hand, *Eye of the Centaur: A Visionary Guide to Past Lives*. Santa Fe, NM: Bear & Company, 1986.

_____, *Heart of the Christos: Starseeding from the Pleiades*. Santa Fe, NM: Bear & Company, 1989.

_____, *The Pleiadian Agenda: A New Cosmology for the Age of Light*. Santa Fe, NM: Bear & Company, 1995.

_____, *Signet of Atlantis: War in Heaven Bypass*. Santa Fe, NM: Bear & Company, 1992.

Feldenkrais, Moshe, *Awareness Through Movement*. San Francisco: Harper Collins, 1991.

_____, *Master Moves*. Cupertino, CA: Meta Publications, 1984.

Fromm, Erich, *The Art of Loving*. New York: Harper Collins, 1974.

Grant, Joan, *Winged Pharoah*. Alpharetta, Ga.: Ariel Press, 1985.

Hurtak, J. J., *The Book of Knowledge: The Keys of Enoch*. Los Gatos, CA: The Academy for Future Sciences, 1977.

Morgan, Marlo, *Mutant Message Down Under*. New York: Harper Collins, 1994.

Redfield, James, *The Celestine Prophecy*. New York: Warner Books, 1993.

Starhawk, *The Fifth Sacred Thing*. New York: Bantam Books, 1993.

GLOSSARY

Akashic Records: (1) collection of all past, present, and future experience and learning for individual beings, collective consciousness, and all of existence; (2) records of all that ever has been, all that is, and all that ever shall be.

Alcyone: central sun of the Pleiades constellation around which Earth and this solar system orbit every 26,000 years; also serves as a "galactic gateway" to the Galactic Center.

An-Ra: one of the Pleiadian Archangelic Tribes of the Light, radiating a clear emerald-green color, and in charge of all plant life, including the plant devic kingdom, in our solar system. Their nature is that of divine compassion and understanding.

archangels: (1) the highest evolutionary level of angelic consciousness still maintaining individuation; (2) self-motivated angels, holding dominion in a particular specialized area, as opposed to serving angels who simply do as instructed by beings on higher evolutionary levels. Examples: Archangel Michael/Michaella is in charge of the Legions of Light who carry the Sword of Truth and protect beings on the physical plane who request it. Archangel Gabriel/Gabriella is a messenger of God and interfaces between dimensions, maintaining communication as needed. They and their helpers also make sure that human free will is honored by etheric beings.

Ascended Master: (1) a being who has lived on Earth in a body and reached enlightenment, experienced either conscious death or full body ascension, and attained Christ consciousness; (2) all of the members of the Great White Brotherhood, including the Sisterhood and Brotherhood of the Ray of the Ascended Christ; (3) beings at this level attained divine alignment through all nine-dimensional aspects of the self simultaneously while still in human form.

ascension: translation of the spirit and physical body together to the fourth or fifth dimension from the third dimension without experiencing physical death—due to a cellular vibrational frequency increase beyond the maximum number of vibrations per second at which the body can remain physical. This is accompanied by a state of spiritual enlightenment and conscious alignment throughout the nine dimensional aspects of the individuated self. In third-dimensional reality, the person *ascending* would simply become invisible and disappear.

astral body: (1) exact etheric double of the physical body which leaves the body while we sleep and travels in the astral and higher planes; (2) connected to the body at all times with a silver cord in the third chakra, or solar plexus. (3) While we sleep, the astral body contains our consciousness and goes into other realms to act out and heal karmic patterns, clear the subconscious, learn from higher beings, create the future, heal the past, interact with other humans, and explore. (4) When we are awake, the astral body is blended with the physical body andbrings psychic protection to the body and aura if it is in healthy condition.

astral planes: (1) nonphysical realms of consciousness corresponding to the physical world but not of it. (2) *Lower-astral planes* are referred to as the "bardos" in Buddhism, or the dark underworld, Hell, and Hades in Western society. They consist of parasitic entities, denied aspects of human consciousness, thoughtform entities (thoughtforms that have become self-aware and self-sustaining), and projections created by negative emotions. The realm of "bogey men," monsters, and your worst-feared agendas. (3) When emotions are held onto and believed to be based in truth instead of being seen simply as emotions, they become negative. Examples: phobias; revenge; lusty sexual fantasies devoid of love and spirit connection; repressed and justified fear, anger, rage, hate, blame, self-pitying victimhood, control, and greed. These energies, as well as physical abuse, rape, drugs, alcohol, indulgence in negative thinking, past-life murder or suicide, and absence of spiritual connectedness, pull humans into the lower-astral planes. (4) There are also *higher-astral planes* that correspond to the physical world such as the geometric plane, causal plane, interlinking communication network, past and future etheric doubles of all physical existence and experience, and the Akashic Records. These realms are generally accessed during sleep by the astral body. (5) the dark polarity of the fourth and fifth dimensions. The beings on these realms impulse humans via their own vices, negative thoughtforms, repressed emotions, and denied or unhealed shadow sides.

aura: the energy field around the body of any living thing which is generated from its light body and form. In a healthy state, an *auric field* can be seen clairvoyantly as filled with clear bright colors of light. Negative and dense energies show up in the aura as dingy or darker contracted areas with little light, if any. Foreign energy, or energy belonging to someone other than the person whom the aura belongs to, appears as dull, milky, and opaque, usually white, but possibly of other colors.

being: the self-aware presence of a spirit capable of conscious thought, projection of thoughts and feelings, and a sense of containment within any given amount of space, though not necessarily in time

Brotherhood of the Ray of the Ascended Christ: males who attained enlightenment and Christ consciousness while on Earth in human bodies; now serving as guides and higher-dimensional teachers to people on Earth who are ready to be initiated into enlightenment and Christ consciousness

cellular spin: the movement pattern of a healthy living cell—not unlike the orbit of a planet around a sun

chakra: (1) an energy center in the body which is formed by a spinning vortex, somewhat like a wheel, which has specific energy distribution and maintenance functions within the overall human system; (2) functions in a connective fashion between the emotional, physical, spiritual, and mental aspects of our wholeness. (3) See illustrations 1a and 1b on pages 78–79. One of seven major energy wheels in the body:

> **seventh chakra:** located on the top of the head, known as the **crown chakra**; brings in all spiritual and cosmic information and energy; regulates and contains our spiritual goals for the current lifetime, as well as what we are here to learn and achieve in the world, which is part of our spirit's learning experience

> **sixth chakra:** located between the brows in the low central area of the forehead, called the **third eye**, or **brow chakra**; rules clairvoyance, self-image, and our perceptions of the reality we see; also regulates how we project our own beliefs and truths onto the world around us

> **fifth chakra:** located in the center of the throat, known as the **throat chakra**; regulates the energy of communications, self-expression, and creative expression

fourth chakra: located in the center of the chest, also called the **heart chakra**; rules self-affinity, self-love, love for and from others, self-worth, deservingness, awareness and experience of your essence, and appreciation of the essence of others; the seat of the soul

third chakra: located in the center of the solar plexus, or diaphragm area; also called the **power chakra, will center,** or **solar plexus center**; holds and regulates all power, dominion, and control energies, whether it be power and control over others, allowing others to control you, or divine power; will, whether it be divine will or lower will; social life and social goals; what you do for others; active expression of emotions; self-respect; self-esteem; ego center

second chakra: located halfway between the navel and groin areas, also called the **sacral chakra**; regulates sexual and sensual energies; self-nurturing and nurturing of others; the feeling nature of emotions; and clairsentience; the creative center in females

first chakra: located at the base of the tailbone, also called the **root chakra**; holds the energies of safety or unsafety; instincts; connection to Earth; relationship to and health of the body; survival needs such as food, shelter, clothing, money (at least in cultures with monetary exchange systems); mobility; and initial instinctual emotional response or reaction

Chambers of Light: (1) energy spaces created by the Pleiadian Emissaries of Light and Christ around the aura and body in which healing, energy-frequency changes, balancing, or states of consciousness can be brought about; (2) a concentrated field of specific light, colors, flow pattern, and frequencies in which etheric, spiritual, physical, emotional, and/or physical change can be facilitated. (3) See chapters 9, 10, 11, and 13 for details about the individual types of chambers listed below:

Ascension Chamber
Divine Axis Alignment Chamber
Dolphin Star-Link Chamber
Emotional Healing Chamber
Integration Acceleration Chamber
Interdimensional Chamber of Light
Ka Balancing Chamber
Love Configuration Chamber

a. Unification

b. Angelic and Archangelic

c. Divine Feminine

d. Divine Masculine

e. Yin/Yang

Multidimensional Healing and Integration Chamber

No Time and Space Chamber

PEMS (physical, emotional, mental, spiritual) **Synchronization Chamber**

Quantum Transfiguration Chamber

Sleep Chamber

Stress Reduction Chamber

Subpersonality Harmonization Chamber

Christ: (1) the Ascended Master who had a lifetime on Earth under the name of **Jesus Christ**; (2) spiritual teacher who taught that all humans are God's children and intended to evolve into full spiritual glory, equality, and enlightenment: "Ye shall do even greater things than I have done." (3) Jesus was known to have miraculous gifts, both for healing and alchemy; his last recorded miracle was to raise himself from the dead and ascend.

Christ consciousness: spiritual evolutionary consciousness of the purity of integrity and action, the mastery of alchemy and ascension, and the ability to know divine truth, wisdom, compassion, forgiveness, peace, and mastery. Beings of Christ consciousness who are incarnate in third-dimensional forms are in their divine alignment throughout all nine-dimensional aspects of the individuated self.

Christ Realm: where the Ascended Master Jesus Christ, Saint Germain, Mother Mary, and all other members of the Great White Brotherhood dwell; connected with the star Sirius and the Dolphin Star consciousness, which is held and emanated by the Light Beings who dwell there or are from there; includes Cities of Light

Christed Self: (1) that aspect of humans who have combined Earth experience, consciousness, and wisdom with that of the Higher Self and Christ consciousness; (2) same as Master Presence; (3) the composite consciousness of all nine-dimensional aspects of the individual having access to third-dimensional consciousness through embodiment of itself in divine alignment in human form

City of Light: (1) fourth- through sixth-dimensional cities of Temples of Light where the Ascended Masters dwell; (2) location of many spiritual initiations, sacred teachings and healings during human dream time, and between-life teaching, review, and healing

clairaudience: (1) the expanded full sensory function of hearing to include physically inaudible sounds such as high frequency tones, or verbal messages from guides or Higher Self; (2) the ability to hear what another person is really thinking when it is different from what he or she is saying

clairsentience: (1) the full sensory perception of feeling to include etheric energies and unexpressed feelings of others beyond what is physically explainable through touch; (2) expanded energy-based feelings as a function of the second chakra

clairvoyance: (1) the full sensory perception of seeing what is not physically visible; (2) third-eye vision as a function of the sixth chakra; (3) ability to see etheric energies such as auras, chakras, energy blocks, guides and angels with the eyes closed, and in some cases open.

cocoons: (1) mummy-like wrapping of energy around the entire aura for the purpose of protection and integration after a healing experience or traumatic emotional release; (2) an etheric structure that completely encloses the auric field in a specific energy frequency such as peace, forgiveness, trust, or innocence; (3) a protective enclosure used to encase and transport damaged lightbodies and souls after a shattering experience. (See illustration 12 on page 239.)

collective consciousness: (1) gathering and uniting of the minds and purposes of a group of beings with common goals, life situations, and location of inhabitance; (2) the "One-Mindedness" of a group of individuals for a common purpose such as evolution of a species, protection of a community, bringing more love to all the inhabitants of a planet, family, community, etc. (3) *Higher collective consciousness* occurs when the intent of a group is aligned for evolutionary, spiritual, or creative purposes. (4) *Lower collective consciousness* exists when a group of beings share identical negative thoughtforms, beliefs, or destructive goals.

cords: etheric, or psychic links between two people for the purpose of exchanging energy, or taking or giving energy to the other person.

Cords can be used for positive sharing, or for manipulation, control, draining life force, or dumping on someone.

Council of Elders: a group of four sixth-dimensional Light Beings who serve as advisors and counselors to beings undergoing incarnations and evolution in the third dimension. They work with the being both in and between lifetimes.

de-cording: process for removing unwanted cords between two people; described fully in chapter 6 in "De-Cording" section

devas: (1) angelic beings who hold a common and specific geometric signature with the plant species, mineral, or element they protect and energize; (2) somewhat like a Higher Self to the plant, mineral, and elemental kingdoms. (Also see Glossary listing for "Overlighting Devas".)

devic kingdom: the realm of consciousness of devas and Overlighting Devas

dimensions: realms of consciousness delineated by vibrational frequency range and nature of form or absence of form. (For a more cosmological understanding, read Barbara Hand Clow's book, *The Pleiadian Agenda: A New Cosmology for the Age of Light.*)

> **first dimension:** the realm of pure minerals as containers for consciousness, but devoid of their own consciousness and self-awareness

> **second dimension:** lower-astral planes on which the consciousnesses perceive themselves as all that exists, are oblivious to spirit, devoid of souls, and totally self-absorbed; also the realm of certain types of elementals that have no consciousness of their own other than is directed by some controlling force; also contains underworld aspect of what is called the bardos in Buddhism, also known as the Hell realms; realm of all plant species

> **third dimension:** physical world and corresponding astral planes; anchored in a linear time- and space-based reality. Anything in this realm exists at a maximum of 9000 vibrations per second. This is the realm in which human consciousness lives.

> **fourth dimension:** Beings retain consciousness as feelings and thoughts based on feelings. This dimension contains both dark and light polarities. The light realms are made up of "Cities of

Light" and those who have reached a vibrational frequency of between 9000 and 12,000 vibrations per second. The consciousness here is the first stage of Christ consciousness following ascension. Many guides, angels, and Ascended Masters impulse the third-dimensional humans who are receptive and available for spiritual growth and evolution. Humans are also impulsed by the dark astral counterpart that exists in this dimension. The dark ones are able to match the lower-vibrational frequency of negative thoughts, vices, repressed emotions, and unhealed or denied-shadow sides of humans—and are able to pull them into the dark side and then control them and feed off their pain, fear, and other dense energies. As humans develop higher-vibrational qualities of being, thinking, feeling, and doing, as well as transcend the karmic tendencies of their own shadow sides, they are magnetized into the fourth-dimensional light impulses and pull free from the dark control and parasitic beings. The dark polarity of this realm is also one of the places where nightmares and astral abuse take place.

fifth dimension: This dimension also has dark and light polarities. Beings retain their etheric forms from the third and fourth dimensions combined, but with refinements and freedom to alter these forms at will. The light aspect of this realm contains most of the personal guides to humans, serving angels, many of the Ascended Masters and members of the Great White Brotherhood, initiatic schools of the intermediate level, the karmic board, Overlighting Devas, and guardian angels. From this dimension and up it is impossible to talk in terms of vibrations per second because it is beyond time and space limitations though interfacing with time and space reality at will. This is also the dimension of actualized Christ and Buddha consciousness immediately after the completion of incarnation, ascension, and transition through the Cities of Light in the fourth dimension. Flying dreams, as well as dreams of healing, higher experiences, and teachings occur in this dimension. This is the dimensional, causal plane relative to humans manifesting and creating in the lower-dimensional worlds during dreamtime. In other words, it is where humans dream their lives into time and space reality, and then wake up and live out the dreams. Higher consciousness, lucid dreaming and white magic happen here. The dark polarity consists of the powerful dark lords of black magic and control. There are dark angels, masters, sorcerers, and rulers of the lower astral planes and underworlds in this realm. If persons develop great psychic powers, and mind control without developing the heart and spiritual integrity, this is where they are ruled by and go during sleep and after leaving their human lives.

sixth dimension: This is the realm of the Higher Council, the archangels who interface with Earth, the Councils of Elders, and the beginning of collective consciousness. From this level on up, the dimensions are exclusively of the Light. The collective consciousness in this realm is that of souls split apart. In other words, if your soul, after being on Earth in one body, decided to split into two or more parts, whether the decision was based on pain or desire for diversity of experience, at the sixth-dimensional level all parts would share the same Higher Self until rejoined in one body again. This is the realm from which the Higher Self communicates with us and connects with us on a soul and spirit level. It is from here that our higher purpose is dictated. Beings on this level can choose to project human-like forms if it serves a purpose, but they actually exist in pure geometric forms which are characteristic of this dimension. In Creation, this is the stage at which thought, color, and sound take on geometric form and numerological significance. When beings on this level wish to communicate with one another, they simply blend their energy fields and consciousnesses. There is a unique grid that is formed by this blending and both beings experience the essential nature of the other mainly by virtue of comparison and what the other has to offer. There is a sense of knowing the other without actually feeling as though you have become the other. Melchizedek consciousness exists on this dimensional level.

seventh dimension: the realm of divine sound and harmonics. All beings on this level exist as expressions of essence through the harmonics of sound, individually and collectively. Form can no longer be projected directly without downstepping dimensionally. Patterns are formed by the sound but are nebulous flows of color and movement. Varying spiral patterns are the only describable forms to be found. When beings on this level wish to communicate with one another they simply combine their sounds, blend colors, and create new patterns. From this experience, both consciousnesses are energized and fully comprehend one another. There is also a greater understanding, which comes from the principle of, "The whole is greater than the sum of its parts." It is the next level of collective consciousness, but this time with other souls as well as different parts of your own. Beings on this level literally hold the key to translating all experience and consciousness into pure sound, carrying frequency and creating flow patterns. These sound frequencies make up the only common lan guage from the seventh dimension down. This is the realm of pure Melchizedek consciousness, as the fifth is of Christ consciousness. Members of same soul family origins have the ability to experience themselves as the same being on this dimension while maintaining the capacity for individuation.

eighth dimension: Pure color and flow patterns are trademarks of this realm. Beings on this dimension exist as self-aware consciousnesses emanating color, light, and movement. When communicating with one another, it is more of a synergistic experience during which neither being can tell the difference in itself and the other. Great love of union and communion takes place here. Because of the absence of sound as an individual expression on this realm, it is also the realm of the void, which in its true purpose is a place to experience one's wholeness and uniqueness as pure essence and consciousness. When fear is absent, it can be a place of solace and deep rest.

ninth dimension: source point of the *Laoesh Shekinah*, the Sacred Pillar of Fire, or Pillar of Light. It is the last dimension on which a Light Being has the capacity to experience consciousness separate from the entire oversoul from whence it came and can also choose to experience that oversoul collective consciousness at will. The only form here is that of the pillar, or parallel strands of very refined light. Everything looks like pure crystalline white light and yet is prismatic, emanating colors to the eighth dimension. This is the dimension of Metatron consciousness. When I was given an experience of this realm once, the only thing I could still differentiate from myself was etheric crystals. I had a collection of quartz crystals on the table in the room where my body was when the experience took place. I was suddenly aware that I could still perceive the crystals as separate from me, although the furniture and people in the room had blended into my consciousness completely. I was told this is as far as a human consciousness can go dimensionally without the body being vaporized.

tenth dimension: All I have been told of this dimension is that all members of original oversoul families experience themselves as merged completely into one consciousness and are no longer aware of their individuation at all. Beyond this point I have been shown and told nothing except that the **thirteenth dimension** is the place of completion and Oneness in which the self is absorbed into All That Is and knows nothing of separation.

divine alignment: the condition in which a person is on their "divine axis" and, therefore, connected through all nine-dimensional aspects of the individuated self; a prerequisite to becoming a being of Christ consciousness

divine axis: (1) the tube of light. See illustration 11 on page 200. (2) a tubular opening that encircles the entire length of the spine, beneath the feet to the base of the aura, and out the crown to the topmost point of the aura and into the higher-dimensional aspects of the individual hologram. (3) It is like a spine that connects the individual to, and through, all the aspects of the self through the ninth dimension and can be used to send energy and communications from one aspect of the self to another. See illustration 15 on page 273.

divine qualities: any attitude or state of existence that is pure and based in God/Goddess sacredness and state of being in all things. Example: Divine love is a pure and unconditional flowing love, whereas selfish love might imply a state of caring about another only for what you stand to gain from that person.

Divine Truth: (1) unchangeable reality based on God-consciousness; (2) absolute knowing about purpose and the nature of reality; (3) absence of thoughts and beliefs that create limitation, destructiveness, or illusion. Example: A person in search of Divine Truth must be willing and able to question every perception of reality at any given moment, no matter how real it appears circumstantially. That all of existence is part of God/Goddess/All That Is is considered to be a Divine Truth.

Dolphin Brain Repatterning: formerly called "Neuro-Muscular-Cortical Repatterning;" consists of hands-on and Dolphin Moves floor movement work, which releases holding patterns in the skeletal, muscular, and neurological systems by teaching the motor cortex of the brain new and more efficient ways of moving without contraction and with spontaneity, freedom, and joy; intended to assist in the restoration of the Dolphin Wave Effect in the body and nervous system

Dolphin Moves: the guided floor movement aspect of Dolphin Brain Repatterning; releases contraction and holding patterns in the nervous, musculature, and skeletal systems, as well as their related behavioral and emotional patterns

Dolphin Star-Linking: an aspect of Pleiadian Lightwork that works on the electrical light body to reactivate and clear inactive, blocked, or damaged circuits in the electrical system. When the circuits are functioning properly, the juncture points in the electrical circuitry are connected to their corresponding stars in this galaxy as the electrical bodies of the dolphins are.

Dolphin Wave Effect: the way energy, sound, and movement translate throughout the body and nervous system when the person or dolphin is in good health, spontaneous, and spiritually aligned. Example: When a dolphin moves its head, the movement translates throughout the rest of its body creating a wave-like effect that is unimpeded by contraction, or holding patterns in the body.

elemental: (1) a nonsouled energy form with movement and purpose, generally created either by obsessive negative focus, a thoughtform becoming self-sustaining and active, or conscious intent. (2) Healers often create *elementals* to achieve certain healing purposes, such as a spinning tornado to clean out a chakra. (3) Elementals can also be projected for negative impact on others, such as in black magic and voodoo. (4) An example of obsessive negative focus is when a person absorbs him/herself in pornographic pictures, movies, and sexual fantasy or experience, the energy around him/her begins to create and/or attract parasitic elementals to feed on and regenerate the negative obsession. (5) Elementals are always second-dimensional forms.

Elohim: the group of Light Beings who are responsible for Creation; also called the Creator Gods and Goddesses

enlightenment: (1) a state of spiritual completion in which all goals for learning and evolution on a specific dimension have been completed; (2) what results when the human consciousness has become totally identified with, and aligned with, the Christed Self or Higher Self in the body; (3) reconnection with the state of impeccability of Oneness, which is sustained and never lost again

erroneous neural pathway: a nervous system circuit in the brain which has been blocked with a *neural plate* that inhibits natural, spontaneous response to sensory input and life experience. See illustration 13 on page 243.

evolutionary consciousness: awareness that our ongoing and overall purpose for existing is to learn, grow, become better and more impeccable in our actions and thoughts, and reunite with God/Goddess/All That Is on all levels

four evolutionary principles: the spiritual understandings that must be presented to every human on Earth before the end of 2012 and embraced by all humans on Earth at that time in order to facilitate the initiation of Earth and her people into their next evolutionary step. The principles are:
    (1) Our purpose here is to evolve physically, emotionally, mentally, and spiritually.
    (2) Every human being has a divine essence made of light and love whose nature is goodness.
    (3) Free will is an absolute universal right; impeccability calls on the self to surrender its free will to divine will in faith and trust.
    (4) All of natural existence is sacred beyond how it serves or meets the needs of the individual self.

full sensory perception: (1) the expanded ability of the five senses to include awareness of etheric, nonphysical energies, beings, feelings, sounds, tastes, smells, and visions; (2) a natural, more complete use of the senses as opposed to the term "extrasensory perception," which would imply that it is unusual or unnatural. 3) See Glossary listings for "clairaudience," "clairsentience," "clairvoyance," and "intuition" for examples of individual full sensory perception.

Galactic Center: (1) the centralmost point of this galaxy; (2) the axis around which the entire galaxy turns, or orbits, constantly

galactic gateway: a location, generally a star or sun, through which beings of fifth-dimensional consciousness and above can pass in order to access points far away in time and space, but immediately accessible when entering the gateway. Travel through these portals is beyond time and space restrictions. For example: (1) with clear intent and focused thought, a higher-dimensional being can move through the Galactic Center and end up in any other place in any galaxy where another galactic gateway exists. (2) Alcyone can be used as a *gateway* to the Galactic Center.

God/Goddess/All That Is: (1) Oneness; (2) the divine in all things; (3) the totality of existence in its purest integrity, which is androgynous and yet includes both genders

God Self: (1) that part of all beings that is aware of its essential nature as being an aspect or part of God/Goddess/All That Is Divine; (2) that which we are in Divine Truth

Great White Brotherhood: (1) Ascended Masters who have lived on Earth as humans and spiritually evolved to become enlightened and then Christed; (2) originally called the Order of the Great White Light, according to the Pleiadian Archangelic spokesperson, Ra; (3) a sacred order dedicated to maintaining Mystery School teachings and assisting in, and guiding, the spiritual awakening of all humans while always honoring individual free will

grounding: (1) being deeply connected as spirit in the physical body and to Earth; (2) a process of running an etheric *grounding cord*, usually between four inches and the width of your hips in diameter—from the first chakra for men and second chakra for women—to the center of Earth for the purpose of being more "in your body." See illustrations 1a and 1b on pages 78–79. (3) anything that makes you more available and present in your body and in life. Example: "That walk in the woods was a *grounding experience* for me," meaning: "I feel more here and more alive in my body by virtue of the experience of walking in the woods." Sex can also be a grounding experience for some people.

Higher Self: multifaceted part of our whole spiritual being who lives in the higher dimensions and guides us toward spiritual growth, evolution, and enlightenment. As we become conscious of this aspect of our bigger selves, we can begin to integrate parts of our Higher Self into our bodies, although certain parts always remain in the higher-dimensional aspects of our hologram.

hologram: anything in third-dimensional form in its all inclusive state as opposed to a two-dimensional image such as a photograph; includes depth, width, height, and form

holographic self: the composite of all aspects of the self throughout all dimensions being in their appropriate alignment and connectedness with one another all at the same time

horizontal alignment: (1) the state of consciousness in which the individual is identified more with the illusions of the physical world and survival needs and fears than with soul and spirit, evolution, and spiritual responsibility for connecting with and illuminating the God Self; (2) completely cut off from Higher Self connection in the body

Infinite Sun: (1) another name for God/Goddess/All That Is, or Oneness, based on the philosophy that everything in existence is connected by and existing within a continual light field which is thirteenth dimensional; (2) that state of existence which includes every thing in existence in its pure essential nature of light

Interdimensional Cone of Light: (See illustration 7 on page 153.) The Interdimensional Cone of Light is the form located at the top of the aura with the point of the cone away from your body. It is composed of rapidly spinning, high-vibrational light frequencies that assist in bringing you into "vertical alignment" and clearing energies released from your body and aura which are not in self-affinity.

intuition: (1) the full sensory perception function of the seventh chakra to include knowing beyond what is rationally explainable. (2) Hunches, feeling guided to do something without knowing why, or "just knowing it was the right thing to do" are examples of intuition.

Ka: (1) the divine double of the physical body that brings in higher-frequency light and life force to the physical; must be fully functional in order for the Master Presence to anchor into the physical body; (2) made up of a vast network of varying-sized *Ka Channels*, including a meridian-like system through which down-stepped higher-frequency energies enter and maintain the etheric light body aspect of your physical existence; (3) the interface between the physical body, higher dimensions, and the Master Presence, also known as the Higher Self, or Christed Self. (4) *Ka energy* is rarefied, down-stepped high-frequency light from the higher-dimensional self.

Ka Template: a horizontal, rectangular, thin etheric center located at the back of the crown chakra which is encoded with information pertinent to the individual's soul goals, body and Ka blueprints, and flow patterns for the Ka energy in the body; shows whether the person is to ascend, consciously die, or experience common death, and how. See illustration 8 on page 156.

karma: (1) the product of life experience which was out of integrity or out of alignment with a person's ethics; (2) a system of learning based on the natural need and tendency of all things in existence to evolve; (3) When action is out of alignment with another person's free will or with the individual's integrity, it magnetizes another similar or polarized life experience through which the person may learn and evolve the original misaligned action into a correct one in present time, which will then remove the *karmic* magnetism created by the original misaligned action.

Lyran Warriors: a group of beings from the star system called Lyra who invaded Orion around 300,000 years ago, enslaved the Orion beings, and took over part of the Orion galactic gateway

Ma-at: one of the Pleiadian Archangelic Tribes of the Light, of the scarlet-red color. Their role is that of the spiritual warriors, and they emanate divine courage that knows no fear.

Master Presence: (1) the Christed Self or Higher Self; (2) what humans become when fully enlightened

Melchizedek: a sixth-dimensional collective consciousness that serves as caretaker of the initiatic realms and teachings for beings in this solar system, and specifically Earth at this time. Priests and priestesses of the **Order of Melchizedek** were known to run mystery schools in Atlantis and ancient Egypt. Jesus Christ studied with members of the **Order of Melchizedek** prior to his initiation in the Egyptian pyramids during his late teens and early twenties.

Merkabah: any vehicle made of light and consciousness in which an individual being or group may travel through or beyond time and space—as opposed to a mechanistic means of transport such as cars, airplanes, or mechanical spaceships

Namaste: an ancient greeting, generally considered Hindi in origin. The palms of the hands are placed together in prayer position beneath the chin, and the head bows and nods toward the person or group for whom the Namaste is intended. It means, "I acknowledge and honor the God in you."

neural pathway: a minuscule nervous system route in the brain which receives sensory input, translates it, determines what action is to be taken based on the input, and then stimulates the body and consciousness to act on the decision. (See illustration 13 on page 243. Also see "Erroneous Neural Pathway" listing in Glossary.)

neural plate: a blockage in the neural pathway of the brain containing self-programming that inhibits natural and spontaneous response to sensory input and life experience. (See illustration 13 on page 243.)

neurotoxin: a substance contained in most commercial detergents, shampoos, hair sprays, aerosols, soaps, perfumes, and any product with chemical scent which attacks the nervous system by clinging to nerve endings and gradually breaking down the integrity of the mucous membranes, nerve sheaths, and brain function

Oneness: (1) the natural state of spiritual connectedness of all things in existence; (2) sometimes used as another name for God/Goddess/All That Is, or the divine in all things

Order of Melchizedek: (1) humans who studied and were initiated in Atlantis and ancient Egypt into the mystery schools of spiritual initiation and ascension. (2) In Atlantis, two sects of the Order became known as the *Gray Robes* and *Black Robes*. The Gray Robes were a specific group of priests and priestesses who specialized and focused on alchemy and divine magic. The Black Robes sprang from this group of alchemists and magicians and became misusers of the special powers, or black magicians and sorcerers. This latter group defied the spiritual protocol and divine laws of the original Order.

Order of the Great White Light: the original name of the Great White Brotherhood as we know it today, according to the Pleiadian Archangelic spokesperson, Ra

Overlighting Deva: (1) very large devic beings who oversee, protect, and energize individual plant and mineral devas. Examples: Overlighting Deva of the Mineral Kingdom, Overlighting Deva of the Diamond-light Healing Matrix, Overlighting Deva of Flowers (2)

large beings who oversee specific functions relative to Earth.
Examples: overseers of weather patterns and Earth changes; overseers
who help keep the planet's orbital cycles in alignment with directives
from the Central Sun; or overseers who maintain and change poles
based on evolutionary and physical time cycles; (3) large devas who
oversee and act upon specific needs of the human race. Examples:
Overlighting Deva of Healing, Overlighting Deva of Mourning,
Overlighting Deva of Childbirth.

paradigm: (1) a concept or model of "reality" generally shared by two
or more people who not only live by the concept and model but who
hold it together; (2) a contextual basis for "reality" versus open-ended
or nebulous "reality" structure; (3) any complete way of thinking and
responding that is predetermined by an existing pattern or belief
structure.

paradigm shift: when a person or group completely drops a way of
thinking, being, or behaving that has previously been set and predictable. Example: When a person breaks away from the group consciousness that says, "You only have one life and all you have to do
is survive it the best way you can" and creates a *new paradigm* for
him/herself based on, "The purpose for all of life is spiritual evolution
and we will continue cycling in and out of lifetimes until that purpose
is fulfilled."

parasitic entity: (1) any conscious or instinctual creature who lives
exclusively off of, and at the expense of, others; (2) one who feeds off
of the energy of another without giving anything in return

photon: (taken from *Webster's New World Dictionary*) "A quantum of
electromagnetic energy having both particle and wave properties; it
has no charge or mass but possesses momentum and energy. . ."

Photon Band: a wide stream of *photonic* light originating at the Galactic
Center in which Alcyone, central sun of the Pleiades, remains at all
times. As Earth and this solar system make their elliptical orbit around
Alcyone every 26,000 years, this entire solar system passes through the
Photon Band for a period of 2000 years every 11,000 years. In other
words, the first 2000 years of each 26,000-year cycle begin with this
solar system immersed in the Photon Band; this is repeated again
after 11,000 years out of the Band, or halfway through the elliptical
orbit for another 2000 years. During the time inside the Band, spiritual

evolution accelerates, planetary poles shift, and the frequency of light coming into the planet's atmosphere is greatly increased. As a result, much emotional, mental, physical, and spiritual clearing and integrity are required in order to withstand the intensity of light and energy coming in from the Galactic Center. The period of time inside the Photon Band is sometimes referred to as "the Age of Light," "the Golden Age," or "the Age of Enlightenment."

Pleiadian Archangelic Tribes of the Light: (1) members of the Pleiadian Emissaries of Light who are guardians and stewards of Earth and our solar system, with many diverse responsibilities. (2) The individual tribes are known as *Ra*, *Ma-at*, *Ptah*, and *An-Ra*. All members of each of the tribes radiate the same color and share the same name. (See individual Glossary listing for each tribe.)

Pleiadian Emissaries of Light: This is the name given to the entire Pleiadian group, including the Pleiadian Archangelic Tribes of the Light, who are my guides and sources of most of the channeled information in this book. The group also includes the etheric psychic surgeons, healers, and general light workers, who work with the life force and evolution throughout the Pleiadian Cluster and our solar system.

Pleiadian Lightwork: a new/old healing modality given to me by the Pleiadian Emissaries of Light and presented in this book, representing a renaissance of ancient Lemurian, Atlantean, and Egyptian healing-temple practices for awakening and strengthening the Ka. The main purpose behind Pleiadian Lightwork is to prepare you for full descension and embodiment of your Master Presence, also called your Higher Self or Christed Self, in preparation for ascension. Spiritual evolution is given as the divine counterpart to the Ka work, for without it, the Christed Self cannot live in the body.

Pleiadian Lightwork Intensive: a training program in Pleiadian Lightwork originally channeled and taught by Amorah Quan Yin; designed for those who wish to become Pleiadian Lightwork practitioners, or simply experience deepening of this work in a group setting

Ptah: (1) the soft-blue Light Beings from the Pleiadian Archangelic Tribes of the Light. Their role is that of protectors and preservers of the eternal nature of life. (2) In ancient Egypt, Ptah was the name given to the Creator and sustainer of life force.

Ra: (1) members of the Pleiadian Archangelic Tribes of the Light who emanate soft golden-yellow light; keepers of divine wisdom as the natural product of life experience; (2) the name of the individual being who speaks to the author bringing all channeled information and teachings; (3) ancient name of the Sun God in Egypt and Atlantis

relative truth: (1) anything that is based solely on everchanging life experience; (2) a perspective on reality based on opinions and beliefs versus Divine Truth. (See Glossary listing for "Divine Truth" for comparison.)

seven solar ring karmic patterns: the major lower qualities of consciousness which must be eliminated from this solar ring in order for planetary spiritual initiation and ascension to take place. The *seven patterns* are: arrogance, addiction, prejudice, hatred, violence, victimhood, and shame.

shaktiput: a dispensation of high-frequency white light that is so concentrated that the person receiving it experiences a few moments of reality in which only white light exists; this is usually accompanied by the third eye being radically opened, and a state of pure ecstasy during and after the experience; usually given to the individual by an enlightened human or Ascended Master who was enlightened while in human form

Sisterhood of the Ray of the Ascended Christ: Females who were enlightened and became Christ-conscious beings while still on the Earth in their bodies; now serving as guides and higher-dimensional teachers for humans ready to become enlightened and initiated into Christ consciousness

solar ring: the term the Pleiadian Emissaries of Light use for "solar system"; includes a sun and all planets that orbit around it, such as our Sun and all of the planets that orbit around it continually (Earth, Mars, Pluto, etc.)

soul: (1) that part of the overall individuated self that exists as a small ball of light like a sun which registers experience and learning as it moves from lifetime to lifetime and beyond; (2) immortal part of the self which contains and emanates the essence of the self

soul matrix: the area approximately one-and-a-half to two inches interior in the body to the center of the heart chakra where the soul anchors into the body for the duration of a lifetime

spirit: that part of the self that is without any form but can choose to inhabit a form, whether physical or etheric. This aspect can blend with anything or anyone and still maintains a sense of self, but without agendas.

tantra or **tantric energy:** sexual energy that is moved upward through the chakras from the sexual organs and lower spine, usually accompanied by the kundalini energy rising up the spine, as opposed to sexual energy that is released only locally in the genital area and lower chakras

thoughtform: a collection of beliefs, pictures, and feelings about a common theme that limits your reality in some way

thoughtform being: (1) a thoughtform that has become so big and so energized that it begins to function as a conscious being with a singular purpose based on the illusion the thoughtform is holding together. This is one type of elemental as described in the Glossary under "elemental" (2) a being found on the second-dimensional level which can be created by an individual or a group consciousness

time-space continuum: the paradigm of connectedness and continuation within a reality in which sequential time and first-through-third-dimensional space exists and seem to be ultimate. The illusion of ultimate reality and physicality only exists in the first through third dimensions, however.

truth: that which is unchanging, divine, and not subject to virtual reality influence

tube of light: the tubular opening that serves as an axis beginning at the apex of the aura beneath the feet, moving through the human body around the spine and out the crown, up and through the apex of the top of the aura and continuing like a spinal axis throughout the higher-dimensional selves all the way to the ninth dimension when the person is in "divine alignment". The higher-dimensional selves send light and energy through the tube when it is opened, which creates a continuum between all of the nine dimensional aspects of the individuated self. (See illustrations 11 and 15 on pages 200 and 273 respectively.)

vertical alignment: (1) the state in which a being is conscious of the difference in the illusion of relative truth and Divine Truth, seeking to

live by Divine Truth and integrity, knows the sacredness of the spirit
and soul in themselves and all beings, and is in connection with the
Higher Self, at least energetically; (2) the condition of being on your
"divine axis." (See Glossary listing for "divine axis.")

ABOUT
THE AUTHOR

Amorah Quan Yin, born November 30, 1950 in a small town in Kentucky, has been a natural healer and psychic since birth. As a child, her clairvoyance, clairaudience, and clairsentience were active, but these gifts gradually shut down when she entered public school and succumbed to peer pressure. At age sixteen, upon the death of her grandmother, once again her full sensory perception, as she prefers to call it, reopened. Sporadic experiences throughout her early adult years finally led to her spiritual awakening in early 1979.

Two years prior to her spiritual awakening, Amorah had been given less than two years to live by a medical doctor and an osteopath due to her extreme allergies that appeared to be untreatable. The specialist did not know about environmental illness at that time and persisted in trying to treat her in conventional ways, leading to a worsening of her allergies and stroke-level high blood pressure. These problems disappeared when she began to meditate, started eating vegetarian whole foods, stopped smoking, eliminated refined sugar from her diet, and altered her ways of thinking and living in the world.

With her spiritual awakening came a natural healing ability. Through books, classes, spiritual work with a teacher, and her own increasing awareness, Amorah broke away from traditional jobs in 1985 and began teaching workshops about using crystals and gemstones for healing and awakening. She also began to make and sell crystal and gemstone jewelry at that time. Private healing sessions and teaching were erratically intermingled with her other work until 1988 when she sold the jewelry company, moved to Mt. Shasta, California, and began building a full-time teaching and spiritual healing practice. Today, Amorah is well respected and known as a very capable and gifted healer, seer, and teacher in the Mt. Shasta area. Her limited private healing practice consists of individual sessions and private intensives done in person. She also does phone readings and distance healing work.

In 1993, she took the name Amorah Quan Yin. This came about as a result of two experiences. In the first, while on a twelve-hour air flight in

1990, an angelic voice sang softly in her left ear, "ah-mo-rah." Later, she learned what the syllables mean: "ah" is the universal sound for divine love; "mo" is the universal sound for mother; "rah" is a universal sound for holy father. Altogether it means beloved of, or divine love of, the Mother Goddess and Father God. The second experience happened in January 1992, when, while Amorah was meditating, the Goddess Quan Yin came to her, sat in front of her, and gave her mudras and a discourse. Quan Yin concluded her teachings by saying, "You are a little piece of me come to Earth to do our work. You are not me. You are the 'ah-mo-rah' part of me." Amorah says that she felt a deep sense of peace and a knowing inside that this was true. Connecting with Quan Yin and her healing energies has always been the easiest and most natural of all of her higher-dimensional connections.